DEMOCRACY
AND
NONVIOLENCE

DEMOCRACY
AND NONVIOLENCE

The Role of the Individual in World Crisis

by
Ralph T. Templin

AN EXTENDING HORIZONS BOOK
PORTER SARGENT PUBLISHER

11 Beacon Street
BOSTON, MASS. 02108

To Anne O'H. Williamson

. . . as friends in India always
said when they welcomed us into
their homes . . .

"This is yours, with gratitude."

Acknowledgment

During the Second World War the writer made two tours
among some of the many Civilian Public Service Camps and
Units on behalf of the education committees, first, of the
Brethren Service Committee, and later, a second tour sponsored
by both the Brethren Service Committee and the American
Friends Service Committee. He spoke on the implications of
nonviolence for Western society and its relation to decentralization of power and to democracy as a "way of life." Discussions of the most lively and searching type always went on
after these presentations and often late into the night. These

young "warriors" in a struggle, "Not with sword's loud clashing, Nor stir of rolling drum," were protesting in positive "socially useful" ways their society's all-out resort to military force "to preserve and extend democracy." This reliance upon force for the extension of democracy became our society's Cold War strategy during the post-World War II decades, a period in which the "conquest of violence" would be deliberately and indefinitely suspended. Would the Meek inherit the earth? Realistically, we would struggle with this problem in our discussions. It is difficult to estimate the sense in which these young visionaries were to become the avant garde of a new awakening. Their discussion would compare favorably with university groups of that or any other period. It is, of course, impossible to measure the author's great indebtedness to the courage, insights, and devotion revealed by these youth in these gatherings all across the country.

His thanks are especially due to two persons who read and commented on the first draft of the manuscript with great care and who gave themselves freely so as to be of the utmost help — Morris T. Keeton, Dean of the Faculty of Antioch College (then College Chaplain and Professor of Philosophy), and Anne O'Hare Williamson, Honorary Editor of the *Journal of Human Relations* (at that time its first editor). Miss Williamson read and re-read the manuscript and helped advise in reorganization and other matters. He is indebted also to Frances E. Hawkins, her sister Evelyn V. Rockhold, Jeanie Strand, and Pauline Pidgeon, who in their spare time helped with the typing, and later, with the proofreading; to Lawrence Templin, printer and specialist in English, for his help on the proofs; also to Central State College and the *Journal of Human Relations,* published by the College, for various help toward financing the research and in other ways. Thanks should also go to the *Christian Century* and the *Journal of Human Relations* for permission to use published articles by the author in adapted form. A special note of gratitude is extended to Mrs. Constance MacMillan who devoted many hours to the organization and preparation of the final manuscript before printing.

Much of a long experience that has gone into the making of this book as background has been most intimately shared by my helper and partner during a large portion of a lifetime,

Lila Templin; and this includes the painful searching of hearts, the convictions reached, and finally, the stands taken on those convictions which at times changed our lives most profoundly.

The author, finally, is indebted to the following publishers and holders of copyrights for their privilege to quote from their published works as noted in each case in the footnotes.

Alfred A. Knopf, Inc., New York
Allahabad, Katabistan, London
American Scholar, The
Association Press, New York
Beacon Press, Boston
Blue Heron Press, New York
Charles H. Kerr and Co., Chicago
Charles Scribner's Sons, New York
Christian Century, The
Community Service, Inc.
Appleton-Century-Crafts, New York
David McKay Co., Inc., New York
Doane Agricultural Service, St. Louis
Doubleday & Co., Inc., Garden City, New York
Duell, Sloan & Pearce, Inc., New York
Encyclopaedia Britannica
Friendship Press, New York
Garden City Pub. Co., New York
Grosset & Dunlap, Inc., New York
Harijan
Harper & Row, Pub., New York
Holt, Rinehart & Winston, Inc., New York
Hodder & Stoughton, London
Houghton Mifflin Co., Boston
John C. Winston Co., Chicago
John Day Co. Inc., New York
Journal of Human Relations
Lyle Stuart, New York
Macmillan Co., New York
Maurice McCracken, written statement
McGraw–Hill Book Co., New York
Modern Library, Inc., New York
Navajivan Pub. Co., Ahmedabud, India
Oxford University Press, Inc., New York
Political Science Quarterly
Prentice-Hall, Inc., New York
Princeton University Press, Princeton
Saturday Review, New York
School Science and Mathematics
Sri Aurobindo Ashram, Pondicherry, India
University of Alabama, Birmingham
Vanguard Press, Inc., New York
Viking Press, New York
Wilfred Wellock "New Horizons" privately published, printed with permission of the author, who is also his own publisher, Wilfred Wellock, "Orchard Lea," New Longton, Preston, England.
William Morrow & Co. Inc., New York
World Pub. Co., New York
W. W. Norton & Co. Inc., New York
Young India

RALPH T. TEMPLIN
Wilberforce, Ohio 1965

Foreword

A. J. MUSTE

There are frequent discussions as to the relation, or lack of relation, between nonviolence as an inward disposition or "way of life," on the one hand, and nonviolence as a means of social protest and instrument of social change, on the other. As I can testify from my own relation with him, the author of this book has been a practitioner of nonviolence as a way of life and has also made notable contributions to nonviolent action movements both in India and the United States. It is fortunate that he has been able to complete his labor of recording his experiences and reflections and that this book is now available.

The Peace Movement is in a period of transition, a period of groping for a valid analysis of the conditions under which we live and for a program based on such an analysis. This is true for all sections of the movement in all countries, East, West, or essentially unaligned. Like the labor and socialist movements of a half century ago which had such great promise and, alas, did not find fulfillment, it is a movement which seeks economic well-being, social justice, humanness in all human relationships, equality and the end of war — all of them together. It believes in man's power to determine his own destiny and to build the beloved community. We need such a movement in our time and it is not easy to see how it can be gathered in such vastly changed circumstances. In this volume, Ralph

Templin has attempted to outline the needed program and to clarify the task that lies ahead of us.

I can only list some comments in this connection which it seems to me are relevant to our situation.

1. We in the Peace Movement should stop being good-natured, easy-going optimists. We have to face and do all we can to get our fellows to face the stark reality of our situation. World War I *did* happen, so did World War II. And World War III will come, unless this generation by the grace of God finds new methods, rallies new forces, to prevent it.

2. We must abandon our fascination with, our worship of the word, of talk, of negotiations, which do not correspond to the realities, which are contradicted by the facts. When the arms race is speeded up while governments talk — even the United Nations talks — about stopping it, or slowing it down, we have to see steadfastly that the arms race is real, the bombs, the germ warfare arsenals are real. The rest is unreal, illusion, salve on a cancer.

3. We have to address ourselves resolutely to finding a fresh approach, calling forth new forces for peace. One factor in this process is to stop thinking that the basic fact of modern life is the conflict pattern — conflict of states, systems, ideologies. The operative concept is, rather, entrapment, mutual entrapment. The United States and the Soviet Union, the West and the East, are trapped by the runaway military technology which they no longer control, trapped by all the attitudes and habits of thinking which may have been applicable in the pre-nuclear age but are not any more. Both worlds, and the so-called underdeveloped and unaligned world also, are trapped in the pattern of nuclear arms race, armed nationalism, dogmatism, suspicion, fear, hate. Neither the "free" nor the underdeveloped world can deal with its problem straightforwardly and effectively while caught in this trap, obsessed with the compulsion to rivalry and conflict, saddled with the mounting financial and human costs of modern war. Real amelioration and solution is not possible within the conflict theory. Looking at it from another direction, we may note that, temporarily at least, a lessening, even in a minor degree, of threat tends to lower defensiveness and hostility in an opponent. This decrease in mutual hostility results in what the diplomats call deténte. If a nation were to have the

strength, courage, and wisdom — perhaps we may add grace — to extricate itself from the trap instead of mauling its neighbor caught in the same trap, miraculously its neighbor might just prove sane and human also. Something of this kind has to be assumed and is in fact implicit in every confrontation, some modicum of reason in the opponent, or no accommodation is possible and we live in a mad-house doomed to extinction.

4. Another aspect of the needed fresh approach is the recognition that if indeed deterrence is no longer to be relied on, then the break with war preparation in this period of history has to be unconditional and the way to disarmament is the unilateralist way. A nation cannot be both in the arms race and not in it, any more than a woman can be partly pregnant and partly not. In a period when "negotiation," what a critic of Sir Stephen King-Hall called "positive international action" takes place in the context of an arms race and the other elements we have noted, King-Hall is right in calling for "positive national action," the unilateral break which might once again make genuine negotiation, i.e., honest confrontation, possible.

5. The individual must take personal responsibility both for participation in political activity and for his attitude toward war preparation. The essentially individualistic moral or religious pacifism, characteristically expressing itself in conscientious objection to war, is no longer a sufficient basis for a thoroughgoing movement. (It has been too little realized that this type of pacifism has been a phenomenon largely confined to the Anglo-Saxon world and to a limited period in history.) This in no sense means that this type of pacifism no longer has a place or that it should be rejected. The one thing we don't have a surplus of in our time is non-conformity, No-saying. Our need of the person who, in C. Wright Mills' arresting phrase, at least affirms himself "as a moral center of responsible decision," is desperate. The development of war into something which is not war in the traditional sense constitutes the decisive new political fact of our time. This is what in immediate political terms the nuclear age means. The survival of mankind and even more its ability to devise a creative life for itself in the nuclear age depend on each of us breaking with war and war preparations unequivocally, breaking with what passes for "realism" now in each of our countries.

The responsibility for the Cold War and the constant threat of nuclear devastation cannot be laid to any nation or any bloc of nations. The fact is that Communism, in so far as it is a malady, is a product of Western civilization. The malady afflicts the body of which we are all a part. If the Communists tried to develop a new breed of Communist or Soviet man, it is now clear that they did not succeed, and we do not constitute a peculiar breed either. Underneath surface appearances mankind as a whole, societies of East and West confront the same problems. The task, basically, is not for the United States to liberate peoples from Russia, or for Russia to liberate peoples from United States imperialism, but for each country to liberate itself and thus help liberate the other and mankind. This has nothing to do with being "soft on Communism," which bothers many Americans, or being "soft on imperialism," which bothers the Stalinists and the Chinese so grievously. And it forbids the assumption that we have a peace bloc (us and our allies) and a war bloc (the enemy, of course). This is also an aspect of Cold War thinking, and diverts attention from the doom which hangs over us all. I submit that the problem of war cannot be solved in the context of the assumptions and attitudes which govern human thinking and behavior today on both sides of the Iron Curtain. It cannot be solved within the existing economic and political structures, for these structures would undergo vast changes if war were actually abolished. And it cannot be solved by means of the instruments now at hand and the procedures which are being employed to stave off war.

There are a number of considerations which make the abolition of war, especially wars of mass destruction, more necessary and in a sense more feasible than fifty years ago. The argument that was made then by Norman Angell seems feeble indeed beside the argument that can be made in the age of atomic weapons in support of the same contention — that war can no longer achieve rational economic and political objectives. To some extent even military men on both sides of the Iron Curtain reckon with the factor of unsupportable and inadmissible losses to be sustained in any major war. Furthermore, in repeated instances as in Korea, Cuba, Vietnam, United States policy-makers are confronted with the fact that nuclear weapons, which are supposedly the embodiment of superior power, cannot be used in combat. (Some use is made of them in the game of "brinkmanship," but even this resort may prove ineffectual if it is generally recognized that the weapons will not actually be used.)

Secondly, modern technology has placed the abolition of poverty and the general elevation of living standards within reach of mankind and thus removed one of the major reasons for war. This could be more or less clearly discerned in 1914. It is self-evident now.

Thirdly, man's knowledge of history, of his evolution, of himself, has greatly increased. The means of communication are vastly improved. Were these factors devoted to solving man's problems, they would provide our generation with an enormous advantage over that of our grandparents.

The world needs a revolution in feeling, in sensitivity, in orientation, in the spirit of man. This is an age in which the world of the physicist has become one of virtually infinite possibility. In every field of research the walls are down. In the realm of human relations, however, of politics in the basic sense, no such break-through has occurred. Here the walls press in upon man. The operative phrase is "the politically possible," which means what is possible within the existing socio-political context, the prevailing frame of thought. It would in fact be more accurate to say the outmoded, rapidly vanishing pre-nuclear age context and frame of thought. As Einstein stated it definitely a decade and a half ago: "The splitting of the atom has changed everything save our modes of thinking, and thus we drift toward unparalleled catastrophe." Similarly, Professor Templin maintains that "We must rethink, reformulate and revitalize our convictions." Whether we like it or not we are compelled to seek a new social ethic, an ethic based on nonviolence.

It is, therefore, a time to weep or turn to nonviolence. Better, a time to weep and turn at last to nonviolence. It is hard for men to achieve the change of focus which would enable them to accept this conclusion. Thus they keep coming back to the contention that the choice is to be brave and fight, even if this means commiting national or racial suicide, or to be cowardly and submit to Communism — or to capitalist enslavement, as the case may be. But this formulation is itself evidence of our mental and moral sickness. The choice is not between war or submission. It is between nonviolence or extinction. We must agree with Professor Templin when he asserts that "A nonviolent war against all aggression . . . will prove more effective than all the world's armies . . . if the nonviolent of the world will put their minds and hearts to the matter. We can stake our future, our society and our lives on this war without violence, for without it there will remain no civilization: violence is no longer possible."

I have since my own youth seen the United States develop from a nation which regarded itself as peaceful in contrast to the nations of the Old World, which looked down on the soldier and had a meager military establishment, into the greatest nuclear-armed power in the world, with a fifty-billion-dollar military budget and all that this entails. Our present military posture is not only a contradiction of our traditional secular heritage, but also an outrage to our religious precepts. Today, multitudes of Christian youth in the West see no contradiction between military service and what they have been taught in the Gospels. How can we change existing conditions? What approaches are open to us?

In seeking a point of reference and social context for popular nonviolent action, Dr. Templin turns to the Gandhian Movement in India, in which he played an active role. Gandhi's application of nonviolence and noncooperation "may well be regarded by future historians as the most practical performance of an age which has called him impractical. Before nuclear threat had demonstrated the necessity of men's controlling their destiny, he proved that men can learn to master their own destiny. He taught, lived by and led others to live by integrity of the human spirit and by active love in operation." Gandhi had an inclusive philosophy and vision. At the same time, he involved himself in public affairs and political struggle as a strategist and popular leader. He was deeply concerned about the "things of the spirit," the inner life of man. He did not think that the quality of the human beings who form a society is a minor matter. Nonviolence was his operative concept, the idea, as Joan Bondurant has set forth so clearly in *Conquest of Violence,* and as Professor Templin has so passionately elaborated in this volume, that the means which men employ in dealing with actual problems, if they be sound or nonviolent or democratic, will shape the society to creative ends, as against the concept of an end, an "ism" which society sets itself and then resorts to such means as it thinks will achieve the end.

13

Gandhi looked at the problem of modern war in this framework. If people were self-centered and acquisitive and the economic and social base organized on class distinction, injustice and power over others, then you would have centralization at the top or center, states based on power and the technique of war. It was, therefore, all-important to develop genuinely democratic and fraternal relationships at the base. Such a society would not need a huge powerful officialdom at the center. It would not have the instruments with which to wage modern war, nor would it need them, largely because it would meet other peoples in the same noncompetitive and fraternal spirit that was characteristic of its own life.

It seems to me that only a moderate amount of reflection is necessary to drive home the conclusion that opposition to (thoroughgoing noncooperation with) war and the building of a nonviolent social base are inseparable. A violent society will wage war, it is true. It is equally true that a society which wages war will not develop a nonviolent social order. The relation here is not a chronological but a dialectical one. We must be under no illusion that waging a war, engaging in an arms build-up and arms race, promoting centralized control which this entails, psychologizing the people for waging war, cutting down in education and social services — all this on the one hand — and instilling nonviolence in the people and building a nonviolent social base can be treated as parts of a single spiritual, social and political whole. The question of war and peace cannot be separated from the questions of political structure, economic exploitation, racial and other forms of oppression. Consequently, we are also involved in struggles for national liberation, racial integration, social justice. In all we seek to apply the method and spirit of nonviolence and recognize that the basic task is building a new, nonviolent society. In the words of the World Peace Brigade statement of principles, we seek "to revolutionize the concept of revolution itself by infusing into the methods of resisting injustice the qualities which ensure the preservation of human dignity and create the conditions necessary for peace."

In this context, Professor Templin fully recognizes the importance of the success of the Civil Rights Movement. In as much as the movement is activated by the technique and spirit of nonviolence, it will form the alternative means which is, as Templin points out, capable of turning us from the nuclear abyss. The acceptance of nonviolence as the method of the Freedom movements is certainly one of the singularly most heartening social phenomena of our time. "Freedom now" is a familiar cry to us now. Sensible people, people of good will, for the most part have recognized that the habit of temporizing and equivocating about civil rights has to be abolished, equality has to be posited as the goal. Doing this has not removed risks. It has not afforded an escape from grief and suffering. It has raised problems difficult to solve. But it was a break which had to be made with the absurd and the anti-human. It stated the real problem and it makes a solution and the blossoming anew of the human possible in our land.

We may here remind ourselves that it is a part of American tradition to hold that freedom cannot be handed to people on a silver platter, that real men and women stand up for their rights. "Don't tread on me" is thought of as a typical American slogan. To be ready to defend your own house and shoot the man who invades it and would perhaps insult or attack your women folk is commonly considered a laudable attitude, especially in the South. Are not Negroes following in this American tradition when they resent being patronized, when they do not have the "feel" of being free until they have taken hold of freedom? One often hears men of standing say that it would be different if Negroes asked (begged?) for their rights, but that "we're not going to be bullied into granting them — don't push us." In much the same way, many Englishmen, of the time of George III, thought of the colonials as upstarts and insolent boors for "demanding" rights and independence. There are many generations of humiliation and oppression behind the upsurge among Negroes and the belligerence now asserting itself. The results are not invariably pleasing. They are often bizarre and in some cases horrible, as revolutions always are. Perhaps we could at least not be so surprised that the familiar accompaniments of mass change manifest themselves in the United States today. We might even take some satisfaction in the realization that once more people are "demanding" that beautiful thing, freedom, and that their leaders are saying: "Let my people go." Perhaps whites could derive a measure of intellectual objectivity and reduce the intensity of their anger by realizing that these things are "happening" to us (as similar surprises, mysteries and disturbances have happened to others in revolutionary periods) rather than being "inflicted" by some mad or evil persons who live in the Negro section or flood out of New York's Harlem to tie up highways to the New York World's Fair.

Any social and radical movement today which thinks that its goal can be achieved by and in an America which does not break sharply with war and devote itself instead to facing its own life problems and helping to advance the emancipation of the disadvantaged masses throughout the world, is deluding itself. It tells its followers in effect that they will attain freedom and peace in an America as it is today, an America which fails to devote itself to freedom and peace for all men.

Since much of Professor Templin's work deals with the sources and forms of revolutionary activity in the developing nations and since his views in this extremely significant area of conflict are very much in accord with my own, let us turn for a moment and consider this revolutionary factor. The revolts of the past decade, in Asia and in Africa, and now in Latin America, have a political aspect — the desire to get rid of a foreign master, and to achieve national dignity. In the economic field the aim of these revolts is to abolish various forms of feudalism and to industrialize rapidly. Finally, there is the critical psychological, racial, or cultural aspect. The contemporary revolutions are revolts of the humiliated against the whites and not least the Anglo-Saxons who have for centuries been the humiliators. We are slow to realize that we are not loved and in fact deeply hated by many in Latin America, Asia and Africa. As a nation we have a strong anti-colonial tradition. We have occasionally irked our allies in recent years by giving some mild support to rebel elements in their colonies and former spheres of influence. Now it is the peoples in these vast reaches of the world who are in revolt — a revolt in part directed against us, and based on the fact that in actuality (though not in form) they have constituted colonies of the U.S. in an economic, military and political sense. We now find ourselves denounced as alien masters. It is difficult for us to accept these charges — easier for us to repeat the error of the European colonial powers when they faced revolts and to charge that the whole problem is a creation of Communist agents.

There is no more point in quarreling with these revolts than in shaking one's fist at a hurricane. Furthermore, it is not possible to quarrel with the basic aims of these revolts. They arise out of human dignity, out of the passion of human beings to be human. Yet it is a fact that Western powers generally, including in a slightly modified degree the U.S., tend to oppose these revolutions, to try to dilute them and slow them down. These revolutions are not manufactured by the Communists. If the Moscow regime did not exist, they would still be a characteristic of our age. It is also a fact, however, that the Soviet Union and the Communists are on hand where these revolts are brewing and — for reasons which we hardly need to elaborate here — are generally on the side of the revolutionaries, though the support is often subject to the exigencies of Soviet power interests. The result is that Communists are quite often in a position to "take over" and do, and although they experience their own difficulties and have bitter disagreements among themselves, by and large, our era is marked by the growth of Communism and of the power of the Soviet bloc and by a lessening of the power of Western nations and of the influence of Western culture and prestige. The revolutionary "class" today consists of the masses among the underdeveloped, mainly colored, peoples of the world. The West, and this includes Russia, dominates them in only a limited sense now. Before very long even the United States and Russia and the rest of Europe combined will not be able to dominate them. If these great sections of mankind are arrayed against each other, then the West will not be able to withstand the rest of the world.

In this context it is pertinent to point out that in so far as one can speak of "responsibility" in such historic developments, the white peoples of West Europe and North America have brought the present situation upon themselves and the rest of mankind. These peoples developed the technology which made large-scale industry possible and revolutionized agriculture. For several centuries, they spread their rule over the world by direct or indirect conquest, while preaching doctrines of freedom, of equality and even of love. They are now developing automation. The white nations are still militarily dominant and the nuclear powers. They made the mistake of engaging, mostly among themselves, in two colossal World Wars during the present century, as a result of which their hold over colonial peoples was broken.

The psychological aspect of white conquest should constantly be kept in mind these days. One of the great chasms in the world is that between the peoples who have known humiliation as peoples and those who have not, but instead have humiliated others. The white peoples are the ones who shoved other peoples, especially the colored, off the sidewalk in Western and in Asian and African countries alike, but no one could push the white master off the sidewalk anywhere.

The tide began to turn some time ago and is now flowing strongly in the other direction. The colored peoples are asserting themselves; the white people are having to make room and to abandon theories and practices of superiority. This is never easy, and seldom if ever has backing down from a position of superiority and domination to one of something near equality been done gracefully. But there come times when it has to be done. One thing that can save the West and the United States in particular is to recognize that their day of power and domination is over; for the United States to avoid interjecting its supposed power interests as over against the Communist "enemy," with whom one nevertheless gladly consorts if it appears to suit one's power interests. In place of this the American people must become sensitive to the world revolution that is sweeping over Asia, Africa and Latin America, and become a humble creative supporter and friend of these efforts of multitudes to rise into physical well-being, political independence, and spiritual freedom.

All believers in nonviolence (and at least some who do not think of themselves in those terms) do not see the task of our age as that of a seizure of power by a new social element and the setting up of a new power structure. They see the task of our age as that of building the beloved community. No one can have a fairly close contact with the Civil Rights Movement and the people in it, including the young people, without feeling that, in spite of all contrary appearance and even realities in the movement, deep near its center is the aspiration for a beloved community and the faith that this is what they are working for and already in a sense realizing now. "O, Freedom, Freedom over me." "Deep in my heart I do believe that we

18

shall overcome some day" — not overcome the white man, but overcome that which stands in the way of man, each man.

In an analysis of this kind, attention must be focused on the white community. I referred earlier to the chasm between the peoples who have known humiliation as peoples and those who have not, but have humiliated others. The latter are the West Europeans and the Americans. The chasm has for the most part kept the (colored and white) peoples separated from each other. It is so no longer. The chasm is going to be bridged somehow. From the side of white men a bridge of understanding, repentance, reconciliation and love might be thrown across the chasm. If this is not done, a bridge of pent-up frustration, vengeance, hate may be thrown across it by the majority of the human race. Those who over centuries dug the chasm would hardly be in a position to quarrel with the effect. But this would not be building the beloved community either. It would be opening another familiar cycle of domination and eventual corruption. This might prove suicidal for all in the nuclear age and because this is so, a nonviolent revolutionary movement has to be international, eventually global, in outlook and scope. Of course, there must be strong movements within each country, but a series of isolated or tenuously related national organizations and movements simply cannot deal intelligently and seriously with the threat of war and the task of building a sane society. There must be international thinking, planning, action.

Only a few years ago nervous discussions about the goals of American society were constantly appearing. They reflected the lack of a sense of direction and of drive. It can be said that the Kennedy and Johnson administrations have witnessed and in some degree produced a change in some areas. The change has been most obvious and dramatic in the field of race relations. It is of considerable significance in relation to Professor Templin's thesis and speculations that the struggle in this field has been consciously and predominantly a nonviolent one. More recently, President Johnson widened the program to take in the problem of poverty in the midst of affluence and has projected the concept of the Great Society.

In dealing with world relations and the problem of war in the nuclear age, American society has so far failed to achieve a decided change of focus and is operating on the basis of traditional concepts of deterrence, negotiation from strength, arms rivalry, fulfillment of "commitments" to intervene militarily in distant situations. The tendency is to "go along" with the policy the Administration devises, on the assumption that in the nuclear age we have to "live with" these things. But it is not reasonable to think that a crisis which would prove catastrophic can be indefinitely postponed, if only because no people can survive, much less flourish in the modern world, in such an atmosphere devoid of direction and hope. There must be something — something else to live *for*, not merely just live *with*. The politics which the American people are now being offered in the area of international relations will prove a politics of bewilderment and despair.

We need a politics "on the other side of despair," a politics based on the conviction that another kind of society must and can be built.

In this work, Ralph Templin offers us a vision of what a new kind of society, a nonviolent society could be like. This vision is presented as a conception of community; a human community based on love; where the problems of existence are solved not by superior force, but by cooperation and mutual aid, where freedom and human dignity no longer need debating, because they are lived; where peace is the wide communication and trust among all peoples, and not merely the quietude of fear.

If we really want to put an end to war, discrimination, inequality and all forms of degradation and human suffering, we do well to listen to what writers like Ralph Templin have to say, and this holds good even though at many points we may not entirely agree with him. This is the case because Templin begins where thinking now has to begin, namely with the recognition that our present attitudes, our patterns of thinking, our very institutions are outmoded. They are associated with man's psychological immaturity and in the nuclear age men will either have to mature or suffer extinction as a species. As Martin Buber has declared: "Ours is not an historically familiar malady in the life of peoples which can eventuate in comfortable recovery. Primal forces are now being summoned to take an active part in an unrepeatable decision between extinction and rebirth."

A. J. Muste
New York 1965

Table of Contents

21

Introduction

JAMES FARMER

How unique and terrifying it is for a social historian to speak with candor. Both democracy and nonviolence have become fair rhetorical game in the recent half-decade; so much so that the singularity of their aims, a true attribution of their meaning in a turbulent moment of history has been very nearly lost. If Dr. Templin's book serves no other purpose, it succeeds, through frank and unembittered prose, in taking the scales from our eyes, unveiling our domestic and foreign tragedy without quarter.

It is simply not enough for us to say (as we all do from every lectern) that this is a revolutionary era. How pointless it is for us to celebrate the anti-colonial surge of Africa without a searing analysis of the political options, democratic and otherwise, these new nations contemplate. How destructive and pointless a civil rights revolution in America becomes without a parallel and constructive criticism of the society from which American Negroes seek redress and *in* which American Negroes seek to prosper. The true intercourse of our century, blooded by war and hate and poverty, is a total dialogue, admitting that "democracy" has been redefined to suit our weaponry and our global appetites.

Dr. Templin's analysis comes, unfortunately, as a surprise.

His candor reminds me of the days immediately following the Freedom Rides that CORE conducted in 1961. Faced with long days in the Mississippi prisons and flushed by television and newspaper citations, the riders sat in their cells and tried, probably for the first time in their lives, to measure the real purpose and meaning of their actions and their tactics. Those who mechanically "bought" the mechanics of nonviolence were stung by its effectiveness and startled by the near-theology of its impact on them. It became, at least for me and many others, not a time for public martyrdom, but rather a contemplative moment in our lives in which the injunctions of Gandhi acquired shape and size . . . and for the first time a word, "nonviolence," left the academic vocabulary and joined the real issue in the real world.

In this same sense, Dr. Templin isolates the word "democracy" from the lingo of the seminar. In a tough, undecorated look, Dr. Templin finds democracy at its best as a fluid, unstable entity, a pliable alternative that disintegrates as it hardens on the anthems of national sovereignty. Democracy, martyred by misuse and misappropriation is, as Dr. Templin sees it, very much like a squeamish Hamlet, changing costumes to suit the scene, now soft and pudgy in the act of love, now armoured in defense against the poisoned sabre. If one reads "Democracy and Nonviolence" with as little predisposition as possible, it becomes a primary text, a McGuffey's primer on how we can and must survive.

A single example might suffice.

After a rigid catechism about the real meaning of "popular sovereignty" and the implications of that phrase, Dr. Templin recalls Clemenceau's injunction at the 1919 peace conference at Versailles. "If we give up all future wars," said the French statesman, "we must give up our empires and all hope of empire . . . peace, is very expensive." Thus Templin strikes directly home at a moral question of our century, i.e. if democracy truly means that *people,* not states, are sovereign, then we must abandon literal, economic and intellectual slavery. We must surrender our rationales of "least evils" via "means and ends." Dr. Templin points out, as the "sovereign state of Mississippi" chains and murders its dissidents, so does the nightmare of Dachau and Budapest murder the future in Europe and Asia. Something is desperately wrong when freedom must come by partition from one's own countrymen and "democracy" is written into the lyrics of battle.

Thus, Dr. Templin *does* take a hard look. A look long overdue in a rapacious world that has forgotten such simple creeds as "all men are created equal."

Further, in his section addressed to the question of nonviolence, Dr. Templin provides a second imperative lesson. He has said that there is no peaceable alternative to nonviolence in an insurgent, violent world. Probably as important, is Dr. Templin's analysis of the effects of nonviolence and the permanence of its impact. The psychology of that impact, becomes, in his view, essential to our understanding and use of the tactic. Nonviolence indeed dispells its antagonist, violence, through a virtual revelation of the stupidity and fruitlessness of retaliation. It has long been time to strip away the canards of "pride" and "self-defense" that have been used to ridicule nonviolence. Not only an act of supreme personal courage, the application of nonviolence represents true historic courage in its reversal of the tide of violence that has stunned two dozen centuries. There is, indeed, no alternative — just as the aspirations of the victims of violence and human enslavement are undeniable.

So we are confronted by an honest and virile reading of our society. Shot through with a near-sentimental ardor for first-principle democracy and militant nonviolence, this book serves the important purgative purpose of either preparing us for, or arming us against, an ultimate tragedy. We must choose between acquiescence in annihilation or Templin's more positive program of systematic and democratic nonviolent resistence to the genocidal tendencies of the age. Which course we choose, is, without question, up to us.

James Farmer
New York 1965

CHAPTER 1

DEMOCRACY AND REVOLUTION

Democracy is on trial for its life. Its survival and the survival of Western civilization are so harshly threatened that no person remains outside the struggle.

Revolution is the order of the day — like it or not, there is no evading this fact. Violent revolutions are affecting larger populations than ever before; nonviolent revolution has become a familiar phenomenon. Scarcely any portion of the globe is free of the fever of revolt. Changes unsought by man, always brought about by revolution, are coming so thick, with such urgent swiftness and such devastating priority, as to raise seriously the questions of man's survival on the earth and his spirit's continued supremacy over his physical environment and his Frankenstein creations.

The West has been aware of the world's rising tide of revolt, but has failed to understand its own principal part in it. If the West is to save itself and its democratic heritage, it must learn the meaning of these revolutions in every part of the world.

At least four popular revolts, each against a separate tyranny, are clear: (1) In Asia, there is revolt against both feudalism and Western colonialism; in Africa, against the latter. (2) In all places where there is war weariness and fear of total destruction, there is increasing revolt against war. (3) In every part of the world there is growing evidence of a revolt against unilateral nationalistic behavior — against the aggressive absolutism of modern nationalism. (4) All over the world, the colored peoples are rising to throw off once and for all their "inferior" status. There is a new and rapidly increasing world solidarity among all nonwhite peoples; it is their refusal to any longer be divided and ruled.

Though we question the Soviet Union in many ways, we cannot question her realism in moving politically with each of these spreading revolts. In Asia, Africa and elsewhere, she encourages popular revolt. In Europe she discourages reliance upon war. In the United Nations, she champions a laying down of arms. Many colored peoples believe she champions their cause of equality. In supporting these revolutionary movements, the Soviet Union hopes to embroil Western nations in protracted crises which are intended not merely to destroy colonialism but substantially to weaken Western alliances and military-strategic capabilities.

In contrast, the Western democracies have not offered any good alternatives to people in revolt against old systems. Amazingly, and to the contrary, Western nations have tended to support and perpetuate ancient feudalisms and decaying imperialisms. They have attempted to whip their citizens into a state of preparedness for a war for which they have only repugnance. Money and political influence are frequently used to aid a white ruling elite holding vast majorities of colored nationals "in their place."

Why is it that Western democracy can present no clear alternative to people aspiring for their freedoms? Why does democracy falter at a time when it might secure the prosperity and political support of awakening nations by offering, unconditionally, its two greatest achievements: liberal egalitarian philosophy and technology?

All existing democracies found their way to freedom through struggle against exploitive or dominant orders. American people who cherish the spirit of the Boston Tea Party face the revolutionary state of the world with understanding. They consider the emerging worldwide revolution of peoples against tyrannies, ancient and modern, as a great new hope — hope for the world, and hope especially for Western society. They view the revolution in their own South in the same light as the revolutions in Africa or the workers' revolts against the workers' state. They realize that the people of the United States, to regain control over their lives and their country, must join the world's revolutions — against economic and political domination by special interest groups, against the danger of wholesale nuclear destruction, against the moral decay that permits indifference to the struggles and the sufferings of other men.

To accomplish a revolution in democracy, we must rethink, reformulate and revitalize our own convictions. Democracy, revolution against entrenched power — democracy, the continuous peaceful shaping and reshaping of governments and society by the people — has been betrayed. It is not too late to return again to the original democratic path.

A second revolution is needed in defense. Increasing

multitudes of the world's people are casting about for a system of adequate defense. They are beginning to realize that there is no hiding place. They know, and so actually do all of their leaders, that the security inherent in a balance of military strength and in diplomatic dealings based on this balance has been blasted by potential nuclear devastation. The kind of policy reformulation going on is utterly inadequate to meet our needs.

The need for at least one other great revolution is indicated — a revolution in moral control. This is crucial to the questions: Can man survive the death-hold his technological achievements have thrust upon him? Can the people regain their democratic sovereignty? Only the people can answer these deeper questions.

The early history of democracy in this country shows that it was conceived as something distinct from, and even opposite in nature to, the competitive, autocratic and highly nationalistic nation-states existing in Europe at that time.

Democratic principles, as they were promulgated by this nation's founders, were universally applicable: all men created equal . . . government by consent. These were not concepts which could be restricted to any segment of mankind or monopolized by a national group. An ethnocentric, aggressive democracy which lives by tyranny and exploitation is blasphemy against our democratic heritage.

In 1953, in an address before a Chicago audience, the late Justice Robert H. Jackson declared that "no nation is more force-minded than our own." He was concerned with the democratic betrayal — the self-contradiction — implied by this force-mindedness. He saw the Western world turning away from reason and legitimacy to the accumulating of instruments of physical power. Can we profess to offer a saving faith to the world, he asked, while engaged in the surrender of belief in law and the rule of law? He pointed out that it is the special function of democratic law to put "rational restraints upon the use of coercive power by those in authority." Such, he noted, is the real mark of distinction between democratic legal philosophy and that of communism which, according to Vishinski, is only "expressing the will of the dominant class . . . the compulsive will of the State."

This precise statement of the legal case between two incompatible ways of life, one of them tracing its roots from the Magna Charta, shows how impossible it is for the force-minded to either preserve or defend democracy. The West's taking, as alternative to the way of law, the way of preponderant military strength, has already dealt slow death to democracy in many nations.

Throughout the United States, a nation calling itself the world's greatest democracy, human rights are sacrificed daily to the material aspirations of dominant sectional, racial and business interests. Laws permitting racial segregation are blatantly immoral. Those fostering or contrived to protect monopolization and the concentration of land and wealth in the hands of a few persons or corporations sanction economic tyranny. Legalizing the operations of an industrial system which provides for the personal enhancement of a few at the expense of the many is as undemocratic as dictatorship.

Set forth in the Constitution of this nation is an expression of the people's sovereign right to exercise control over every level of constituted authority. All phases of citizenship — local, state and national — were to be experienced and practiced simultaneously. No authority at any level was to be regarded as final. The regulatory agencies of government were to serve the people, not hinder and restrain them. Individual members of the society retain the constitutional right to modify, manipulate and even to overthrow government authority. This belief and practice the new nation was prepared to make secure as its basic way of life.

Today, in sharp contradistinction, both conservatives and liberals tell us that a vast system of national interests and defense commitments extending into every part of the world must be maintained to defend our way of life. And this is too often directed against aroused and resisting peoples who are striving to emulate our original ideals and who proclaim their right to cast off foreign domination and gain or regain self-determination. These far-flung national interests must be defended at all cost, despite democratic opposition at home. American capitalism is now a way to be preferred above democracy itself, and the right of sovereign citizenship with which we began this nation may have to be sacrificed.

Fear of communism is both a pretext for the subversion of this truly American ideal and something that opponents of democracy have seized upon when pursuing contrary and often selfish or totalitarian ends. The two major objectives sought by antidemocratic factions within our society are the arousing of nationalistic emotions and aspirations and the overruling and subsequent elimination of opposition.

That which became ascendent as this nation's founding ideology, which made her greatness, attested to her distinctiveness, and validated her mission to all peoples of the world is not today ascendent or predominant. Our present weakness in a faltering world leadership, our chief aid to the expansion of international communism, issues forth from this serious lapse: a subversion of our nation's original democratic precepts.

The cold war has been a period in which the Soviet Union has been able to call almost every tune, initiate practically every crisis, be always on the offensive, and place the Western bloc almost invariably in the role of following her lead. The United States has led the West in a purely negative policy; everything said or done has been cast into the negative mold of anticommunism. Years of belligerent posture on the part of the United States have served Soviet purposes and tended to detract from American popularity among the peoples of developing nations, while swelling the ranks of Soviet sympathizers.

The nations of the West took the name United Nations in the united pursuit of their aims in World War II. If, having won that war, they had then used this concept of solidarity to set forth for all men a strong, positive assertion of democracy of universal application, how very different could have been the outcome. We could then have retained our position as the champion of freedom through the establishment of universal democracy. We could have so busied ourselves with the positive task of helping to establish world democracy under the United Nations that we would have had neither use nor time for the follies of a cold war. The United Nations would have quickly had the added support of all newly independent nations, of all the noncommitted nations, of all those aspiring to independent or equal status, and of what is now the Western bloc. In 1945, it might still have been possible for such a policy to win China over to the position of genuinely free peoples and away from international communism. With a policy which embraced nothing more positive or democratic than anticommunism, or cold war, or later, Red China's exclusion from the United Nations, a constructive approach was, of course, impossible.

Why did the West fail then, as now, to work actively for the expansion of democracy? Because this would have meant the forthright end of every brand of Western imperialism, which even while only slightly colonial in form is a contradiction of democratic equalitarian principles.

Chiang Kai-shek is supported, protected and maintained in the United Nations under the auspices of the United States not for any intrinsically ethical reasons but rather for his value as a market for American business interests. Recognizing the exploit potential of the Chinese situation, American industrialists have brought pressure to bear upon irresponsible politicians and have in this way helped shape our present status-quo policy on China in the U.N., in spite of overwhelming opposition at home and abroad. And so it seems to the peoples of foreign nations that our supposedly democratic government has denied representation to over 600 millions of the earth's inhabitants in the name of democratic justice.

Instead of leading all who would follow in the quest for democracy and world law under the United Nations, we have unilaterally sought collective defense in our own interest and at the expense of millions; we have unilaterally engaged in the negativism of cold war. In following these self-centered patterns of behavior we have probably done more to advance the cause of communism in China, Cuba, Africa and elsewhere than the Soviet Union.

Dwight D. Eisenhower started this nation on a search for new objectives when he appointed the President's Commission on National Goals.[1] At the time of his retirement from the presidency, he warned against the danger of the power alliance of business and military leaders which he saw foreshadowed and indicated that he realized the urgency of pressing toward new goals.

The National Goals report returns with nostalgic hope, but little suggestion of application, to the early European liberalism from which this nation took direction and out of which all Western democracy arose. The report moves within the framework of subverted applications of those early democratic principles; it overlooks the fact that the liberalism of the present is not historically American. The report overlooks also our failure as a nation to manifest and perpetuate the eighteenth century egalitarian philosophy which is the source of our original democratic ideals and documents.

That philosophy has, in fact, scarcely been tried even within this nation. It has been surrendered for more rigid ways of life. Such rigidity is not the way of the original liberalism of democracy, nor is true democracy within the way of the liberalism of the present.

What is the possibility of the New Frontier for all humanity proposed by the late President John F. Kennedy? We assume that this means a goal of free association among all nations, established on international law in justice and concern in a human community of the world. Democratic peoples can settle for no less than this.

The term "free association" appears in the modified development of the Congressional "Organic Act" under which, within strict and arbitrary limits, the Puerto Rican people were permitted to write their present Constitution. The free association was intended to serve as a pilot undertaking, pointing the way to possible future relationships with all the Latin American peoples. It was intended specifically to suggest to Latin America and to the world that political or economic independence from the North American industrial-financial colossus is not the basic ingredient of genuine human freedoms.

These words are high-sounding. What are the realities behind them? Are free associations of all nations, and the New Frontier of all freedoms for all peoples, just words?

Puerto Rico, without a single vote in Washington but legislated for and controlled by Washington, symbolizes the weakness of democracy in our foreign relations. Puerto Rico is a doorstep into the world for whatever "American way" is advanced from Washington. Pre-Castro Cuba was probably even more limited and controlled in her self-expression than Puerto Rico is today under her "modified colonialism." In these places very close to our shores, the blessings of our free ways should have extended long ago and should have made any kind of contention for supremacy from the outside impossible.

A basic weakness is here revealed in the leadership of the United States toward a free world. A majority of the Latin American people repudiate our professions of sincere concern for human welfare. Why? Is this not because any policy of limited and controlled self-expression is incompatible with any profession of free association? A world bonded by free association under world authority can make possible world order and world peace. But what is the reality of free association within the United Nations? What, among peoples anywhere? Is a New Frontier possible under the present organization of all of Western society?

John Lear, Science Editor of *Saturday Review*, wrote during the Kennedy Administration that it makes a great deal of difference how America may try to export the

American Revolution. The ways in which we have "packaged" this great American offering in the past

> . . . frustrated Woodrow Wilson in Europe. They blighted the good neighbor policy in the Western Hemisphere. They paralyzed the "Atoms for Peace" crusade of Dwight D. Eisenhower. And now they stare enigmatically in the face of John Fitzgerald Kennedy who has determined . . . to push the export of the American Revolution.[2]

John Lear was commenting on Kennedy's foreign policy as interpreted by scientist Max Millikan, Director of the Massachusetts Institute of Technology Center for International Studies. This interpretation is excellent for its application of a broadly scientific approach.

But it contains no indication that this new ship, readied for the voyage to the New Frontier, will be any the less laden with the freight which has bogged down every former attempt to export the American Revolution. The groups which have imposed all those barriers in the past not only remain in their controlling positions, they remain unchanged in their view that a good foreign policy is simply one which is in our own national interests.

It is not scientists nor the administrative bureaucracy that hold the balance of power in government. The real power passes from party to party, finding one party as effective as the other for its major purposes, and most often the power operates through a bipartisanship which is not far from a one-party state system. This power group succeeds through an association of "conservatives" and "liberals" with enough common desires and purposes to make solidarity possible, even though a national fiction of democratic opposition is maintained.[3]

This strange association of conservatives and liberals works to prevent all serious attempts to extend the offering of democracy through a League of Nations, a United Nations, a Good Neighbor Policy, or any other way. The tendencies of conservatism not to conserve and of liberalism no longer to liberalize represent shifts from the positions of origin to their opposites.

Conservatives begin by wanting to conserve something from something else — for example, to conserve the unrestricted nature of profit-seeking from democratic controls. Historically, however, conservatism ends by practically never conserving anything. Instead, conservatives become indirectly responsible for the most radical social changes.

In early America, the banker-business circles were the reactionary opposition; the liberals of the time were able to chart the new democratic course. It was the banker-merchant conservatives who tried at one point to have Washington crowned king.[4]

Later, through Jeffersonianism and against very great odds, the liberals were able to fix the new ship of state on its originally declared course. But the merchant-banker conservatives never rested. In subtle but tangible ways, they spread their empire, already more than a hundred years older than the new nation. They learned how to favor and employ for their purposes the new façade of the exciting frontier politics, in which log cabins and hard cider could easily be made the major issues.[5]

"A Conservative government is an organized hypocrisy," said Disraeli in a speech to the House of Commons. Conservatives are often those most subversive of their society's original mythos (its religious-cultural idealism). An example is the American conservatives' embracing of the

European spirit of nationalism and method of a balance of military power which our early American spirit and method sharply repudiated.

American conservatives today, calling that early American spirit and attitude isolationism (the very opposite of its meaning), take the way of the international anarchy of the European scene, the way of the chaos which their nation originally repudiated in order to take its democratic way of law. They exalt going it alone; they exalt expanding the American empire. Many conservatives are joining forces to suppress all opposition to untrammeled exploitation and enslavement of peoples in many parts of the world, including the United States, by an ethnocentric reactionary oligarchy whose principle tools and objectives are political conformity and superindustrialization.

And what of the liberals who charted the course of our new nation? Liberalism, born of an awakening, has discarded wakefulness. Having produced assertion of popular sovereignty, liberalism today disavows the people's control even of themselves or their parties; having encouraged people in their own responsibilities, liberalism now denies them opportunities for human fulfillment. Liberalism offers no redress for the totalitarian drift to either left or right; it produces no alternative to the frank and ruthless advancement of a police-war state in the West.

Today it is not uncommon for people calling themselves liberals to insist on the necessity of preserving at all cost the particular (though largely nonexistent) socio-economic system called free-enterprise capitalism. Some of these people stress the importance of preserving this way of life even at the expense of restricting civil liberties and due process. Their civil liberties committees, established to champion civil liberties for every man, have turned toward the "now necessary task" of determining the limits of civil liberties. Such is the emerging mentality of much of present liberalism throughout the West.

In the processes of history, both this conservatism and this liberalism have completed circles which bring them together in the long-range subversion of democratic values. This is true not only in the United States; it is the prevailing Western cultural predicament. For example, it is difficult to find any important difference between the Laborites and the Conservatives in England today.

American bipartisan interests find it increasingly easy to pass from the Democratic Party to the Republican Party, and back again when the surface political pressures require. Cold war subversion of the original solidarity-upon-law of our Union, "domestic anticommunist" subversion of our original diversity-within-union, and persecution of any opposition to these policies are palatable to both parties. Both parties, accepting the leadership of the financial-industrial machine behind government, equally betray the basic legal foundation upon which early American security, ideals, well-being, and peace rested. Within both parties, liberals and conservatives are united in the surrender of this early national heritage of democratic law to national interests, advantages, power, gunboat diplomacy, reliance upon balancing our power with all other nationalistic powers, and the quest for "American world destiny" in the "American Century."

"Progressives" can no longer be merely liberal; they have to be radical in order to remain progressive. They also have to be radical to be conservative of any of the significant values contained in our democratic origins.

We have failed to understand and assist in the development of the United Nations, our only authentic offspring in the international field except the abortive League of Nations. We by-pass it when it does not go our way; we try to forge it as a tool for our foreign policies. Every other nation is trying to do the same. There is no leadership toward the realization or fulfillment of our original democratic purposes in international relations.[6] We set no example of democracy before any of the peoples now newly free or striving for independence. The democratic basis of supremacy of human dignity has not been supreme above material conquests; exploitation of people has not been replaced by the concept of people exercising control over their social, economic and political institutions. Democracy has some reality of existence, but not in an international application.

In all the places beyond our borders, our national interests have been the precise opposite of those of the original American way. The framework within which international relations have existed or developed is that of the war system and the diplomacy of the national agencies, which is based upon the war system. A United Nations organization cannot change this fact until certain areas of national authority are surrendered to it — until nations use the United Nations for something more than settlement of differences. The very philosophy, spirit and attitude of the present role of this country in the United Nations are subversive of the principles of our original democracy. Without power to adjudicate, the United Nations remains a part of the great hypocrisy of nationalism so well illustrated by the double-talking slogan which hangs on American military walls, "Peace is our profession."

What might we Americans have become as a people had we been able to live during all the life of our country the wisdom, the statesmanship, the constructive community building implicit in the universal principles solemnly vowed as we formed this nation?

From the first, unfortunately, we have been spiritually illiterate bunglers. As a people we tend to be self-deceived. Our deception leads us to deny, and even resist, both within and beyond our borders, that which we made our democratic political formula and way of life: the sovereignty of citizens at all levels of authority. Our denial of this principle is leading to speedy curtailment of this way of life. At present we can still enslave while granting independence (as in the Philippines), while inducting into statehood (as with Hawaii), or while introducing a new formula (as in the Puerto Rican "commonwealth").

Even within our land of liberty, such freedoms as voting, educational and job opportunities, and choice of living accommodations are withheld from millions. When we realize, with some appropriate searching of soul, how far we are from making some of these first and most essential applications of democracy even in the freest parts of the free world, we can be charitable toward others: charitable even toward some of the most resistant to the nonviolent Freedom Movement in our own country.

Democracy's signal failure has been the failure to trust democratic consent. It was in this failure that fascism in Europe arose. When the ruling elite could no longer trust ballots, it turned to bullets, justifying the move to dictatorship by saying, "But these people wanted revolution." Yes, they did. That was what our fore-fathers wanted. It is what our forefathers had. It is what every free spirit aspires to.

The twentieth-century world is one wherein social revolution is long overdue. This world revolutionary situation must be tempered through democratic reform and social change; democracy probably faces a necessity for the greatest forward movement for people's freedom in its history. It can survive only by taking the way of freedom for every last person on earth.

There can be no way or status quo which is preferable to democracy itself as the popular assertion of freedom, and the only way democracy can survive is by trusting the people. Democracy inheres not in military strength, in coercion, in intimidation, in dollar diplomacy, nor in usurpation or coalition of power, but in the strength and the will of the people. Democracy alone has the answer to the present upsurge of peoples all over the world, but democratic values are not furthered by a militarized bloc of nations, however loosely held together. We falsely worship power, centralization, efficiency! But democratic power is the power of the people.

It is time, therefore, that the people undertake their own moral and spiritual revolution to regain the controls which their government leaders, in a kind of demented fury of international piracy, are now flinging to the winds in utter disregard of all the things that are needed by the human race. No democracy exists on either side of arbitrary governmental acts — on the side of the receivers or the side of the dispensers of tyranny. It is important that people on both sides of the tyranny refuse to obey its demands.

Popular revolution by some effective method is the

very essence of democracy; most democracy in the world today originated in popular revolt against tyranny. Some form of revolt born of a need for social revision has spawned whatever Western democracy has existed. Every American schoolchild knows that our democracy began with our Revolutionary War, the War of Independence.

What is not so often recognized is that revolution has traditionally been the principle means for implementing democratic reform everywhere. Also, democracy is twice revolution: after being initiated by assertion of popular control, democracy next establishes itself as a political system, a legal framework for popular conquest of governmental power through peaceful conquest of public opinion. This absorption of governmental apparatus and authority by the popular will and its expression for the general well-being of all is the legal provision for continuous revolution through the method of peaceful persuasion. The degree of availability of this provision for peaceful and, if desired by the people, radical change of government is the basic criterion for determining the degree in which democracy can be realized under a particular political arrangement; democracy means that instruments of social and cultural revision rest in the hands of the common people.

Our country's mission should be that of leadership in bringing about a democratic world. As a whole, the nation vaguely conceives of that as her destiny. In heart and mind we Americans are still colonial. Before us lies all of the real American Frontier — a national and international realization of the original American spirit or dream.

We are fumbling in the eyes of the world, however; we have not been clear in our idea of democracy for other peoples because we are no longer clear in our idea of democracy for ourselves. The examination of our original great dream and of the present degree of realization of that dream can lead us into a new, vital and timely consideration of what it means to be democratic — for people, for states, for a world of nations.

FOOTNOTES CHAPTER ONE

1. *Goals for Americans: The Report of the President's Commission on National Goals* (New York: Prentice Hall, 1960).

2. "Exporting the American Revolution," *Saturday Review*, October 2, 1961, p. 49.

3. C. Wright Mills, *The Power Elite* (New York: Oxford University Press, 1956).

4. Francis Rufus Bellamy, "Washington's Answer to the Proposal That He Be Made King," in *We Hold These Truths* (New York: Grosset & Dunlap, 1942), p. 62.

5. W. E. Woodward, *A New American History* (New York: Garden City Pub. Co., 1938), pp. 427-432.

6. For a critical account of our international affairs, read Harry Elmer Barnes and Oreen M. Ruedi, "International Relations: Problems of Peace and War," in *The American Way of Life* (New York: Prentice Hall, 1950), pp. 433-455.

CHAPTER 2

THE AMERICAN DREAM

In Boston in 1773, a small group of colonial leaders met to wrestle with the problem of their diminishing freedom. Tyranny was hedging in the young colonies more and more; now Britain had added another insult by levying a tax on their tea. The people had decided at a town meeting to send back, still loaded, the British ship which had brought the tea, but the governor had refused to order the cargo returned.

After four hours, a sense of utter futility settled over the meeting. If the tea were unloaded at the Boston harbor, there would be those who — careless of their liberty, caring only that the price of this first shipment of taxed tea had been set low enough to make the tax more palatable — would buy it. Then one more link would be forged in the chain of oppression. How long would they continue to accept taxation without representation? How long would they continue to allow the will of the people, expressed at their town meeting, to be ignored by their government?

Finally a Negro in the group who had remained silent — it was Crispus Attucks, later the first American patriot killed in the Revolution — arose and said, "I have been sitting here all the time you have been talking, wondering how that tea would mix with salt water." The Boston

Tea Party was thus conceived; that long meeting turned from passive despair to active planning and led into our forefathers' dynamic pursuit of truth.

Hardship, tribulation, anguish and death in the Revolution that followed were the birth pangs of a nation that would embrace diversity in a spirit of unity — "a new nation, conceived in liberty." This Revolution was a seven-year Passion in Violence, Manhattan Island its Gethsemane and Valley Forge its Calvary. The spirit which led dedicated men through the suffering of that terrible winter of 1776-1777 was that of "the cross that turns not back."

That spirit was never better described than by Thomas Paine who, as a private at Valley Forge, inscribed it upon a drumhead.

> These are the times that try men's souls. The summer soldier and the sunshine patriot will, in this crisis, shrink from the service of his country; but he that stands it now, deserves the love and thanks of man and woman. Up and help us; lay your shoulder to the wheel . . . The heart that feels not now, is dead.[1]

Such was the dedication of these rebels to a new way called democracy which existed initially as a supreme faith — a faith called the American dream.

The dreams of men, pursued for the truth they possess, lead to practical historical performances. To confuse dreams with reality, however, is a danger; such confusion is the root of mental illness. In this sense, nations can be as ill as persons. Deep and realistic probing may help the patient or the nation to recognize the difference between the dream and the reality — the first step in the restoration of health.

We Americans need this realistic understanding; the tendency to confuse our ideals with reality is widespread. Many Americans believe that democracy is something already achieved. They think all that remains is to export democracy to other countries — by force, if necessary!

This assumption that democracy is a reality hinders the fulfillment of the dream. Progress toward the realization of democracy requires that the ideal not be confused with the facts, which have to be faced. To know the ideal is our responsibility; we must know our dream of freedom for what it is. We must also know how far we are from realizing this dream and what is keeping us from democratic realization. We must understand the plight of democracy and the crisis which faces it. This knowledge will enable us to get on with the business of fashioning a democratic world.

The American dream is a noble one. It is the vision of the ultimate realization for all mankind of equality, brotherhood and liberty under law. It sprang not from mere national patriotism, but from the determination of visionary men to achieve emancipation from all the fetters which can bind the human spirit — fetters of ignorance, fear, servility, deprivation, greed and shame.

In its nature, the democracy of the dream is applicable to every person. It was never thought of as something to be confined to any one nation, however great, because it is a goal for people — all people. It is a spirit and way which recognizes that no one is free while even one person is not free. Thus democracy can be fully realized only when extended to the last man and into every area of man's life.

This universality of application was emphasized in early American documents and writings. Thomas Jefferson recognized that the closest practical application of the original conception of democratic universality in his time existed in his own country. Abraham Lincoln, whom most students rank nearest Jefferson in the understanding of the ideology of original American democracy, made essentially the same observation. When Lincoln said that our fathers had "brought forth on this continent a new nation, conceived in liberty and dedicated to the proposition that all men are created equal," he was not using idle words. It was a statement of fact.

In its Declaration of Independence and its Constitution, the United States blazed a new and different trail for all nations, basing government on the strength of popular law. Several governments were provided for in the same Constitution, each to be servant in its own sphere of service to the people — local government, state government and national government. The American thus became a multicitizen and the only "sovereign" with respect to all his governments.

Although this dream of democracy is cherished in America, we seem unable to think democratically. Consider the way we call democratic countries "sovereign nations," even though our democratic credo begins with the assertion that there is no sovereignty save that of the people. Lincoln stated that when the government assumed sovereignty it should be destroyed by its citizens. He expressed the intention of the architects of democracy: government of the people, by the people and for the people.

Democracy in America thus started was far more than mere ideological conquest of the minds of men. It represented a basic switch in political thinking and implementation.

The new nation made another basic change in traditional political structures with its unique contribution of federalism. According to Felix S. Cohen, a leading authority on the American Indians, both Jefferson and Franklin derived their ideas of unity in diversity, which were incorporated into our governmental federalism, from their observations of the Five Nation Confederation.[2] Jefferson particularly was much impressed by the Iroquois' admirable system of government which, he pointed out, bore no resemblance to the modern European state.

This federation of Indian tribes — launched, according to legend, by the great sage and statesman, Hiawatha — remained hardy and maintained peace among the Iroquois along the Eastern Seaboard for three hundred years. Our federalism is similarly conducive to our national peace. We would consider it impossible for a loyal Ohioan to war against people of West Virginia or make border raids into Kentucky. Our federal type of organization of democracy has thus preserved for us some of the original universality of the great idea of democracy, but in a definitely limited measure of application.

Our approach to the issue of state and federal rights is another indication of our strange inability to think democratically. When the thirteen colonies created the federal government, they did not put the federal government above the individual colonies in a "sovereign" sense. Nor were the colonies above the federal government, even though they had existed before it and brought it into being. The states, as they came to be called, reserved to themselves on behalf of their people every area of responsibility that was not specifically assigned to the new national authority.[3]

The fact that we can argue which of these authorities, state or national, should be "sovereign" indicates how far we have drifted from the concept of democracy under which our federal system was created. The ideas we now discuss — that this authority is supreme, or the other authority, or that world authority may mean the surrender of some sovereignty — are precisely the difficulties from which the framers of the Constitution were trying to save us. They intended the national, state and local governments to be servants of the sovereign people, each in its own area prescribed constitutionally by law or conventionally by usage.

If we had preserved this basic principle of the original American dream, it would now be possible for us to grasp the present urgent need to assign the tasks of the additional area — democracy in world affairs — to a new servant, a world authority. Our inability to think democratically betrays us at this stage.

There is a school of historical realism led by some of the ablest political scientists of the last generation. Franz Oppenheimer in his valuable classic, *The State*,[4] and Albert J. Nock in his New Deal critique, *Our Enemy the State*,[5] represent this school at its best. These men use the term *government* to describe the people's democratic rule of law, which they distinguish from the modern state.

Oppenheimer traces the evolution of the state through the primitive and feudal states to the modern state. The position taken is that when one does not begin with some theory of the state's origin, as did both Rousseau and Marx, but simply examines the facts, the state is found to have evolved as the political instrument of power. Various exploiting groups snatched political power as a means of holding themselves in privilege and others in subjugation. The modern state, this school holds, is no exception to this development; indeed, it has enhanced the power of the political instrument through totalitarian development.

These historical realists agree with Thomas Jefferson's distinction between what he termed the jungle of states of Europe and the spirit of the young government in the new world. The idea of a government's existing for people, rather than for national power, wealth and fame, is relatively new and is still rare.

The distinction between the state as it historically evolved and the new kind of government, democracy, becomes clear from a study of the relation of the individual to the state. English democratic ideologists differ sharply from Americans in their approach to this relationship. The British attitude is that the people are in opposition to the state; this view assumes the validity of the sovereignty of rulers and ruling factions — a kind of carry-over of the "divine right" into democratic theory.

Human rights are not considered inalienable, but exist as concessions wrested from the always reluctant sovereign. Until won by the subjects, these rights inhered in the sovereign. They gradually became enshrined in laws, beginning with the Magna Charta, finally gaining ascendancy over the sovereign by virtue of the power gained by organized opposition.

The people as sovereign is a concept nonexistent in the prevailing English theory and practice of statecraft,

though it is to be found in some English writings.
Throughout the writings of Hobbes, the opposition of
the subjects to their state is implicit. Even Locke's *Two
Treatises on Government* was intended, he said, to "establish the throne . . . in the consent of the people."[6] The
people's revolutionary alertness to wrest additional rights
from the sovereign, and their eternal vigilance to keep
those won is, according to this view, the historically realistic foundation upon which democracy rests.

The English regard their concept of democratic theory as realistic and ours as idealistic. J. H. Morgan, an
English authority on constitutional law, writes:

> The sacramental words, "We, the people of the
> United States . . ." do not confer sovereignty on
> the people. The people who ordained and estab-
> lished the Constitution have no power to change it;
> a majority of the State Legislatures alone can do
> that. . . . Popular sovereignty is therefore apt to
> resolve itself, legally speaking, into a myth in any
> organized society. It is a purely primitive idea, be-
> longing to the days when . . . freemen of the German
> tribes decided every question with a loud shout and,
> we may surmise, by knocking the minority on the
> head. We may also find the idea of popular sov-
> ereignty in the Anglo-Saxon folkmote and the
> *Landesgemeinde* of the forest cantons of Switzer-
> land: we shall find it nowhere else."[7]

The British political scientist tends to regard as unreal
and sentimental the American concept that man alone
is sovereign, and that all just power resides with the
people and derives from their consent.

In contrast with the British view, Americans regard

themselves as sovereign rather than subject. In practice, we have drifted from our credo; in theory, the idea of the supremacy of the individual remains and is generally recognized. The American view of the state begins with the individual, in whom all sovereign power is inalienable. His rights are natural rights, inherent in the structure of human life and society. The American pictures his government as having no representatives but his own, no officials but his servants, no authority except that which he grants, and no will and destiny but the people's will and destiny. This remains the prevailing, if not realistic, view of the American citizen's relation to his state.

That human rights are inalienable because their origin is in man's natural state is the American democratic contention. Man lives uniquely by asserting his controlling character in relation to his environment and by gaining strength and security within social groups. From these two characteristics of natural man — his uniqueness as the controlling creature and his uniqueness as the social or community creature — four natural laws are evident. They may be stated as follows:

(1) *Man has a right to conscientious assertion.* The individual must be able conscientiously to assert his personal inner integrity, and conscientiously to object to whatever sullies his inner integrity or thwarts his growth. Such assertion is the psychological source of all human freedoms, obligations and — hence — development.

(2) *Man has a right to personal access.* The individual must have access to the means and materials necessary for the production of all the goods and services needed for fullest life, health and security;

and the fruits of men's labor must be shared in equity.

(3) *Man has a right to self-realization.* The individual must have the freedom and opportunity to be, to improve and to express himself.

(4) *Man has a right to socialization.* Human beings must be able voluntarily to associate (or dissociate) in extending group control over arrangements for shared enterprises.

These freedoms — to associate freely and organize mutual endeavor, to live and grow normally, to be "at home" on one's own earth, and to struggle to overthrow whatever defiles or annuls these rights — are the basis for democracy's basic concept: personal sovereignty extended through organization and protected by "revolution."

America has a tradition of partial acceptance of some of the rights implicit in these basic laws. Regarding conscientious assertion (in its negative form of conscientious objection), we began as a nation by claiming the democratic right of rebellion against arbitrary authority. We made no mention of this fundamental right in our Constitution or laws, however.

We did provide the democratic due processes by which the people can peacefully rid themselves of their unfaithful servants — arbitrary or irresponsible government administrations. This is in line with the first democratic right that we as a nation asserted — the right of overthrow — but in our Constitution and tradition this right is partial.[8] Our imaginations could conceive no possibility of extralegal resistance, even if and when this right became the only way remaining to free men, except the bloody kind of struggle out of which we as a nation emerged. We therefore were not prepared to give to conscientious assertion of the human spirit — the basic psychological democracy — a recognized place and dignity in our laws. This right was provided with constitutional legalization by the new Government of free India.

Lincoln, Jefferson and other great American statesmen have declared that it is not only our right but our duty to rise up and overthrow any government which is no longer responsive to the people's will. We are probably far less prepared today to meet this requirement, so fundamental to democracy, than we were when our nation began. At least partially, then, we have denied in our law that which made possible the birth of our nation.

The right of personal access was also never specifically recognized in our laws. At first, rights of access to earth, like the right to vote, was reserved to a few property owners. Duties and a modest share in the rewards were benevolently extended to a defenseless consuming public — the hireling class. The serious omission from our Constitution of this vast and crucial area of human rights remain to this day. We were initially saved from the disastrous results of this great defect by the availability of free land and an open frontier, but we made no legal provision to keep the earth available and accessible to man. On the contrary, we provided legally for its accumulation in large holdings, until land monopoly has become one of the most destructive monopolies to our economy and to the fulfillment of the American dream.

The third right, that of self-realization, was largely considered by our forefathers as a luxury for a privileged aristocracy. It was not enshrined in the Constitution except in fragmentary and innocuous form in the

Bill of Rights; to the domestic slaves of that day, even these moderate rights were denied, as they are still denied to many Americans. Accidental democracy existed in this area as long as the frontier alleviated this omission by offering some opportunities for self-realization. Our country is not now without such opportunities, but they are neither available to all citizens nor protected by law.

Early America did express the fourth freedom, the right to socialization, in its early local organizations. We still have extensive and influential voluntary associations of many kinds. Nevertheless, the early reality and hardiness of our American society has tended to fade out. No provision for the fulfillment of this right of intimate human association was enshrined in fundamental law; vital community, left to the hazard of circumstance in an age of centralization, has tended to give way to a nation of joiners and of mass-motivated people. In an age mainly careless of human values, the blind forces of centralization, militarization, urbanization and imperialism have turned us, along with all the West, away from individual participation in socialization to the use of mass media, mass processes, mass action and mass organization. The majority of people are therefore susceptible to mass psychology.

It is clear that only failure to think in terms of the basic principles of democracy could generate the common illusion that majority rule is democracy in action. The fact is that democracy now quails before this dangerous inner foe — the dictatorial majority.

Jefferson expressed his concern about this problem in his First Inaugural Address. He said that the new nation could retain the sacred principle of the will of the majority but that to be rightful, this will must be reasonable in permitting minorities to possess equal rights under law. The violation of minority rights would be oppression.[9]

It is easier to keep alive the majority than the minority in a democracy, but it is more important to keep the minority alive; without it, democracy is impossible. A majority can preserve the democracy which brought it into power only by maintaining the rights of each minority which may desire to overthrow the majority. This basic principle of democracy applies to all, including members of the Communist Party and those of the John Birch Society. To destroy democratic processes for any is to destroy those processes for all.

William James, whom Horace Kallen calls the "most renowned and representative of the thinkers of America,"[10] found his answer to this problem of democracy in a common habit of the democracy of English descent — "the habit of trained and disciplined good temper toward the opposite party when it fairly wins its innings."[11] The training and good discipline called democracy allow the opposition, the minority, all the advantages the majority had and used to achieve its position. No democratic people can close the democratic way to anyone. Those who gain power must keep open the way for loss of it, or lose democracy itself.

It is deceptive to think that this dilemma of democracy is a product of the developing complexity of society or of changing modern demands. Many of Jefferson's contemporaries were not ready to trust democracy. There were those at that time who were bent, out of their natural fears and as a matter of necessary defense, upon the abandoning of the republican form of government almost as soon as it was created.

European powers had territorial possessions and armies on this continent. Danger from these forces was imminent and real. Some who were responsible for the young nation were afraid to entrust her to a people's government. Jefferson's fiercest opponents held some things dearer than democracy and wanted to protect these things from the people. Some were in the imperial business of world trade; some were profiting from the slave traffic; for these and other reasons, they feared to trust government in the hands of the people.

The basis of these fears was expressed by Thomas Paine in *The Rights of Man.*

> No sooner did the American governments display themselves to the world than despotism felt a shock. and man began to contemplate redress. . . . What Archimedes said of the mechanical powers may be applied to reason and liberty: "Had we," he said, "a place to stand upon, we might raise the world. . . ." The revolution in America presented in politics what was only theory in mechanics. So deeply rooted were all the governments of the Old World, and so effectually had the tyranny and the antiquity of habit been established over the mind, that no beginning could be made in Asia, Africa or Europe to reform the political condition of man. Freedom had been hunted round the globe; reason was considered as rebellion; and slavery of fear had made men afraid to think.[12]

Jefferson was full of confidence in the great idea of democracy. He was called upon to jail dissenters — to preserve the new nation by using the protective measures of a police state. He could have taken the step which appears all too attractive today: the rounding up of the threatening violators or the leaders of the opposition. That course, while protecting the country from foreign invasion and domestic enemies, would not have been the democratic answer. That course would have dissolved the democracy it was intended to save and started a national career similar to those of certain other "republics" which have never known real democracy.

We may be thankful that the wisdom of Jefferson prevailed over the unwise counsel of those who sought to defend the new nation with other than democratic security measures. In his First Inaugural Address he said,

> During the throes and convulsions of the ancient world, during the agonizing spasms of infuriated man seeking through blood and slaughter his long-lost liberty, it was not wonderful that the agitation of the billows (from Europe's stormy ocean) should reach even this distant and peaceful shore; that this should be more felt and feared by some and less by others, and should divide opinions as to measures of safety. . . . If there be any among us who would wish to dissolve this union or to change its republican form, let them stand undisturbed as monuments of the safety with which error of opinion may be tolerated where reason is left free to combat it.[13]

How can we resist, except with Jefferson's way of preserving democracy itself, "the midnight knock on the door and the total disappearance into the night?" Oppressions are the result of betrayals from within, the abuses of authority. Any one-party or one-idea authority is on the road to totalitarianism.

Totalitarianism is the temptation of the majority; it is the majority's betrayal of its democratic faith. In its numerous forms, totalitarianism seeks to eliminate political opposition to the policies of those in power. Fascism, an expression of this form of government, is a relatively new name applied to an old tyranny. This tyranny was practically universal in the "republics" of the West at the time democracy "brought forth on this continent a new nation, conceived in liberty . . ."

Unlike fascism and other statisms, democracy never remains in static condition. Many seem to consider democracy a set of fixed cultural patterns which can be defended across boundaries and extended by invasion, seizure, occupation, thought control and so on, just as imperial or totalitarian control is extended over people.

Democracy can never be equated with any static way of life. Any rigid way of living is sure to result in the curtailment of certain civil rights. The persons whose civil rights are diminished are invariably the ones who oppose policies regarded as more important than democracy itself. This lessening of civil rights for some groups or persons is accomplished by the coercive powers of the state for the sake of national security, national advancement, or another generally accepted cause.

Historically, this sequence of events has always been the camel's nose of fascism in the democratic tent. Even those majorities who have gained power democratically tend to change the democracy by degrees, under subtle pressures of "emergencies," into a police state. This temptation of the majority is an inner betrayal more to be feared than all enemies from without. The basic perjury is the claim to be defending democracy by withholding civil liberties. The elimination of opposition is as basic to all brands of totalitarianism as is the right of opposition to every possible arrangement of democracy.

A society wherein a few have power to determine a way of life for other people while calling itself a democracy is self-contradictory. It is not a democracy, whether the power elite is of the capitalist bankers, militarists, or bureaucrats, or of all of them, or whether the power elite are called proletarians.

Both fascism and communism are now making spurious use of the term democracy. Fascism presents capitalism and says, "This is it." Communism presents socialism (state capitalism) and says, "This is it." Both remove all choice from the people; both deny the essence of democracy: popular sovereignty, freedom of the people to choose their own methods, and the reign of law over all governmental powers and procedures.

Not only such ideologies as communism and fascism are dangerous. The very idea of a blueprint for living is the major menace, because it is a contradiction of democracy. Democracy is not an absolutism of any kind. Democracy is the way of freedom from all absolutisms which might fetter the human spirit. If the people do not choose or cannot change their way of life, they do not enjoy true democracy. This menace has been no respecter of governments on either side of any iron curtain.

Historically, democracy has resulted in political and economic eclecticism; it has chosen from whatever source it could without fear or favor. Democracy is not a substance or content of any way of life; it is a method, determined by popular experimentation. It is people experimenting on their own behalf. The people's freedom to experiment, choose, change, discard and experiment again is the only political democracy. We the people are the only America.

The American dream is not a political concept but a vision of the potential of the human spirit. In its democracy, it sees free man organizing himself as a responsible citizen within his free institutions, master of his own destiny. It sees him shaping his society, developing his methods as he experiments and learns. In his freely chosen means to his freely chosen goals, it sees those "invisible molecular moral forces that work from individual to individual . . . which, if you give them time, will rend the hardest monuments of man's pride."[14]

When Jefferson preserved the democracy of the American dream with full confidence in its inherent strength and rightness, he was facing strong threats at home and from Europe. Are we confronting some menace in our day which makes it impossible to hold to the principles which gave birth to and sustained democracy? By what path have we strayed so far from the vision of freedom and fulfillment for all men which was our origin, our greatness and our pride?

FOOTNOTES CHAPTER TWO

1. Francis Rufus Bellamy, *We Hold These Truths* (New York: Grosset & Dunlap, 1942), p. 43.

2. Felix S. Cohen, "Americanizing the White Man," *The American Scholar,* Spring 1952, pp. 177-191.

3. See Articles IX and X (Amendments to the Constitution), the last two of the original Bill of Rights.

4. Franz Oppenheimer, *The State* (New York: Vanguard Press, 1926).

5. Albert Jay Nock, *Our Enemy the State* (New York: William Morrow & Co., 1935). This is one of the most scientific criticisms of the centralist tendencies of some New Deal experiments.

6. Encyclopaedia Britannica (14th ed.), XIV, 271.

7. J. H. Morgan, "Constitution and Constitution Law," Encyclopaedia Britannica (14th ed.), VI, 317.

8. The order of logic with which Americans supported their rebellion in the Revolutionary War is (1) the state of nature, (2) the social contract, (3) the broken contract (government arbitrary or on its own), and (4) the right of revolution. For a good summary see Mosher and Associates, *Responsible Citizenship* (New York: Henry Holt & Co., 1941), pp. 647-653 and 665-667.

9. Bellamy, *op. cit.,* p. 43.

10. Horace Meyer Kallen, "William James," Encyclopedia Britannica (14th ed.), XXI, 883.

11. Kallen, *The Philosophy of William James* (New York: Random House, undated), pp. 312-315.

12. Bellamy, *op. cit.,* pp. 44-45.

13. *Ibid.,* p. 106.

14. Kallen, *The Philosophy of William James,* p. 310.

CHAPTER 3

LIBERALISM AND TOTALITARIANISM

The West as we know it today was brought into being through a great spiritual awakening. This awakening was responsible for the features that mark the West as modern; its prevailing characteristic was liberalism. The original spirit and purpose of this liberalism contrast strongly with its historic development; from the first, the awakening was harassed and distracted by ancient tyrannies.

Liberalism, the great mother spirit of the time, both brought to birth her own children of the new age and took into her family the inherited scapegraces of an earlier lineage. The history of her household is the record of two diverse families under one roof. Her early enthusiasms and formulations were concerned with her favorites, the children of her own being — democracy, free enterprise, and the quest for truth in science and religion. But her most influential children were those of the ancient stock, taken by adoption into the new family — class consciousness, imperialism, absolute nationalism, the *Herrenvolk* mind, violence, coercion, and religious conformity.

These adopted children, older and better known, came steadily to the fore, increasingly shaping the family fortunes. They busied themselves with confining the awakening world to the old ways, while liberalism was preoccupied with the development of her own favorite offspring. Thus it was inevitable that the outlook of liberalism should become dichotomous. The Western world suffered the contradiction between the way of life of liberalism's inherited brood and the way of thought of the genuine spirit and children of liberalism.

Under liberalism's administration, there was neither rethinking nor reformulating of her ideology in spite of a century of increasing conflict. Nor did her family seem to learn anything from the revolts against their disorderliness. There were great souls who saw all that was happening, but their warnings went unheeded. India's success in using nonviolence as a new and democratic method for overthrowing tyranny apparently meant nothing to liberalism. Her children snubbed socialism's concept of broadening the application of democracy to include economics and drove socialism into the arms of the totalitarian left. Totalitarianism of the right then emerged out of fear of the totalitarian left, and out of fear that people might be led to take democracy seriously.

Liberalism's far-flung family never bridged the chasm between their ways of life and liberalism's ideology. Instead, early ideals were elevated into a great and cherished dream, while their ways of life grew ever more distant from their announced intentions. The complexity, collectivism, and centralization to which liberalism's brood of alien spirits led have now even caused liberalism to waver between the continued cherishing of her great dream and its outright abandonment.

This crisis of internecine and fratricidal strife is rooted in the national versus international struggle peculiar to this age. The birthright children of liberalism are universals. The search for truth in science and religion, democracy, and free enterprise are for all men; they lead to freedom for the whole human community. The inherited, feuding members of liberalism's family are of more parochial lineage.

Meanwhile, time itself has joined forces with the genuine offspring of liberalism: today's realities are international realities, while whipped-up fictions of national concerns — still psychologically potent — are survivals of a past which tolerated them at its own great expense.

The popular revolution that was liberalism's own way of gaining ascendancy has burst and showered into manifold revolt against her overbearing brood in every part of the world: national revolt against imperialism, international revolt against nationalism, nonviolent revolt against irresponsible authority, socialist revolt against tyrannical economics, religious revolt against neopaganism and irrelevant hope, and revolt of the colored peoples against the arrogant superiority and domination of the white race.

Democracy, born of liberalism and nourished by American pioneers, was under particular attack from the adopted members who could not thrive if democracy grew strong and healthy. Based on the new spirit and outlook of liberalism, democracy tried against overwhelming odds to usher in a great new age which is still in the future. We tend to confuse this democracy of the great American dream with a political emergence of history.

At the time of the awakening from which liberalism

sprang, the Western world was the competitive, nationalistic world of modern imperialism, great trade rivalries and living by wars — of looting, pillaging and enslavement. Europe was a bedlam of competing and often warring states; their competitions had already extended into the New World.

Modern Western democracy came into such a world and was made an instrument of existing institutions and practices. The modern world was already set and rigidly fixed by preponderance of influence. Instead of being able to replace the old order as its inevitable opposite, the new order was able to survive in slight measure in Europe and in a greater measure in England and the United States only by accommodating itself within the old order. Thus aggressive, expansionistic states chiefly determined the future of political democracy as well as the structure and processes of modern Western society.

The modern West's initial deviation from democratic processes was the admission to its governing processes of the spirit of autocracy, the special evil which democracy had originally sought to expel from affairs of governments. This political power over people assumed new and enhanced forms and strengths, some no longer regarded as governmental. The autocracy in government arose out of Europe, which had already sent forth into every land another greater and more determining tradition, the trading company.

What we call imperialism preceded both capitalism and democracy and furnished the mold in which both were cast. European patriots, fleeing from tyranny of both church and state, were settled in America by trading companies which had already carved out their spheres of domination, and which were the international agencies of the very tyrannies from which the people were fleeing. The same ships brought free men on upper decks and men in bondage in their holds; aristocrats and slaves were among the immigrants to the New World.

While some of our forefathers were urging universal fulfillment of democracy, enterprising settlers preferred to make the new nation into an expansionistic businessman's empire. (Later they proposed that it should ultimately rival all the other empires of earth.) This obsession was enhanced by the pioneering fever to get rich.

The self-contradiction that brought slaves to the land of liberty arose from the West's divided nature and continues to hamper the noble experiment of Western democracy. The ideal of democracy was to fulfill human brotherhood in all the organizations of all the people. As in all nations, however, such democracy as has developed in this country has been limited: democracy for European invaders but not for the native American Indians; democracy for the whites but not for the Africans seized and imported as booty; democracy for domestic capitalistic economic empires but not for the foreign places of their investments and exploitations. Every institution of our social order is implicated in this fundamental contradiction. We deal out indifference, unequal opportunity and exploitation with one hand and with the other, aid and compassion.

William James perceived that the crisis of democracy, already apparent during the Civil War, was an inevitable result of the self-contradiction imbedded in Western culture. This evil, James said, because not dealt with in time, had "wrought until at last the only alternative for the nation was to fight or die."[1] Lincoln reminded Americans that this nation was trying to do two utterly incompatible things: to defend — in his own striking figure — freedom for the fox and the rabbit at the same time.

The twentieth century is facing on an international scale the same crisis that produced our Civil War. It is the crisis of Western self-contradiction. Today this world contest is not between democracy and communism. It is between democracy and totalitarianism. The democracies face totalitarianism on both their left and right. They have not yet found a democratic answer to this threat, for to line up with either totalitarianism of left or right against the other, or to employ their methods, is to fall with them into the same ditch.

In this age, characterized by a preference for force over either law or peace, it is crucial to see revolution of left, counterrevolution of right, and democracy's own revolution — the worldwide revolt of peoples — in their true perspectives.

Revolution on the left and counterrevolution from the right appeared in the second and third decades of this century as outcomes of the First World War. Although they appear to be monstrous opposite extremes in the present crisis, both are contenders for dictatorial or undemocratic power; neither is a popular democratic revolution. Both surrender claim to being defenders of the democratic tradition or way of life because the objective of each is to seize political control in terms of a state supreme over the people; both thus deny the sovereignty of the people. Neither is popular in the sense that it trusts the people. Both are totalitarian by definition, despite the names they use, because both use force to regiment people, to stifle the spirit of opposition, and to destroy the means for making opposition effective in government. Fascist capitalism and Soviet communism are seemingly ideological opposites. They are alike, however, in that each prefers its ideological absolute and its particular way of life to the democratic tradition and way.

Dr. Eddy Asirvathan, India's outstanding international expert, said that in his opinion the Soviet Union does not represent an ideology distinctly different from that of the West. He said that the best term for the economic structure of the Soviet Union is bureaucratic capitalism. Politically, the Soviet Union has developed national totalitarianism; only this political development could make the economic one possible. The attempt to define what the Soviet Union has become presents many semantic difficulties; it is clear, however, that Soviet communism has over the years become so like Nazism and fascism as to result in essentially the same kind of state, albeit beginning on the left instead of on the right: the same strong man in control, the same single party, the same stifling of all opposition to the power elite, the same whipped-up chauvinism, the same nationalistic aggressions and dominations.

Neither one of these destructive forces — fascism or communism — has ever been limited to particular nations or areas; both are within the class-ridden nature of Western culture. Both are enemies of democracy, and the use by both of the name democracy must be repudiated.

We have now reached a stage in history when both attack democracy, one on its right and one on its left flank. They are so much alike in both structure and method that they probably could meet in their common desire to end democratic rights, particularly the basic democratic idea that both law and the popular will must be above the state. Such accord between these opposite extremes did occur briefly in the early part of the Second World War; it might have continued but for Hitler's sudden and inexplicable change of heart. It may be supposed that it was agreed that Europe should be united under an iron heel in order to stamp out the last remnant of democracy. And why not? Fascism holds democracy in utmost contempt, as was made clear in Hitler's book, *Mein Kampf;* communism regards democracy as bourgeois, hypocritical and decadent.

It cannot be too strongly emphasized that both of these monstrous evils, in both method (the use of state's powers to coerce and regiment people) and form (the dictatorial state), are outside the streams of historic democratic tradition. They put themselves outside that tradition by the substitution of force for law and the assumption of centralized power over people. Each is making its attack upon democracy from outside that tradition, from the side of its particular class interests.

To the left, communism would establish a social order professing to be for the people by using the coercive powers of a totalitarian state in betrayal of government by the people. Slavery has always been for people but never by them. To the right, by the same betrayal of government by and for the people, fascism would defend itself against the menace of communism's claim to popular revolution. The John Birch Society is showing our nation the danger of choosing the totalitarian way on the right simply from a fear of communism.

It was in this supposed defense against the menace of communism that Nazism and Fascism arose on the continent of Europe. In the same supposed defense of Europe, the democracies, freely offering collaboration under the policy called nonintervention, permitted Nazism and fascism to destroy the legitimate government in Spain and to replace it with a fascist government.

Europe practically surrendered to fascism in this strange defense against communism; later, during a great wave of artificially maneuvered and spurious anticommunism, most of the armed forces of the West were used to stamp out legitimate revolt in every part of the world. Fascism was conceived and brought to birth by the frankest betrayers of democracy, by governments which particularly rose to power by going all out for this illusion of defense. What they defended, of course, could no longer be democracy, but totalitarianism. The way of democratic law and the way of security by war are philosophical incompatibles.

Even communism can be regarded as a direct outgrowth of the general betrayal of the democratic faith. Steadily, democracies have been destroying themselves and their democracy by shifting their base of security from people to states. Steadily, they have been shifting from faith in people and reliance upon the power which is ultimately only in the people, to faith in and reliance upon arbitrary power imposed upon the people. There is less and less difference, in this shift from law as the final arbiter to force as the final arbiter, between those nations calling themselves democracies and those frankly asserting themselves to be dictatorial.

Democracy is thus steadily being forced to find another line which it can draw and another kind of bulwark for its defense than that sought by nations which strive for security through developing preponderant force. Security through collective power is probably the supreme fallacy of the West. It is advanced only to fore-stall the necessity of extending democracy where it has not yet gone: into geographical and human waste-lands of man's inhumanity. Withholding democracy is its destruction; extending it is its only defense. Though difficult for the force-minded to grasp, this is neverthe-less the basic reality about democracy. It can be saved only by its realistic extension both geographically where it has not been known and socially where it has not been applied. If democracy had been fully realized in only one of the great nations that have called themselves dem-ocratic, the whole story of the first half of the twentieth century might have been very different.

We tend to think that certain evils which we call totalitarianism are far from our shores. We say we in-tend to keep them there with our sheer brute strength. But as we go all out for this strength, and because we do so, totalitarianism, a menace of all liberties, appears and grows strong within our borders.

The modern West has betrayed its original purpose. It has arrived at its present reckless course toward self-annihilation through aberration from the spirit, method, and substance of its own democratic liberalism which gave birth to its basic way of life. The modern West is now driven on its course by great machine-like, super-collective systems which are the result of its default and not inevitable outcomes of technology and complex modernization.

In an era of encroaching centralized organizations, the challenge to democratic nations demands that com-mon man keep himself sufficiently alert and intelligent to govern himself. Can planning be assumed by responsible citizens where they associate in their common responsibilities? Many, if not most, of the trends of Western society are in significant ways running counter to the operation of any organization of people which would seriously attempt to implement democracy as a way of life. If many of these trends, such as Pentagon influence upon foreign policy and upon higher education and scientific research, are not curtailed or eliminated altogether, this nation will, with other Western nations, continue steadily toward various forms of totalitarianism — its concentration camps, its total conscription, its Gestapo, its police-state inquisition, and the surrender of democratic rule of law to reliance upon physical force. Each of these we have already had in fairly well-developed forms within the United States.

The conformity apparent in education is closely allied with the desire of the ruling elite to eliminate opposition. Conformity has had its normal place in all societies, but in Western society the drive to inculcate conformity is absorbing more and more of the energies of those in control. Seldom has conformity reached such a degree of perverted use as that which now pervades great areas of modern education. It replaces preparation for democratic citizenship with a forced uniformity of mentality and habits. As the student becomes less like himself, not knowing what he knows nor what he is able to do, he becomes more capable of acting only as the crowd will act. Strange preparation for democratic citizenship!

In making "state control of education" a shibboleth in the name of democracy, we have forgotten that dictatorial rulers in Europe began that very use of education long before their bold snatching of the political instrument of power. We have forgotten, too, that democratic education has always provided the key to its own nature in the right of personal, family and group choice of education as fundamental to all other freedoms involving choice. Denmark has for many years supported the famous "folk high schools." The funds for education go with the pupil to the school of his choice. These schools are all private, but they rise and fall with the popular support of a "folk movement."

The right of educational dissent from the will of any imposed authority is the most basic element in democratic education. To it all other important elements, such as separation of church from state, are merely supplementary. Hitler presumably separated his state education from all religion; the value in this for democracy was nil. Dealing with educational problems on superficial levels instead of in terms of democratic principles leads to much sound and fury signifying little for the enlightenment of people and still less for the strengthening of democracy.

In the West, the state's education is tending to become one of the revolving parts in the mass production of human beings. There are some who would now like to complete this changeover in short order and end all dissent. Such an educational system would operate on the principle that man exists for the institution, not the institution for man.

The great hope is now dead that the West can have a democratic world and a tyrannical world at the same time. It will not help us to continue to deceive ourselves that we are the champions of liberty elsewhere, as we rapidly surrender liberty at home. Western man cannot serve two masters. If he cares for democracy's rule of law, he will have to repudiate autocracy's rule of force.

He cannot cleave to the latter in defense of the former; the only bulwark of freedom is its inner integrity.

At a time when popular revolt against tyranny is in order as never before in democracy's history, it becomes increasingly impossible to carry through that revolt with violence, without further strengthening the great destroyers of the people's freedoms. By use of violence, people automatically put themselves in one of the enemy camps and destroy their own liberties. This struggle is in our world, within our nation, and within every American citizen. Every one of us has to answer whether we want to take the way of the totalitarian elimination of all opposition to a single predetermined blueprint for society.

There is a tendency for nations or peoples to become like that which they resist. The strength of the tendency is proportionate to the strength of the resistance, and the characteristics taken on tend to be those most disapproved in the antagonist. This tendency recurs in human history and probably relates to every type of human antagonism. The nations which have gone the way of total war are those which have been most involved in putting down totalitarian, or total war, states.

Note the present likenesses between the United States and her cold war opponent: reliance upon force instead of law, abandonment of reliance upon popular consent, elimination of opposition, use of intimidation and fear, reliance upon secret police and espionage agencies, pressures upon the judiciary, and finally, marshalling of the people into the increasing controls, levies and regimentations of the totalitarian and collective state regime. All of these, most deplored by us in other nations, we have already in some measure assimilated.

To some degree, every nation in the Western world is taking on the same frightening aspect. Gandhi referred to this fact in his open letter to Britain on the eve of World War II: "You cannot destroy Hitlerism by its indifferent adoption." Vast machine-states, in their opposition to one another for survival through world supremacy, have become so like each other that they have used capitalism, imperialism, democracy, socialism, communism, totalitarianism and collectivism as terms to be hurled indiscriminately as shibboleths or as missiles, not as words to convey intelligent meaning.

Karl Marx said that the state, as it grew into the superstate, would destroy itself; the superstate tends to destroy itself whether of capitalist, communist, or any other persuasion. This age is one of collective, leviathan blocs of states, as indicated by the rise of both the totalitarianism of the right and the totalitarianism of the left. Such powers are self-destructive because they exist upon the great self-contradiction of denying within their systems whatever strength they have actually relied upon.

Because their method is force, they do not want international order based on law. The collectivism is thus only a colossal expansion of monolithic unilateralism which robs others, with itself, of that which makes free association in a society of nations possible. Such dominant powers fear granting even a little independence.

What we call neutralism is a desire to shake off all relations with any such circling monster. The prospect of a final battle of such giants is not a happy one, for with nuclear missiles the possibility of self-destruction is spelled out.

Nowhere in the world can people be expected to

give their lives willingly to uphold this battle of power giants. As people's understanding of the situation increases, it will require more and more coercion to induce them to support their own or other people's enslavement. We see now the adoption of a new order of defense which disregards the people. Regimentation of all the people, compulsory employment, the secret political police, loyalty tests, legal banning of strikes and the final, frank elimination of all popular opposition — these are its symptoms.

This new order of defense is now common, in varying measure, in all parts of the West. The United States has peace-time conscription, ever-extending secret political police, loyalty oaths, inquisition-type investigating bodies which negate due processes, and concentration camps in readiness in various parts of the country to take care of prison overflow in time of "emergency."

Centralized control over man is the many-headed monster which now stands astride our world. Only by liberalizing all our institutions, including our government, making them exist only of, by and for the people, can we return to or conserve anything of value which democracy historically set forth. And it is only when one starts with determination on this journey of the mind that one can know how very far Western society has drifted from its original liberalism and her distinguished offspring — democracy, free enterprise, and the search for truth in science and religion.

FOOTNOTES CHAPTER THREE

    1. *Ibid.,* pp. 312-315.

CHAPTER 4

NATIONALISM AND PERSONAL ALLEGIANCE

Nationalism is a significant human value. To be sure, it is tarnished with the aggressions, dominations and militarisms of an ancient, outmoded age. Further, it is now threatened by self-destruction; the nations are their own worst enemies.

The highest responsibility of a citizen has become the act of trying to save his nation from itself; saving nations from their present suicidal madness is the great new meaning of modern democratic citizenship. This is the national loyalty of significance today; this only the world's people can do. That this loyalty aligns itself with loyalty to humanity is but a fruit issuing from the realities of the present world situation.

Nationalism exists best when free of all aggressiveness; such nationalism is, in fact, the only building material out of which an effective internationalism can be created. The purposes of all nations can best be served through a cooperative world order maintained as unity in great diversity, and by and for all mankind.

The West is offering its people no alternative to the prevailing political outlook which thwarts them in their attempt to rise above today's national barriers to world order and peace. The people cannot serve two masters. They cannot work for world government and at the same time support their nation's unilateral power-quest and struggle. Nationalism itself is not at fault and can be strengthened by the union afforded in a genuine world association.

Nationalism has never been inconsistent with either internationalism or worldwide cooperation. As Gandhi often said, no country that has not attained its national-ism is able to make any contribution to internationalism. He also said that the country that restrains other nations from attaining nationalism is even less able to make any contribution to internationalism, because free asso-ciation is possible only among nations of equal status. Historically, some of the noblest and most robust nations have demonstrated that a genuine, strong nationalism can also be internationalistic — consider Sweden, Switzer-land and Denmark, among others.

It is the use to which Western culture has put na-tionalism — making it absolute, competitive, aggressive against others, and unilateral in its decisions — which has halted democracy at national boundaries. While the realities of our age make for an international oneness of the whole human family, nationalism is being used to set artificial limits and maintain old barriers. It is being used to interfere with those things which help men know and understand each other. Trade, science, invention, communication, travel, art, education, industry — all are potential battering rams for use against the barriers which divide men. But all such internationalizing agencies are themselves thwarted continuously, crammed into the old aggressively racialistic and nationalistic molds.

In spite of a measure of voluntary cooperation of nations through the United Nations, chaos reigns in international affairs. People are forbidden democratic struggle or expression that looks toward the end of the false uses being made of their nationalisms. Forms of collective action for security, or advantage through power blocs which struggle to accumulate influence in their own favor, intensify the chaos in the world. No alternative is being presented to the each-against-all basic nature of Western aggressive nationalism. Although democracy wants more than anything else to prevail in the world, it has been barred from fulfillment both abroad and at home by having its popular strength confined within geographical nationalisms.

Democracy cannot support the nationalism which shows itself in devastating application as a *Herrenvolk* aberration, capable of existing in fury within the minds of men who are mass-controlled by centralized authority. Nor can democracy support nationalism which expands with inevitable drives for maximum inequality in the nation's own favor, for exploitation of the weak, for domination and tyranny, for trade conquest, for military preeminence, for wars and cold wars, and for all the other elements of nationalistic aggression. For democracy, these are self-contradictions. For the war state abroad, no self-contradiction is involved, but the war state abroad inevitably becomes the police state at home. Within such a state we can observe the steady erosion of democracy where it once may have thrived. The freedoms are shelved as "inadequate for the necessary security."

The centralized nationalism of the Western democratic powers has reached an ominous circle of evil which may now have to be broken if either democracy or Western civilization is to survive. Despite all specious pretense and even use of world organization, the competitive nature of nationalisms has been whipped up as never before. The current sense of crisis leads toward maximum centralization of governmental power, the utmost efficiency, of course, being in a one-man reign. Thus we have had the return of the West to autocracy and dictatorship. Trigger-action efficiency requires total preparedness; total preparedness demands regimentation of the people. It also requires that any opposition be crushed by the police power of the state.

This process always begins with loyalty oaths and inquisitorial bodies which enable the government to keep up a show of due processes in courts after the substance of democracy has disintegrated. Strategic materials in every part of the world must be controlled in order to keep them from the enemy; strategic bases all over the world must be acquired. Far-flung influence and alliances must be developed. Local governments must be manipulated and, in some cases, populations expelled against their will. Artificial crisis situations were developed for such manipulative purposes in Vieques (Puerto Rico), Guatemala, Iran, Greece, British Guiana, East Pakistan, Okinawa and other places.

Of course, all is in the interest of "defense" — as someone put it, "defense against existence." Our confusion is indicated by the fact that we can talk "coexistence" and "massive retaliation" at the same time, while rationalizing our schizophrenia by terming it "negotiation through strength." But we ourselves do not know what we mean.

The heart of this circle of evil is fear of opposition;

fear of the democratic processes normally fulfilling themselves in world terms; fear of what will happen if people really assert sovereign control over the organization of their lives and of society. Some people never felt safe with democracy even while it remained a ready instrument for gaining benefits for themselves. The stepped-up madness of this circle of evil arises from the desperate attempt on the part of various absolutistic social systems to do the same thing that the older theological absolutism did before: to crush all opposition. All the modern political absolutisms have in common the belief that "thus saith the State" is the means of their dominance. All alike fear democracy. Toynbee described the nation-state as the man-made idol of the West before which its maker, Western man, offers himself as human sacrifice.

If this circle of evil of Western society is examined, not a single element can be found which centers in people and their importance, their influence or their sovereignty. The core of this philosophy is that the individual exists for the institution, not the institution for the individual, even that the institution is the repository of democracy!

The conclusion is that totalitarianism, both Bismarckian (German imperial) and Marxist (scientific socialist), arose out of the same Hegelian conception of the state as "consummation of man as finite,"[1] and is but the natural and inevitable offspring of the madness which led the West into the present world crisis.

National imperialism, the term used by historian Carlton Hayes, developed throughout the nineteenth century as Europe's way of life.[2] The New World faced it deep within its own folkways. The whole world had become the European white man's empire; the early American Colonies were no exception. Fear mounted that these intense and extensive rivalries would erupt into terrible wars in Europe.

A result of this prevailing fear was the development of the Concert of Europe by the great powers. The Concert was designed to facilitate worldwide conquests without incurring devastating wars. It is ironical that even the Geneva Convention and the International Red Cross were intended by the Concert to institute merciful arrangements on the battlefields of the future wars which they regarded as inevitable. On the popular front, however, they encouraged a "peace deceit" to grow; it became almost universal by the end of the century. Many even thought the Concert would grow into a parliament of the world and that wars would be no more. Yet all that time, almost uninterrupted aggression was carried to the very ends of the earth. Nevertheless, by a brutally frank booty-swapping policy, the Concert did succeed over a considerable period in Asia, Africa and the Middle East in achieving its twofold end of carving up most of the rest of the world while maintaining "peace" at home and abroad.

The feared inevitable began to emerge before the end of the century while millions were still dreaming of the coming age foretold by the prophets. The Concert gave way to competitive militarization (for national defense in each country, of course), and this, in turn, to the struggle for power which exploded into World War I. This and the following one were world wars because the systems being defended were world systems. Great as was the fear of war, the reluctance to surrender empire systems as the condition of international organization and peace was far greater. It still is.

There is plenty of evidence to support the incompatibility of selfish national interests with truly democratic interests. Because of business interests, democracy has been withheld from important areas of fulfillment. For example, industry is autocratic, for the most part, and democracy has had to inch its way — for the very few inches it has penetrated — into this stronghold of reaction and tyranny. Further, because of business interests, democracy has also been withheld politically and economically in every geographical area where business empires sought to establish their favorable inequalities of advantages, concessions, holdings (not in equity), and essentially forced labor. Arthur Morgan, famous engineer, educator and community sociologist, has set forth clearly this picture of affairs in today's world:

> Today three social orders are struggling for world supremacy. One of these is democracy, one is communist dictatorship, and the third is special privilege. If each of these systems should stand and be judged by itself, pure and unadulterated, men would have no trouble in choosing, and I have no doubt they would choose democracy.[3]

If it be true that at one stage in certain areas of the world this special privilege deliberately hired international gangsters to develop for them their Axis powers (one of them wrote a book titled *I Paid Hitler*), then we begin to see how complete on both the right and the left may be the abandonment of any democratic way. We see how dangerous is our position while we stand, as if paralyzed, nationalistically balked by our hesitations from establishing the universal concept of democracy in its final and full application — a democratic world order.

The clashing ideologies of this age may be contenders for national ascendancy in this or that place, but all of them now regard their goal in terms of one world. Each gives evidence of growing worldwide pressure against national policies and politics: today the battle of the ideologies is on a world front. The Registry of World Citizens, with its millions in over fifty countries, and the various organizations of the World Government movement are a further indication of this reality.

Because this is now one world, democracy can no longer be confined to national borders. All the significant aspects of nationalism, if they are to be preserved, must be made meaningful in international relationships. The only international way is the way of law, producing solidarity amidst variance — our original unity in diversity. This is the American way which frank repudiation of the European way brought forth upon our shores. We cannot now fulfill or even keep that American way except through its application in all international affairs. This also is the only possible way of saving from destruction whatever national qualities are worth saving.

The original democratic ideal included the concept of multicitizenship — the simultaneous experiencing of local, state and national citizenship. In the light of today's realities, the remaining logical step, world citizenship, seems the one hopeful political alternative to the cold war power struggle. The highest possible American patriotism can be realized as world democratic citizenship; how can we be good United States citizens if we resist becoming good world citizens? Democracy is not a special private possession for a chosen people! If we aspire to democracy for the world, we cannot limit our citizenship to a geographical nationality by refusing to surrender "sovereignty" over international matters to a higher representative body. To do so is to deny that democracy can exist outside of our borders or that it is a universally applicable concept.

That democratic citizenship is in essence world citizenship has been indicated from the beginning by the creed which begins, "We hold these truths to be self-evident, that all men are created equal and that they are endowed by their creator with certain inalienable rights; that among these are life, liberty and the pursuit of happiness." All that is new is the urgency with which we are called upon to fulfill our democratic citizenship by recognizing its world obligations and implications.

The world of the future will be a people's world, not a world of powers whether political or economic, capitalistic or communistic. It will be the most relaxed world the West has known in all of its history, with people working together in organizations operating within minimum areas. The federal world government will associate the most diverse kinds of ideologies and oligarchies, exactly as United States federalism has been able to do throughout its history, ranging from slave states to free states, from totalitarianism of right through oligarchies of favored elites (like the present oligarchies of some of the states of the Deep South) to totalitarianism of the left.

Historical accounts of that future day will note with amazement that we ever battled over states' rights versus national rights or small versus large industrial operations or even over private versus public enterprise.

These will seem trivial, because people will then be seeking what is humanly advantageous and not what increases institutional or political power.

The peoples of the world are ready for this new age of international law and peaceful pursuits. Given the chance, free men and rising millions who have been slaves of imperialism, and other millions who are still her slaves, will seize the offering of an organized world gladly and cherish all the freedoms under its law as fervently as did we ourselves in the beginning of our nation. Probably two-thirds of the world's people are utterly wearied and impatient with the European method of balance of power and are looking to the United Nations for security — even for survival.

Such is the democratic task in today's world. It is not a task for national governments which are, in their nature, incapable of establishing any higher authority than themselves. It is a task for the world's people.

FOOTNOTES CHAPTER FOUR

1. J. B. Baillie and William Wallace, "Hegelian Philosophy," Encyclopaedia Britannica (14th ed.), XI, 383.

2. Carlton J. H. Hayes, *A Political and Social History of Modern Europe* (New York: Macmillan Co., 1921), pp. 454 ff.

3. Arthur Morgan, "The Essence of Community," *Community Service News,* March-April 1948, p. 34.

CHAPTER 5

DEMOCRACY BETRAYED:
U.S. FOREIGN POLICY

Throughout her history, the United States has had certain clearly distinguishable strands of foreign policy. They have varied in their influences, gaining or losing dominance, but none have ever wholly faded out or been replaced. In the order of their historic introduction into international relations, these strands of foreign policy are as follows:

1) Colonial-Imperial Expansion
2) Security Resting upon Constitutional Law
3) Hemispheric Protection
4) Hemispheric Monopoly
5) Open World Expansionism

This nation began as an empire. As Bernard De-Voto, the great chronicler of this aspect of American development, clearly stated, for more than a hundred years we were colonials, just as there are colons, as we now say, in Kenya, East Africa and South Africa today. The first two volumes of DeVoto's famous trilogy[1] are the story of the first and second stages of our expansion across the continent at the expense of the original inhabitants. A good deal of this history is of the long struggles against the Indians and against other colonial powers in rivalry with the American colonies for the conquest of the North American Continent.

DeVoto's third volume is the story of the whole period of expansionism, including the continuing Open World Expansionism which began when national economic expansion terminated at the beginning of the twentieth century. According to his recording of this development, this original American empire still exists in a more economic and less political form. Its importance can be measured in part by the fact that it "is older than the United States."

Open World Expansionism has more or less dominated this country's foreign policy for about the last seventy-five years. A part of the expansion achieved under this policy has been colonial territory frankly possessed outright, "belonging to but not a part of the United States," in the words of a Supreme Court decision. Most consistent, however, has been the United States' noncolonial expansion in other nations: their markets, deposits of natural resources, and finance-capital establishments. Such nations become "clients," defined in international law as one step removed from the subserviency of being under colonial rule. Such countries must vote as the dominant power dictates — in all United Nations issues, for instance. This is what Jawaharlal Nehru called "the invisible empire of the United States."[2]

Pre-Castro Cuba, with steady development since the United States relinquished its military occupation, was an example of an American client nation and of the invisible empire of which Nehru spoke. Puerto Rico, still dominated by Washington and administered as "commonwealth" under our Department of the Interior, is an example of colonial expansionism, continuing even in this day of the ascendency of the noncolonial type of expansion.

The domestic need for the American economy to expand was a basic motivation in Open World Expansionism. In 1914, to the National Council of Foreign Trade, Secretary of Commerce Redfield of the Wilson cabinet said, "Because we are strong, we are going out into the markets of the world to get our share." Secretary of State Bryan followed in the conference, reminding his audience of investment bankers and manufacturers that Woodrow Wilson's foreign policy was to "open the doors of all the weaker countries to an invasion of American capital and enterprise." He added, "My department is your department; the ambassadors, the ministers, and the consuls are all yours. It is their business to look after your interests and to guard your rights." Later that day, speaking to the same Conference, President Wilson himself heartily supported these strong assurances by declaring that his government would seek their cooperation in bringing about "the righteous conquest of foreign markets." This, he said, is "one of the things we hold nearest to our heart."[3] Woodrow Wilson was not different in this respect from other leaders during this period of expansionism, even though he was the most idealistic of them.

To the business elite anticipating the achievement of the "American Century," Virgil Jordan, President of the National Industrial Conference Board of the National Association of Manufacturers, said in 1940:

> Whatever the outcome of the war, America has embarked on a career of imperialism in world affairs . . . At best England will become a junior partner in a new Anglo-Saxon imperialism . . . World events . . . have provided us not only with

the occasion but with the economic tools, the social attitudes, and now the political manners and customs of the modern imperialism.[4]

Jefferson observed in his First Inaugural Address that "nations . . . feel power and forget right." Imperialism, even of the mildest order, is incompatible with the original democratic spirit and idea. This country's late and usually milder orders of expansionism are a definite betrayal of the American faith. Yet such betrayal has been one of the chief characteristics of political democracies in all their commercial dealings with exploitable peoples throughout the history of Western democracy.

Imperialism, the essential order of the earlier mercantilism and older than democracy and capitalism, was an important part of the inherited mold into which the newer democracy was cast. Imperialism might well be called an international extension of the caste dominance which prevailed on the continent of Europe at the time democracy arose. The resulting realignment of rigid class distinctions was similar, though milder, in England and the United States.

If we give the term *imperialism* a broad application, yet use it with accurate connotation in its narrower political application, we find that people are imperialistic when for any reason, or with any cultural pretext of superiority (personal, class, trusteeship, benevolence or otherwise), they seek to manage other people and the affairs of other people on the assumption that those people cannot properly manage themselves; or when for reasons of their deep-seated inferiority, they simply downgrade others in order to upgrade themselves. Imperialism is initially psychological and is usually a mixture of these two: the concern to influence other people and the working out of unconscious inferiority.

We can understand, then, how imperialism works out from its human center in many forms — national, race, class, religious, economic, social, institutional or purely mental — and in such strange mixtures of parts that it is sometimes difficult to distinguish the pretext of superiority from the end value being sought. Everything from Europe was from the first considered superior to whatever counterpart existed in any other part of the world. This idea is still prevalent in the West.

The following of the European way continues to be the chief barrier to achievement of democratic law and order in international relations. Nations called democracies behave undemocratically when abroad; millions of people in the world are so deceived by this self-contradiction that they assume that democracy is like a conquered and stored-up booty which can be snatched or attacked or defended across national boundaries or across some parallel.

Some political democracies have, in places distant from their shores, notoriously revealed all the aggressive characteristics of the modern state at its worst. They have followed trade with gunboats, and where possible, captured both people and resources. Millions are still enslaved under such "republics" in many parts of the earth. These nations are still forcing concessions favorable to themselves and condoning and supporting the slavery of other peoples in order to protect their own superior standards and ways of life; an example is South Africa's treatment of all colored peoples.

Some of these nations have used their "protection"

exactly as racketeers in cities use their "protection." By establishing money empires, they have excluded from great areas of the world's markets and resources, nations with a more natural right to that trade and those resources than their own right.

Lacking understanding, we have thought that underdeveloped areas in Asia and elsewhere possessed inherent weaknesses which made them fall a ready victim before any expanding ideology. We could not grasp the fact that Western society had modeled them in its own weakness. Some of our leaders may have used duplicity to camouflage their real intentions. Imperial policies have supported unpopular, artificially bolstered governments upheld by hated foreign allies or dominant powers. This weakness existed before communism, fascism or Nazism appeared. Asia's weakness before Japan and the British weakness before nonviolent India are outstanding examples of the weakness inherent not in underdeveloped areas, but in the imperialistic order established by the West. Imperialism can possess no popular support.

In 1937, when Western financial leaders were overtly or covertly encouraging, bolstering or financing the rising fascism in Germany, Italy, Spain and Japan, in the undoubted hope that fascism would furnish an impregnable barrier against communist encroachment in Europe or elsewhere, Jawaharlal Nehru wrote,

> Imperialism and fascism are close of kin and one merges into the other. Sometimes imperialism has two faces — a domestic one talking the language of democracy, and a colonial one verging into fascism. Of the two the dominant one is the latter and it ultimately governs larger policies. . . .

Empire and democracy are two incompatibles; one must swallow the other. And in the political and social conditions of the modern world, empire must either liquidate itself or drift to fascism, and, in so drifting, carry its domestic structure with it.[5]

Gandhi knew that no empire could ever liquidate itself. He saw more clearly, perhaps, than any one else those political and social conditions of the modern world which were bringing this international confrontation of the two incompatibles to the climax of a great world crisis. Democracy might free itself from imperialism of whatever kind, but only if people everywhere would democratically rise up to overthrow empire exactly as they did when the thirteen British colonies of North America secured their self-rule.

Colonial-Imperial Expansion and Open World Expansionism were brought into the New World along with the rest of Europe's culture, combining the European policy of expansionism with its essential defense of all such expanded national empire systems. The United States came into being, however, as an association for solidarity, security, defense, well-being, and continental development. The new nation deliberately turned its back upon the European way by establishing its solidarity upon a written constitution. Its way of security, peace and well-being resting upon law constitutes an original repudiation of all unilateralism in national world behavior: a repudiation of isolationism.

The strand of foreign policy called Security Resting upon Constitutional Law can be termed the American way because it began whatever was unique in the constitutional launching of our ship of state. Lincoln understood the universal character of what was achieved when he called this "a new nation conceived in liberty and dedicated to the proposition that all men are created equal." The original American spirit was not nationalistic, but international in both outlook and proposal. Here, long before the League of Nations came into being, was a foreign policy leading the way to international unity and order.

This strand of influence has come down through United States history and has been responsible for both the League of Nations and the United Nations, which similarly set forth an alternative to the European way of expanding and protecting each nation's own interests in a completely competitive world. Because this new American way necessarily entailed turning the nation's back upon the European way, the inaccurate term isolationism has been used to describe it. In *The Tragedy of American Diplomacy*,[6] William Williams thoroughly destroys the myth of modern isolationism and exposes its hypocrisy (nobody really wanted America to stay at home). The so-called "George Washington isolationism" is also a myth; our forefathers were the great universalists, the great internationalists, of their time. That is what the ideal of democracy means and always has meant. These visionary men wanted to demonstrate how a continent could lead itself out of nationalistic strife into the peace of internationalistic solidarity and cooperation, out of bitter rivalry and war to the democratic way of law.

The truth is that assertion of nationalism is the great isolationism. Unilateralism in decisions and actions — going it alone in matters like Cuba, Laos, and Vietnam — make any nation solitary in world affairs. They make any nation feared. The fear they invoke is in direct proportion to the power which they assert in the grandeur of their posture of isolation. The original way of the United States was precisely the opposite of this.

Tragically, the United States is not now leading anyone in the political way of life her early leaders chose. We have surrendered the peace, security and order that rest upon the solidarity of law, and accepted the insecurity, disorder and continuous threat of war inherent in the European system of balance of power. In spite of our own authentic leadership through a League of Nations and a United Nations, we seem to have lost our original purpose to establish democratic law on all the earth.

The results of this failure are tragic for our own nation. The trigger-action efficiency required by this nationalistic, competitive struggle to balance power skillfully is slowly but surely corroding our democracy. The mentality which accepts domination by industrial and military leadership as the defense of freedom, or the conquest of world peace at the price of conscripting its youth for war and of making the nation into a police state, is a more basic and dangerous subversion than any our Justice Department has ever singled out. Jefferson referred to faith in the people — the idea that the people can be trusted when reason is free — as the world's best hope. Today it may be the world's only hope.

The strand of foreign policy called Hemispheric Protection began with the Monroe Doctrine. At that time, the protective motivation was probably dominant. The new federal government genuinely wanted, for very good reasons, to keep Europe out. As a matter of fact, Europe was not out. The colonial agencies, including

English colonialism, were still on the continent; the new nation would again lock horns with Britain in the War of 1812. The need for protection of the new nation was natural and inevitable. Bad as they were, conditions could have been far worse if European nations had not been firmly told that they must keep their empire quarrels in their own hemisphere. In addition to this, during this early period the United States had more than enough room for its expansion on its own continent.

After economic expansion within the United States had reached a state of approximate saturation and the nation had experienced a serious economic recession near the end of the nineteenth century, Hemispheric Protection gave way imperceptibly to its present modification, Hemispheric Monopoly. The element of protection remains, but predominant today is the desire to keep other nations out of our economy's most favorable places of profit.

The dominant strands which now characterize our foreign policy are economic expansion and protection of American markets. This foreign policy is not determined by military interests, involvements, or purposes. Rather, the military is a means to the achievement of our foreign policy aims.

We say that our aim is to put down communism in order to preserve and strengthen democracy everywhere for the establishment of a free world. But we propose to do this not by establishing and strengthening a free world based upon law and the security of solidarity. Instead we are leading a militarized bloc of nations which will aid us in bringing all the world under our influence — for freedom, as we say. In order to do this, however, we are surrendering even our own freedoms. Outside our nation, we are trying to use force to whip peoples into the free world camp but, by the time we whip them into our camp, it cannot any longer be the free world.

Why are we adverse to establishing a democratic world order based upon law? What is it that the Western nations still want that they cannot have without war? Are we still propelled in our world affairs by national self-interests, pursued unilaterally, and secured or defended by sheer military might? These questions are pertinent, but the answers are not clear because we are ambivalent in our attitudes and policies. We are a confused people trying to lead the world to freedom.

We want a world order that will support the interests of the West. The Soviet Union wants a world order that will support the interests of the Eastern bloc. But a democratic world order could support only the interests of humanity as a whole. We do not understand the difference between the American world and the free world, although we can easily see the difference between the Soviet world and the free world.

For the most part, a free world is still a dream. Woodrow Wilson called upon us to make the world safe for democracy. The author rallied with millions of other youth, leaving pulpit and classroom, volunteering even though exempt, because Wilson made that dream of an ordered world so vivid and so beautiful and so real that hope for its achievement inspired us to offer our lives. Later Franklin Roosevelt set forth the same great dream during another world war: the nations of the world uniting as the United Nations could become a free world establishing its security and its order upon the realities of international constitutional law.

Why is it impossible for such dreamed-of and hoped-for use of a United Nations to be realized? First, because nations still persist in acting unilaterally; they do this in their national interests. Second, nations insist that this is necessary and inevitable because they have no way of trusting each other, and no strength but their own and that of their allies to rely upon. When nations have no world order to rely upon, they must go to war; because they go to war to maintàin national interests, they can have no world order resting upon law.

The United Nations languishes because we insist on accomplishing that which is in line with our national self-interest. In the same way, the Soviet Union by-passes the United Nations because only by going it alone can she pursue ends in her self-interest. It was exactly in this way — the great powers' by-passing of the League of Nations — that the League was destroyed.

Our confusing the American world with the free world has been responsible for a tragic era and makes us resistant to the truth that could free us. This confusion is maintained by two widely held assumptions: (1) Since American economics itself is the "free way of life," the American world would be the free world if American economics were expanded. (2) This requires the second assumption, that some sort of political mastery must be asserted for this expansion of American economics.

Although these assumptions have been advanced as crucial to our concept of a free world, they are exact opposites of what would be required for the free world of Woodrow Wilson and Franklin Roosevelt. Their free world would have to be (1) internationally organized; (2) egalitarian in respect to all human rights, opportunities, treatments, etc.; and (3) protective of the last and least political unit from exploitation by even the strongest power on earth, protective of the resources of all the earth from exploitation by any power, and protective of the use of resources for the good of all men. This free world is still in the dream stage, but it would be more practical now than the present way of nationalistic competition and conflict.

We cannot lead the free world — a free world organized and established upon law — until we want a world order based upon law. We want things we cannot have in that kind of world, want them for ourselves, as Americans, in our national interests, to maintain our higher standards, to continue to hold the bulk of the world's resources. We expand our economy with a moral weakness that paralyzes the strength and destroys the integrity we need to win friends in Asia and Africa and the Americas. Our leadership depends upon a most precarious and dangerous balancing of military power. We have been induced by our national interests, idealistic and glamorous as we can possibly make them, to turn our back upon our original way of security and peace established upon law. This has been the great subversion of our history.

Our present policy of economic expansion and hemispheric dominance has made us a leader of European nations, long accustomed to extending nationalistic interests and balancing military power for defense and security. This European technique of balancing military power has now come to mean the balancing of nuclear power. It is a way which is leading us not to security but to insecurity, not to defense but to threat of destruction, not to a following of free peoples but to the steady loss of whatever friends we have had.

Historian René Albrecht Carrie holds that the West planted the "seeds of its own nationalism" throughout the East, beginning as early as "the turn from the fifteenth to the sixteenth century."[7] He adds that the strength of the growth of nationalism is always in its fresh fervency. In this sense, Europe and the West are generally seen largely as examples of "burnt-out" nationalism. He sees Europe in the decline, Asia in the ascendency of the democratic era. Today he would see Asia, Africa, South America and the islands of the seas in the ascendency. He would see the Western democracies everywhere in the world trying to clamp the lid upon the same kind of revolts against feudalism and tyranny which brought them into being.

The balance of world power and the future of the world are no longer with Europe or with the West; they are with neither of the militarized blocs. The power and the future are already with the peoples everywhere who are rising against tyrannies, old and new, and demanding justice within a new world to be established upon law. The United States can afford to by-pass Europe and go out now in another direction — without arms but with all the instruments of equality and justice — into this new world which is taking shape. We can ill afford to continue what we have been doing for over seventy years: following Europe's way or leading Europe down her own path of balancing military power — the path to insecurity, national anarchy, futility, destruction and death.

Europe's method of balancing power by military strength has failed and is out of date, entirely aside from atomic weapons. Those nations with conscription systems and reliance upon armed might did not win the victory in either world war. The United States was probably the determining factor in the victory of those wars and is, therefore, the most consistent example of this superiority of moral preparedness over military regimentation. England is also a unique example, especially in World War II, of where the superiority lies in the long run.

The ultimate power is always in people — in their will to resist. Even in military achievement, the sense of morality is not an unimportant factor. Further, nuclear weapons will turn the tide of military fortunes against all participants.

Military victory itself has failed as a practical reality in resolving conflict of any kind. When we try to get behind the superficiality of military defeat or victory in either of the world wars to the question of whether any basic issue was solved by it, we find still greater failure. Militarism has not, throughout all this era of the world wars, shown itself as a way to the successful resolution of any basic evil. In the First World War, we sought to put down the last of authoritarianism in governments, only to produce the worst authoritarianism the world has ever known. In the Second World War, we sought to put down the totalitarianism that resulted from the First World War.

Today we think we face a greater totalitarianism; we are in fact facing the encroaching of fascist attitudes and methods in all our Western countries as the direct result of the last war and its aftermath. Nuclear methods only accentuate what is already clear — the failure of war to achieve anything of real value to man.

If war does not solve basic conflicts, why then has it been so often resorted to? The answer is strikingly revealed in the story of some dramatic moments at the Paris Peace Conference in 1919, as told by Lincoln Steffens in his *Autobiography.*

Clemenceau, the Tiger of France, usually seen as villain of that conference, was speaking. "One moment, gentlemen," he said. "I have been hearing much talk about a permanent peace. There has been a great deal of talk about a peace to end war forever, and I am interested in that. But I would like to know whether you mean it, this permanent peace."

He looked at his colleagues, and they nodded. "And you have counted the cost of such peace?" he asked. Then there was some hesitation.

"Well," continued Clemenceau, "if we give up all future wars, we must give up our empires and all hope of empire. You, Mr. Lloyd George, will have to come out of India; we French will have to come out of Africa; you Americans, Mr. President, must get out of the Philippines and Puerto Rico and leave Cuba alone, and Mexico. We shall have to tear down our tariff walls and open the whole world to free trade and traffic. These are some of the costs of permanent peace; there are other sacrifices we, the dominant powers, will have to make. It is very expensive, peace. We French are willing, but are you willing, to pay the price, all these costs of no more war in the world?"

The President and the premiers began to protest that they did not mean all that, that it was not necessary, not all at once. No, they had not meant exactly that.

"Then," said Clemenceau, sitting up straight and striking the table sharply, "talk as you may, you don't mean peace. You mean war!"

And Lincoln Steffens concludes: "We do not want

war; nobody wants war; but some of us want the things we cannot have without war. We will not give up the things that cause wars."

The two competing, conflicting blocs now militarized and scattering throughout the world their nuclear, push-button methods are terrifying and menacing all the peoples of the world. Each person is as much afraid of his own nation's nuclear weapons as he is of any from outside; he is aware that it is his own nation's bombs and missiles which place him in continuous peril, not just from the attacking nation but from the combination of great fear and possible error.

Even apart from any new urgency brought by nuclear armament and its threat of total destruction, the need for a radical change in America's foreign policy is apparent and urgent, both for America's own defense and security and for the future welfare and survival of all peoples. The change needed is a swing back from our present European attitude and posture in foreign affairs to our original American attitude of seeking the elimination of war through political solidarity established upon law. This original American way may be coming into its own in a world sense for the first time. It probably offers the one hope available for the future of Western civilization. The organization of the world around law and order as the final condition for the survival of any nation is emerging as an important political issue which may bring the breath of life into the American political arena.

When we took our nuclear-armed U. S. Sixth Fleet within thirty miles of the Soviet satellite, Bulgaria, for naval maneuvers, there was one who was overwhelmed by the responsibility for that Operation Deep Water.

Vice Admiral Charles R. Brown, who was in charge, expressed his great misgivings and said, "We have got to get another formula. . . . When our power to destroy the world, to commit suicide — when that comes, I don't know. The decision is beyond the President and it is beyond Congress. Humanity has to make this decision."

Taking those words seriously, how does humanity make this or any decision? Will it make the right decision, while supporting its nations in their war preparations and war-making? Where and how does humanity bring its pressure to bear? Can it provide those necessary pressures if it has failed to develop the forms through which its pressures may be assembled and made effective?

Our present world task is to build a new order within the context of the present world, and to prepare it for its tasks when it shall finally take over. These are the people's tasks, and it is the people's awareness and strength that have to be developed.

Unfortunately the structures of today's world are not available to the people for appropriate immediate action, not even within the United Nations. Assuming that we could bring popular pressure upon our government, which is the limited meaning of political democracy, how can we make the United Nations as now constituted more than an association of national state departments? How can we make it more than a sounding board for national foreign policies? How can we bring our popular pressure to bear in the international arena where it is so important but where, as the people, we have no representation?

We have to begin with this hard fact: the people will have to develop themselves and their new world within old arrangements which provide no democratic procedures to the people under democratic law. Whatever is available to them within their nations is unavailable to them beyond their borders in international affairs. Among nations, the final arbiter is always unilateral resort to war and threat of war. International law is still little more than a concept.

The hope of the free world is not the flinging about of military power or its use for posturing against one another as nations. It is not in a struggle, cold or hot, to put down anything. It is not in a blueprint for a way of life.

The hope of the free world is in democracy, in the people's experimenting, using law for their general welfare only. How can this be brought about? I can think of only one way. There must be an uprising of peoples of all nations who will force their governments to abandon the pursuit of national self-interest, and through the United Nations to employ only world law and the adequate enforcement of world law in all matters of international conflict and universal human need.

FOOTNOTES CHAPTER FIVE

1.   Bernard A. DeVoto, *Across the Wide Missouri* (1947), *The Year of Decision, 1846* (1950) and *The Course of Empire* (1952) (Boston: Houghton Mifflin Co.).

2.   Jawaharlal Nehru, *Glimpses of World History* (New York: John Day Co., 1942), p. 567.

3.   William A. Williams, *The Tragedy of American Diplomacy* (New York: World Pub. Co., 1959), p. 71.

4.   Victor Perlo, *American Imperialism* (New York: International, 1951), pp. 122-123.

5.   Jawaharlal Nehru, *Eighteen Months in India* (London: Allahabad, Kitabistan, 1938), pp. 124-125.

6.   Williams, *op. cit.,* p. 71.

7.   René Albrecht Carrie, "Some Reflections on the Rising of Subject Peoples," Reprinted with permission from *Political Science Quarterly,* LXV, No. 2, June 1950, pp. 193-213.

CHAPTER 6

THE GREAT MACHINE: NATURE AND SCOPE OF AN ECONOMIC TYRANNY

A democracy which seeks to be political while refraining from being economic is thrusting the poniard into its own breast. The democratic approach to economics is not capitalism, socialism, communism or any other economic blueprint; it is popular experimentation in all economic matters. Are we so obsessed by the white of theoretical free enterprise and the black of theoretical communism that we no longer search for an adequate economic theory?

The measure of a democracy can be taken by the extent to which economic decisions are in the general welfare. The most successful democracies have invariably experimented with organizational forms, fearing neither errors nor radical innovations, in an attempt to discover the best methods for general well-being. A democratic economic system is thus certain to result in a flexible eclecticism.

The United States has never merely imitated the economic systems of Europe. We have combined enterprise with every kind of ownership: private, public, corporate, cooperative. We have restricted monopoly in some enterprises while arranging for monopolization in others (public utilities, for example). One major enterprise, the postal system, is federally owned and operated on a pay-as-you-go basis. Two other great systems, highways and public schools, are also owned governmentally; they are operated by taxing those of material means to provide services for all.

Democracy's philosophical core is that institutions must exist for man, not man for institutions. A free people can remain free, however, only by shaping and regulating its own institutions, economic as well as political. Popular control of economic processes must not, however, be confused with *laissez faire* economics which places society at the disposal of large business interests.

Western liberalism has historically been torn between two contradictory concepts: the people's freedom to control their institutions and the businessman's freedom to exploit people. "Hands off" meant no restraint by either the people or their governments on the specially favored capitalist institutions. This strange association of mutually warring bedfellows, democracy and *laissez faire* economics, reveals a schism inherent in our culture and illustrates the dichotomy that early divorced politics from business. Since the nature of freedom was considered political, people's emotions were to be engaged on the levels of patriotism, warmaking, electioneering and the like. Meanwhile, basic forces within both business and government began to coalesce, each attempting to mold the other to suit its ends, to such an extent that regulation of both was withdrawn from the people at large. *Laissez faire* gradually came to mean "the people cannot be trusted." The ensuing conflict between democratic control and unregulated exploitation has determined the nature of the current crisis of the West — a crisis involving all aspects of life and values. Our contemporary way of life, so fraught with conflict and fear, sanctioned by an ethics of ambiguity, is the natural manifestation of a "Great Machine" fashioned by an economic and political elite. This "Machine" is a conglomerate of vast business empires and concomitant bureaucratic structures of national states which function as mediators, protectors and extenders of these empires. Today the interests of business and government are so inextricably interwoven that national policy is tailored to safeguard the equilibrium of political-economic interdependency with cynical disregard for democratic values, peace and justice. Domestic and foreign issues are examined and decided in the light of expediency to bureaucratic organization and corporate-industrial expansion. Purveyors of the "American democratic tradition" in underdeveloped Latin America are principally in the employ of Sears, Roebuck, the Texas Oil Company or the United Fruit Company. European and American aid commitments in Africa and Asia are whimsically tossed about in the conference rooms of industrial contract negotiators.

The characteristic method of the "Great Machine" has been called the political means, under which arrangements of power are sanctioned so as to appropriate and concentrate wealth in the hands of a few mammoth corporations and "advanced" nations.[1]

Radical changes have been made in the system called capitalism, some by voluntary rearrangement and others as a result of governmental pressure. Some changes, especially those favorable to the Great Machine and brought about by legislation, have been revolutionary.

The industrial revolution led to unfettered private or free-enterprise capitalism. This brand of capitalism is a thing of the past. A more recent phase of the industrial revolution has seen a shift from private ownership to bureaucratic and corporate managerial ownership.[2] This reorganization of the economic structure has aggravated the disfranchisement of the individual, politically and economically. The possibility of popular determination and participation in economic planning and regulation is more remote now than at any time in the history of our country.

Four elements present in capitalist economies are (1) private use of capital, (2) competition, (3) the profit motive, and (4) relative freedom of business operation. In free play, these elements insidiously gain ascendency over other forms of societal order and eventually take control of people, their tools, their resources and their political prerogative. Capitalism, upon usurping the political and economic rights of men during the course of its natural development, finally emerges as a corporate machine which, working through political and legal institutions, sanctions its own activities by bringing into existence those laws which justify and assure its continued opportunity to exploit. A philosophy of domination now arises which expresses itself concretely in accumulation of maximum material possessions, power and privilege. When exported, this way of life becomes known as imperialism or colonialism.

No organization of nations can permanently endure while the Great Machine of Western culture continues to work its way and will throughout the world. International peace and order require the dismantling of the apparatus which has subjugated huge segments of the world's population. Whatever the purpose of domination, occupation and exploitation by this Machine, its termination will put an end to imperialism abroad and social and economic inequality at home. This is the first condition for a sane and stable human society.

The uprooting of firmly entrenched institutions and systems of belief which protect and perpetuate the Machine will be no mean task. The orthodoxy of Western national imperialism is more ironclad and inflexible than the old orthodoxy of medieval Western theology which sought to turn all the people of the world into Christians.

The philosophy of the Machine, with its attendant evils, corruption, exploitation and waste is deeply implanted in the bosom of our culture. In an earlier period, America's conquest of her own western lands evinced what one rural sociologist has called our "folkway of land use, which was to exhaust it and leave it."[3] Material resources and privileges were not to be conserved and shared, but to be fought for and wrested. This spirit continues to spread a basic irresponsibility in the corporate capitalism of today.

In the main, labor is similarly motivated. Historically, the American labor movement has been selfishly particularistic. It reached its present form and status not out of a struggle between two classes, the rich and the poor; it developed as an instrument for obtaining wealth and privilege for small classes at the expense of all other groups and persons. Today the evil of man's inhumanity to man is the collectivized evil of a mass society which has fashioned itself into a mechanical horde, the members of which are becoming less and less responsible as human beings.

The private use of capital in most western democracies is practiced largely by a few great capital corporations and industries. Although it is not used by an authoritarian state, neither is it controlled by the people; nor do the people exercise control over the tools of their labor and the deposits of natural resources upon which they are dependent for life. The exception to this is in the Scandinavian countries, where people have made their freedoms real, where capital is used to some degree by a democratic state on behalf of all persons, and is controlled to a considerable extent by the people at large.

The second element of capitalism is that of competition or what has been called social Darwinism. There was a time when competition and struggle were frankly for wealth. This previous competitiveness, pursued by individuals for what Ruskin describes as "maximum inequality in one's own favor," has given way to a form of competition which threatens not merely political liberty and domestic, economic well-being, but, at the international level, the future of humanity. National military power, centralized authority and the vast corporate empires channel competition into the production of items ranging from the most absurd banalities to the most profound nuclear weapon systems; blithely they pave the road to oblivion.

Competition is no longer an individualized social activity. For most people it is a struggle against the Great Machine itself — a battle to retain a mere foothold, to keep on paying the bills.

The profit motive is an essential element of capitalist economy. Profit provides the means by which corporate business solidifies its dominant position. Working through the bureaucratic tentacles of federal and state government, it tightens its grip on the economy. By concentrating the nation's wealth it is able to manipulate government policy and condition most forms of social behavior.

Finally, behind the absence of economic planning and the refusal by those who control the major portion of the nation's wealth to utilize it in a manner beneficial to the majority, is an outmoded theory of economics. Though different in outward appearance and terminology, the philosophy of *laissez faire,* as enunciated by Adam Smith three centuries ago, perpetuates itself in the denial of controlling interests to yield to the interests of society, to plan ahead so as to avoid war, unemployment, waste and poverty. It is a basic fallacy of this economic doctrine that purports to show that an unregulated economy will, in the final analysis, attain equilibrium and further the cause of social justice.

A fundamental revision is called for, one which will ameliorate existing social ills at home and abroad by releasing society from the grasp of a machine which methodically and relentlessly grinds to dust all sparks of creative endeavor, deviation from established norms, pride of spirit and all types of opposition while subjugating millions throughout the world by enthroning a rule of economic tyranny and military force.

Today a spirit of servility feeds and strengthens the Great Machine. There are two ways to make slaves of men. One is to own them like domestic animals. The other is less heinous but equally effective. It is to own all the tools and materials with which men must labor. Save open revolt, men can obtain the material necessities for keeping themselves alive only by remaining servile. The organization of laborers for bargaining is necessitated by this subservient relationship. Labor, fragmented and reduced to bargaining for particularistic interests, perpetuates social and economic instability which inevitably leads to even greater usurpation of power and control by the corporate, bureaucratic elite. As a corollary, man's increasing servitude leads to the elite's elimination of opposition to its policies and programs. Common to both fascism and communism, this intolerance to opposition has increasingly pervaded the modern West; consider the regimentation, intimidation, and persecution of nonconformity on every hand. The Great Machine cannot trust people to seek a personal way of life free from harassment and bureaucratic control. Nor must the façade of our monolithic society become besmirched by open inquiry into the purposes, functions and failings of its mechanisms.

The Great Machine's need, of course, is a more and more tractable tool — a labor force which will understand little more than that a great gulf is fixed between itself and its specialist-managers; one which will accept its own futility in doing anything about it; and which will, in time, come to expect and hope for little more than a slave's security.

The enormity of influence exerted by the Machine over man and society is frightening. Prevailing ethical standards sanction the use of men as tools. When men cease to accept the necessity for the tyrannical machinery which rules them, society will be free to examine its holdings and plot its future according to the light of reason and compassion. That could mean greater industrialization, more invention, new technology and a greater flow of and availability of goods to all. But it would also entail exposition and extinction of industrial exploitation.

* * *

Freedom can never be static. We have not sufficiently realized that the freedom of yesterday can become the slavery of today. It was the right to be unemployed (in the Thirteenth Amendment to the Constitution) that struck the shackles of domestic slavery from every man in the United States. The right to be employed bestowed freedom of another sort at the time it was granted. In the first instance, we are assured the traditional freedom to choose our own way of life; in the second, we are assured freedom from poverty and want.

During the Great Depression the freedom to be unemployed was a meaningless right. Unemployment became a horrible reality for millions; for other millions of employed it became a threat to the foundation of life and security. What was once freedom became oppression. It was a day when swift thinking and experimentation were the only ways of continuing the struggle, even for capitalists themselves. It is significant that Owen D. Young of General Electric was among the first to call for a "new deal" for the workers, and that the United States Chamber of Commerce seconded this proposal in short order.

During the Great Depression, the United States had present in abundance all the factors or resources necessary for a perfectly harmonizing and operating economy — except one. For that missing one, the Great Machine, the supreme achievement of the West, was not designed. It was a lack of sincere purpose to alleviate misery by distributing wealth. The depression was international and colossal because the Machine was international and colossal. Accumulated capital could not find an outlet. Idle factories were everywhere. Abundant material resources for production were going to waste and even being destroyed to produce scarcity. Millions of people, desperate for a chance to help themselves, rotted amid well-intentioned but ill-conceived benevolence. More millions of people in want — some starving or freezing to death — could have furnished a market for all the goods that could possibly have been produced. At the very height of its success as an economic system, the Great Machine had stalled, and no help in the form of modification or adjustment was possible from within its snarled mechanism. Remedial action had to be forced upon it from without. It has not since that time been restored to balance. It has been shored up and perpetuated by means of artificial subsidization through public works, world war, cold war, disaster and subsequent repair, and financial manipulation.

It is interesting that during this period of turmoil, the most significant and far-reaching developments of the New Deal palliatives were also the shortest lived. These were the "Production Units" of Dayton, Ohio, and the somewhat similar "self-help, barter and scrip movements which . . . (sprang) up all over the country . . . an experiment in production for use as against production for sales . . . "[4] These movements were all based upon the stern necessity for setting aside the Great Machine, momentarily at least, and reestablishing the appropriate relationships among the abundant elements of production which were present but nonfunctioning. In doing this, the people involved recovered direct control of the economic processes. The use of printed scrip in some places by self-help cooperatives showed that freeing the economic process did not mean getting along without money, credit, capital, banking or any other of the elements necessary to a modern economy.

The Great Machine could not long tolerate these palliatives; to do so would have been to relinquish its economic and political supremacy. Neither has it demonstrated over the years its capacity to return to normal operation.

Today, brought to the low level of tending the Great Machine that is their own undoing, increasing multitudes suffer a blackout of human liberty. They squander their leisure, trying with innumerable devices to drown the boredom and purposelessness of their treadmill lives. Their recreational and cultural forms for the most part are neither self-made nor creatively inspiring, but are ludicrous, commercial appendages of the Machine which tend to stifle true creativity.

Our society is machine-like not because of the invention and use of machinery, but because its constituent parts — organizations, inventions, advertising, government, education, religion — have not been developed to promote the growth and fulfillment of its human members. These institutional parts merely assist the Machine to pour out, as if from an assembly line, conforming beings who no longer care to call their souls their own.

An age which blindly worships progress comes to interpret progress in material terms; such progress is almost certain to move to the all-organizational extreme. The establishment of centralized power over people sets in operation principles the opposite of those which lead to socialization and results not in social man and human community but in mass man, mass movements, mass methods, social disintegration and ultimately, if persisted in, mass death.

Monstrous urban aggregations of human beings
have been pyramided. These metropolitan congeries are
destroying culture and humanity at once. One of our
leading sociologists, Robert Lynd, writes in his book
Knowledge for What?[5]:

> As a culture we are accumulating our disabilities
> and the resulting strains incident to daily living at
> a rate faster than social legislation, education and
> all the agencies for reform are managing to harness
> our new knowledge in the reduction of these dis-
> abilities. We are becoming culturally illiterate
> faster than all these agencies are managing to make
> us literate in the use of the potentialities of the
> culture.

The evidences of disintegration are undeniable. Frag-
mentation is the foremost external characteristic of the
present age. The resulting psychological and sociological
evils affecting man include nihilism, mass ennui, frustration, neuroticism, anomic violence, degenerative disease,
confusion, ethical ambiguity, insecurity, apathy, despair,
insanity. Sociologists estimate that one-tenth of all
Americans will see the inside of a mental institution in
their lifetime and that another two-tenths will skirt the
fringes of insanity but not be admitted to hospitals.

Operating with the characteristic indirection of its
political instrument, the complex machinery of our economy, instead of satisfying human needs and desires
with the goods it is capable of creating, separates the people from their material resources so that millions
can make no contact with the stuff of existence. Life has
become detached from the soil that nourishes it.

In the past, social alienation has brought decay and

death to great city civilizations, the material markers of which lie strewn across the world. Sociologists have attributed the downfall of Rome and other once strong civilizations to an extended period of soil erosion. It is much more likely that soil erosion has practically always been preceded by the human erosion caused by social alienation, of which urbanization and exploitation are mere symbols. Civilized arrangements have never been able to circumvent the conclusion made by Oliver Goldsmith in *The Deserted Village:*

> Ill fares the land, to hastening ills a prey,
> Where wealth accumulates, and men decay.

No civilization before ours has had equal mentality and facilities for destroying itself with dispatch.

* * *

The Great Machine is dependent for its survival, at least in part, on urban life. What can be done toward facilitating some degree of population dispersion? Both to restore independence to individuals and to effect a decentralization of our grotesque cities, we must return the community to society — a community small enough to give the human person a sense of belonging and of being a participant. Remaining urban centers must then be restructured so as to incorporate communal atmosphere. The Great Machine has, to a large degree, robbed man of that combined sense of being the intelligent initiating and responsible controlling unit of society which is implicit in all varieties of democratic theory. Loss of this sense has led mass man to his need for authoritarian manipulation and to the attitude that community and democracy are impossible in our age. This has been well expressed by Canon V. A. Demant of London, one of Christendom's keenest observers of the modern scene:

> When the sense of belonging to a community sags, men will not work their civilisation except by compulsion. The naked individual confronts the naked state, with no community in between. It is no use saying men will get a wider loyalty . . . when their sense of loyalty is undermined in the smaller areas of life.
>
> It is a question of . . . how much of these things (mass tendencies of a Machine Civilization) can the living community which rears them stand without wilting?
>
> But you may ask, is that bound to happen? Yes, there comes a point in any civilisation when the rational and constructed equipment, instead of supplementing the biological and spiritual life of man out of which it comes, begins to prey on it as a tumor does on the body.[6]

The power of the small vital community to adjust man to his earth seems to have been the crux of all past economic and social progress. The community and the society educate more powerfully than the school. From this there is no escape. The social disorganization peculiar to the age of the Great Machine is only the fuller fruit of a tendency which in its incipiency was ably described by Pestalozzi, the "father of modern education" in Europe, as indicating widespread neglect of community culture.

> On the one hand, an immense height has been reached in science and art; on the other, the very foundations of a natural culture for the mass of people have been lost. Just as no part of the world has ever risen so high, so none has ever fallen so low. Our continent is like the Colossus spoken of by the prophet; its head of gold reaches to the clouds, but its feet which should support it are of clay.[7]

Such is the picture of an age, which began to cry for what it regarded as socialization while denying genuine socialization at every turn by its resort to antisocial methods and forms.

The true human community educates because the community, like the human personality, exists in a process of growth. The educational factors out of which community is fashioned are interest, understanding, devotion, self-help, and self-control converging upon at least one mutually sought goal. The individual's relationship with his fellows in understanding and controlling the group's social-economic destiny is the fundamental element in community and the sum of all the educative factors.

The tendency of our age to merge the quantitatively lesser divisions in society with the larger divisions (consider the modern obsession with bigness in organization) undermines society. Local community, like its extension into society, is a quality of life rather than anything quantitative. It exists in persons as their experiences and in their continuous outward expansion of these experiences into the larger environment. This socialization consists of a set of processes opposite from those which result in regimentation and conformity.

Real education is always self-education; it results from the learner's experiencing. This is why sharing in community experiences is real education. The establishment of the appropriate setting, inclusive of materials, subject matter and techniques, which can provide the desired experiences for adults as well as children, calls for communities small enough to allow the intimacy and mutuality of self-help processes to grow. Here are both the sowing and the seedbed of a democratic society. The partial, fragmented outlook of our age needs this corrective of education in community, with its citizens locally studying, planning, acting and controlling all the matters of their living.[8]

FOOTNOTES CHAPTER SIX

1. For a thorough exposition of the distinction between economic means and political means, read Nock, *op. cit.,* pp. 59 ff.

2. Industrial bureaucracy is not the only bureaucracy in modern society. Labor is close behind, and government is perhaps out in front of the trend. For a brief account, see Arnold W. Green, "Bureaucracy in Modern America: Structure and the Problems" in *Sociology: An Analysis of Life in Modern Society* (New York: McGraw Hill Book Co., 1956).

3. Bruce L. Melvin, "Man's Relation to the Land," *School Science and Mathematics,* April 1941, p. 362.

4. Ralph Borsodi, *Flight from the City* (New York: Harper & Bros., 1933), p. 154.

5. Robert Lynd, *Knowledge for What? The Place of Social Science in American Culture* (Princeton, N. J.: Princeton University Press, 1948), p. 109.

6. V. A. Demant, "The Breakdown of a Civilization," *Christian Century,* September 10, 1947, p. 1074.

7. Johann H. Pestalozzi, *How Gertrude Teaches Her Children.*

8. For a further elaboration of this philosophy of community in education, see Ralph Templin, "Dewey, Gandhi and the Community in Education," *Journal of Human Relations,* I, No. 2 (Autumn 1952), 55-61.

CHAPTER 7

CENTRALIZATION, FREEDOM AND EXPERIMENTAL ECONOMICS

Does the existence of the Great Machine mean that democracy has failed? The truth is that democracy has never been tried. Political democracy has been attempted by an industrialized, nationalistic West which tends to discard even that diluted form of democracy whenever it fails to support the orthodoxy of capitalism. The West has never known really intelligent planning; its way has advanced from ugly ruggedness through collective madness to the threat of ultimate self-destruction. We still have to take democracy seriously enough to test whether such men as Jefferson and Lincoln were right about reliance upon the common man.

Democracy is hemmed in between equally destructive counterrevolutions to the left and to the right. What place has a people's government on either side of this struggle for control of man's future? Modern society requires planning; how can a complex society be turned over to the people?

Who is it that can plan the human community well? Is it the highly centralized governments of our time, whether capitalists or bureaucratic — these aggregations of power with their vast conscription systems arranging many details of the common man's life in the interest of the state's power and dominance? This is a pattern that seems about to become universal.

Yet it has still to be proved that a managerial or bureaucratic class can plan intelligently for apathetic, security-seeking people. We can see the great failure of our age in the flight of democratic liberalism — in the retreat of modern man from the freedoms he once cherished to a security bought at the price of the surrender of his freedoms to the political leader who will promise most. We have already reached governments of "bread and circuses."

Bureaucratic control of the economic process is not a free people's answer to the need for democracy in this area. Free enterprise has been surrendered within an economic system which is more political than it is industrial; "economic man" is a myth in a political-power age. By confusing his mastery of nature with political mastery of others, man has cumbered the economic process and fashioned the Great Machine which is his own undoing.

The fashioning of injustice and inequality to favor certain interests would be impossible if man did not surrender his birthright of liberty by accepting his own slavery. Mass control of people is the basis of all the industrial collectivism of the West; this began with its earliest form, the collectivization of capitalism.

The survival of democracy may be bound up in the ability of the people to plan wisely for themselves. Even some conservatives assume that only experts can plan — that democratically controlled planning is impractical and unrealistic. These are serious considerations. All that can be said is that planning by the people has never been attempted, and that when the people do not hasten to make it their planning, the "experts" hasten to make it theirs. We must begin with trust in the people's intelligence and integrity even if they advocate, within due process, a complete overhaul of the national economy.

The economic process must be freed from the legalized powers granting to a few control of the system. To free the economic process, people must understand and use that process within the present system, but quite independently of the operations of the Great Machine. This is a distinction we need to hold within our minds and allow to grow upon our understanding. Efforts to distinguish between the economic and the political processes and to employ them separately, in more democratic ways, will lead to a better understanding of their complex interrelations and mutual involvements in present economic arrangements. Any serious popular effort to employ the economic process within the present system will inevitably lead to greater popular effort to strengthen all democratic processes. These are two sides of a single democratic task — man's mastery of his destiny.

To free the economic process, a broad distribution of economic control must be brought about. This begins in the people's consciousness — in their understanding of the meaning and importance of the consumer principle in economics. The result of this awareness will be the people's knowledge that there can be nothing called economics which is outside of them or beyond their influence. As soon as it is understood that the dynamic source of all economics is in human nature, people will have the power of life or death over every economic arrangement. The inequalities and injustices that have been legislated into existence must be removed by the people. A democracy cannot fulfill itself without evolving laws of ownership, banking, credit, employment, contracting, and the like, which operate only in the people's general interest. There are within the present system several ways in which people can employ and have employed the economic process with a considerable degree of freedom and to further their own greater freedom; it is important to examine these ways carefully.

The consumer principle can be applied by one family or by small groups on the land as "homesteading," in a new and modern use of that term.[1] The home is the natural, primary human cooperative association. Homesteading, in the modern usage, means the family's furnishing of some of its needs by the most direct possible employment of the economic process. A homestead has been defined by Ralph Borsodi and Monsignor L. G. Ligutti as "a home on a plot of land where the family, maintaining the natural bonds of unity, lives and works. It is the direct source of the food, clothing and shelter of its members — the scene of integral living."[2]

The family's goal in homesteading is the production of as many things as are convenient in view of the family's size: an assortment of do-it-yourself projects such as a flock of chickens, small orchard, garden, goat or cow, bees and so on. Children return to an important place in the society and are no longer economic liabilities. Members learn many forgotten arts along with the basic human dignity — independence.

During the Great Depression, a number of communities of homesteading families were settled on small holdings of land. Some of them were settled by church and private agencies; the Department of the Interior of the United States Government also settled some of these homesteading communities of unemployed workingmen's families as a part of the New Deal's rehabilitation program. This may be the only act of the New Deal which created specific human values sufficiently abiding to be studied. In Alabama, Dr. Paul W. Wagner studied five of the government-established homesteading communities; they had been flourishing for fifteen years.[3] His purpose was "to determine the potentialities and limitations of a pattern of life which combines industrial employment with part-time farming." About 70 per cent of the 697 families studied showed genuine disposition or talent for part-time farming, and their success "showed surprisingly little correlation with previous farm experience or . . . farm background." Dr. Wagner's findings are valuable for those who would propose the establishment of homesteading communities as an alternative to relief in the event of a future depression.

It is also possible to extend the conscious and direct use of the consumer principle through the people's own organization of all economics. Consumer cooperation does not propose an additional or different kind of society. The beauty of consumer cooperatives is that people simply put themselves to work through organization of themselves in the business of competitive buying, selling, producing, credit control, financing, land settlement, and all the other aspects of the original capitalist economy.

Consumer cooperation is voluntary association of the people for the purpose of economic competition. In the countries where this method has advanced to its apparent maximum development (around 25 to 35 per cent of the total economy), interesting outcomes begin to appear. The organized cooperation of the consumer reaches a point of saturation at around that percentage of achievement. The consumer's original sense of need, which led to the expanding of his organization, no longer exists. The old aggressive and exploitative forms of enterprise no longer exist to spur on and profit their enterprises.

Consumer cooperation thus serves in the total system much as a governor serves in restraining a machine. It has revealed the power to revive the economic system by restoring sanity to the society and by returning it to both morality and democracy. The people's voluntary organization for competing with the existing system therefore becomes an instrument for effective control by the people of the whole of the economic process. It is the only effective means toward industrial democracy so far tried in the West. It should be encouraged, protected and sought by every Western nation interested in the survival of its existing free-enterprise economy. The economic good of a fully developed human society is to be discovered by human beings intelligently and responsibly applying the consumer principle through its appropriate method — voluntary cooperation — to the whole range of industry, finance and trade.

The importance to free-enterprise economics of the cooperative movement is no longer theory; its beneficial influence can be studied in actual operation in various parts of the world. By organizing in consumer cooperatives to furnish themselves with goods and services, people have been able to restore to themselves control not only over the whole of their economy but also over their government. This has been partially accomplished in Sweden, Denmark and Finland.

In Copenhagen, Denmark, in an industrial area in need of low-cost housing, the people long ago decided that they could furnish themselves with suitable housing at a cost which was well within their range. They could turn to the government because, through alert and responsible citizenship, they had made the government their servant. They used the cooperative means with which they were familiar. The new kind of instrument fashioned was called the "debtors' association." The result was a most successful project in low-cost housing.

By associating for their indebtedness, and with the instrumentality of government providing capital and all other necessary assistance, the people were able to extend their amortization to society over several generations. This extension of amortization over more than one lifetime is precisely what the Western governments are doing for the corrupt purpose of carrying their huge burdens of armaments. The people of Copenhagen made use of this method for an incorrupt purpose.

This system of voluntary association and action in a competitive society is one application in a special area of the democratic and economic processes. In making and unmaking laws with intelligence and purpose, the consumer cooperatives of Denmark employed the political instrument of power on their own behalf — what we have always intended by democracy. Developing their own housing projects was a simple, direct use of the economic process.

The political and the economic instruments are obviously complementary in their hands, but it should be noted that well over a hundred years ago the people of Denmark began to develop their alert, intelligent and responsible control by attacking their economic problems with the consumer cooperative organization. Their democracy, or the Danish people's control of their government, resulted from their organization to set free and use the economic process.

India began to develop self-government in this same manner, by gaining control over the economic process and extending its development all over India. She finally gained her political independence largely because, through intelligent and responsible action, she had already taken the economic process out of Britain's hands.

Sweden is probably the best country in which to study the total effect upon a society — government, economics and all other matters — of the development of a bloc of well-balanced cooperative enterprises. Examining this effect throws much light on the methods and possibility of the fulfillment of democracy in a typically Western culture.

H. W. Culbreth, a sociologist assigned by the Rosenwald Fund to make a study of Western democracies, after two years decided that Sweden was the most democratic nation in the West.[4] This is because the country has been made by its people a laboratory for their own experiments in how to live. To apply to Sweden the name of any absolutism such as capitalism, socialism or communism is entirely misleading, but she combines carefully selected elements of all of these. The way to her greater freedom was through the development of consumer-producer cooperation within a vitalized democracy. Though the organized consumers operate probably not more than a quarter of the nation's economy, they have been able, by means of their substantial bloc of buying power, to tame and control the whole of the economy, as well as to fashion perhaps the world's most completely democratic society.

Laborers in Sweden, working also as consumer co-operators, have been able to achieve more progress toward permanent labor reform than in any country where the usual class-conscious organization for bargaining is relied upon. It is as consumers that they have written their own labor code. Since their interests are those of the economics of the whole nation, they have not developed their reforms in the narrow context of the wage-taking factory worker.

In this respect, labor can learn something from consumer cooperative organization. Bargaining should be studied in terms of what it is that enhances power for bargaining. Both business and labor have power to bargain; the source of that power is not merely through big organization. On the side of big business, the principal source is the control of the economic process. On the other side, it is labor's conscious organization. When labor adds to its present power that which can grow out of consumer-producer consciousness and organization, it will be able to deal in equality with big business.

Labor in the United States has alienated itself needlessly from a helpful way of life by its own refusal to employ the economic process. Unions have been prevented by their narrowness of class concept from understanding and practicing methods which could give them far greater bargaining power than they now command. Where bargaining is the accepted method in trade, one learns by necessity the value of indifference, feigned or real. The one who persists in indifference most successfully wins this interesting game which has often delighted the soul of the Western traveler in the Orient. When indifference in bargaining can be real — the customer does not need or want the article or the merchant does not choose to sell it — bargaining power reaches its maximum.

Labor cannot change a system of economics overnight nor suddenly scrap techniques already developed. But labor can learn to build without delay its own economic power and control within the economic system of the present. The organizational forms for such control already exist. Important elements within labor's possible economy are such methods as land, housing and land-use programs, training for productive use of land as a source of self-employment, and all wider cooperative techniques such as cooperative financing (credit and banking), cooperative security (insurance), and cooperative enterprise (production, distribution, wholesaling and retailing). In addition, labor's cooperative strength can be the pooled strength of all cooperators and of the entire cooperative system throughout the world.

Labor can add to the bargaining strength of this ever more real indifference a new and presently unknown strength in this country's labor movement — that coming from the control of a decisive bloc of buying power. The Freedom Movement has proved the effectiveness of this technique. This way of freedom can be established on foundations of organization already laid, and its philosophical basis — that all wealth results from the application of labor to natural resources — belongs peculiarly to labor. As Abraham Lincoln expressed it, "Labor is prior to and independent of capital. Capital is only the fruit of labor, could never have existed if labor had not first existed. Labor is the superior of capital and deserves much the higher consideration."[5] It is labor's opinion of its own first place and importance that is the beginning of labor's freedom and security.

The consumer cooperative movement, warring against monopolistic price fixing, control of consumer impulse, and centralized control over human beings, was opposed by socialist movements in its earlier history as being against a workers' revolution. Radical workers' movements have opposed consumer cooperatives, sometimes bitterly, as a countermovement which would make capitalism acceptable to all human beings.

Strangely and unfortunately, leaders of the present economic system in almost every area have tended to confuse cooperatives with socialism or with communism. Nothing could be further from the truth. Consumer cooperation is actually the protector of capitalist principles by its tendency to minimize the various self-contradictory factors in state and corporate capitalism.

The evidence derived from investigations carried out in Russia by George S. Counts of Teachers College, Columbia University, identifies the nature of socialist opposition to Western developments, and is revealing.[6] He questioned all the exponents of dialectical materialism he could find, asking what they thought about capitalistic developments and what, if any, threat to their revolution they recognized. The reply to the first question was invariably that increasing centralization of control over people, developing everywhere under capitalism, was all in a direction which favored their revolution, as centralization of control made it a simple matter for the workers to take over at the top. To the second question, the uniform reply was that the only threat to the revolution was the method of nonviolence of the Gandhian movement in India.

Consumer cooperation simply means that by organizing themselves for enterprise within the existing system, people can go beyond consumer consciousness and control. All the basic economic principles — such as self-help, self-service, "vertical diversification" (Doane's term for further processing of goods),[7] and increasing correlation of production, distribution and consumption — remain the same as in homesteading, modified only by the greater complexity and obvious loss of directness entailed by bigness.

It is only fair to say that what is now called democratic socialism has diverged so far from scientific socialism (the Marxist brand) as to be something entirely different. This can be seen on the negative side as the fiercest anticommunism in existence in the West. But of some importance are the facts on the positive side: (1) that democratic socialism in every part of the world is increasingly stressing the family farm for agriculture and private ownership of all consumer goods, including homes and land around them, and favoring the development of all kinds of cooperatives and small businesses in a competitive system; and (2) that it proposes to rely only upon the democratic method of peaceful persuasion to gain its ends.

Thus democratic socialism is revolutionary only in the sense that the cooperative movement is revolutionary; both are revolutionary only in the sense that democracy itself is the original popular revolution. The subtle or creeping nature which has been attributed to modern socialism is probably nothing more nor less than the democratic process of the people's experimentation at work, somewhat evolutionary in character, according to the basic nature of democracy.

Consumer cooperative organization is the most apt democratic instrument for the use of socialism in achieving its goal of an economy of, by, and for the people — a "cooperative commonwealth." It is capable of embracing the most complicated and extensive economic arrangements. Through their Farm Bureau cooperative, the farmers of northern Kansas developed their own oil empire; it now serves farmers all over the nation. Through it, these farmers compete successfully with all the other oil empires in the United States. Some of the best long-time international trade relationships between nations have been worked out through cooperative organization.[8]

In addition to homesteading and consumer cooperative organization, another way to use the consumer principle consciously, a way that is basic economically, is the establishment of man's use-right of land. (Ownership of land is inclusive of so much that is subversive of human equality that the term use-right, expressive of the inherent democratic right to land, has been coined.) Inheritance right, as a part of use-right, is also basic.

Use-right of the land does not mean farming, though it includes it; the establishment of man's use-right of land does mean restoring the spirit of husbandry to the whole of society. Land is the people's own, the sole source of the people's physical well-being. No hypothetical or legally provided "right" must be allowed to remove this basic, natural use-right of the people in their land.

Governments have always claimed eminent domain, democratic governments being no exception. This is the right to appropriate private lands for public use with compensation. Therefore, although land is the basic natural resource and the basis of the material substance of all economics including finance, its use is always legally defined. In other words, private ownership is merely a political device.

This is one of the clearest illustrations of how the political instrument becomes preeminent in what is called an economic system. There is actually nothing economic about ownership in and of itself. It is simply a matter of governmental definition. Ownership may be defined so as to thwart, to saddle and ride, to plunder, even to destroy the economic process, and all this as a part of the political instrument of power over people. But such legal prostitution of fundamental human rights becomes possible only because a servile people make themselves exploitable. Millions have already been led by the Great Machine to love the slave's security more than liberty; more, even, than life itself. People have been more dignified and freer in concentration camps.

The right of eminent domain claimed by any government — the right to assume ownership in terms favorable to itself or to an elite which wields its power — is the basic and only ultimate "socialism." Democracy cannot advanced by a socialism achieved as the political instrument of acquisition of power over people. A basic implication of democracy is that the eminent domain must be the people's domain.

The rethinking and redefining of man's use of land, including ownership and tenantry, is absolutely fundamental to control of the economic process by the people. There is no possible way of evading this if democracy is to advance further in the modern world. A definition of ownership of land which includes the right to speculate with land or for any other reason to hold it out of man's use, to destroy or waste its resources, or to exclude people — dependent upon land for livelihood — from access to and use of land, is not a democratic definition. A society which so defines ownership of land has not begun to make itself democratic in fact as well as in name, has not yet taken the first step toward human freedoms.

We must see that there is no one-sided palliative or cure for our society's ills. People have been enslaved while living in small intimate communities and even while living as tenants on the land they till. It is *how* people, in possession of their rights, relate themselves to land and to their use of it in creative purposes, and it is *how* they make themselves masters of their destiny, which are the basic determinants of freedom. These go beyond mere living on the land or living in community and beyond the exercise of citizenship as now narrowly conceived in democratic ideology. Increasingly, some are calling for community living, others for cooperation, and most of the people for political reform or labor reform; all these have their place. No one of them is by itself the way of the struggle for new and fuller human freedoms.

Democracy, the people's experimental search for the best method, is the only answer. It is a way spiritually ennobling, revolutionary and universal. It is spiritual because man has no more important spiritual business than extending his sovereign control over all of the works of his hand. It is revolutionary, because in extending his control, man is up against, and diverting certain of the basic energies of, the Great Machine. It is universal because democracy began as an ideal system which projected into Western thought and practice the qualities of a universal human community.

When men cry no more for liberty, equality and fraternity, but rather for security under managerial control, it is time for a new declaration of independence. It is through a producer-consumer organized society which embraces experimentally all ownership, production, financing and distributing of natural wealth of, by, and for common man that freedom can be restored. The coward may flee to the security of a known way. Free men seek to fulfill the vision of democracy; the greatest forward movement for freedom still lies before humanity. The human spirit's ascendency over nature and control of human nature cannot be achieved through any kind of regimentation or mass control of human beings under capitalism or any kind of statism.

The cause of the individual or of the group is always bound up with the cause of all humanity. It will require a classless struggle in common cause of all the worker-consumers of the earth to bring about an age of democracy and economic justice. This is a task of science, of technology, of religion and of morality. The real foes are foes of all humanity. They are the legalized predacities which have drained the common treasury of wealth, and which now threaten our common inheritance with total destruction.

FOOTNOTES CHAPTER SEVEN

1. For the author's personal experience in a homestead community illustrative of democratic planning, see Appendix I.

2. Mildred Jensen Loomis, "The Return of the Productive Home," *The Christian Century,* Nov. 26, 1941, p. 1469.

3. Paul W. Wagner, *One Foot on the Soil,* Birmingham. Alabama, University of Alabama, 1945, pp. 206 & 214.

4. Harry W. Culbreth, "What Is the Future of Democracy Following Present Trends?" (Report to Ohio Welfare Conference, Columbus, Ohio, Oct. 18, 1940), pp. 7-14.

5. Nathaniel Wright Stephenson, *Selections from Lincoln* (New York: Charles Scribner's Sons, 1927), p. 235.

6. Presented in his course "Education and Nationalism," Teachers College, Columbia University, 1932-33.

7. D. Howard Doane, "Vertical Farm Diversification" (St. Louis: Doane Agricultural Service, 5579 Pershing Ave., undated).

8. As examples, see James P. Warbasse, *Co-operation as a Way of Peace* (New York: Harper & Bros., 1939), pp. 57-71; Toyohiko Kagawa, *Brotherhood Economics* (New York: Harper & Bros., 1936), chaps. 1, 6, 9.

CHAPTER 8

RACISM AND INTEGRATION
IN WESTERN CULTURE

There was a time when the idea of universal brotherhood was considered sentimental. It is now the world's practical necessity, the key to human survival. Harry Emerson Fosdick, at the time of the Hiroshima bombing and the ushering in of the atomic era, succinctly expressed the situation of modern man: "Either we cooperate or we are sunk."

The explosive nature of our world has made brotherhood a practical core of future reality. It is as essential to the survival of democracy as to the survival of mankind, for to exist, democracy must expand beyond national borders and function in world affairs.

Interracial brotherhood is one aspect of world brotherhood. As Dr. W. E. B. Du Bois indicated sixty years ago, "The problem of the twentieth century is the color problem."[1] People did not choose this problem. History presented it and demanded that it be dealt with. Whether people take positive action, do nothing or try a way of escape, their decisions will have a bearing upon the outcome.

Because of the matter of world leadership, the emergence of integration of the races as a great crisis cannot be escaped by the West, particularly by the United

States. If democracy is to survive in the West, all race inequalities must go; that is a condition basic to success. The other threatening problems of the West — potential nuclear destruction and economic injustice — only make the one of race more central and acute. This issue has only lately been distinguishable as the crux of humanity's next great step upward.

In this crisis of integration, the modern West perhaps faces judgment all the more inexorable because of the opportunity afforded it to bring democracy to all peoples. The following passage of George Adam Smith echoes the relentless tide of history when moral opportunities are shunned by a people in any time of great decision.

It is a peal of thunder we hear. It is, in a moment, the explosion and discharge of the full storm of prophecy. As when from a burst cloud the streams immediately below rise suddenly and all their banks are overflowed, so the prophecies that follow surge and rise clear of the old limits . . . by the unconfined, unmeasured flood of heaven's justice . . . Now, once for all, are submerged the lines of custom and tradition within which the course of religion has hitherto flowed; and, as it were, the surface of the world is altered. It is a crisis which has happened more than once again in history: when helpless man has felt the absolute relentlessness of the moral issues of life; their renunciation of the past, however much they have helped to form it; their sacrifice of every development however costly, and of every hope however pure; their deafness to prayer, their indifference to penitence; when no faith saves a Church, no courage a people, no culture or prestige even the most exalted order of men; but at the bare hands of a judgment, uncouth of voice and often unconscious of a Divine mission, the results of a great civilisation are for its sins swept remorselessly away.[2]

Such is the nature of the integration crisis of the twentieth century. It is like an international flash flood whose moral truth will carry everything else before it.

The integration crisis taken in a world sense does not mean only the Negro or African color problem. It means the color problem that has been politically created by the West, and it includes all the colored peoples of the earth — of Asia, of Africa, of the Americas and of the islands of the seas.

Certain sociologists have made much of recent anthropological conclusions that the Asian Indians are included among the whites. Some use this theory in order to offset the numerical impressiveness of the alarmist doctrine of a "rising tide of color." In such a setting, the theory strikes one as wishful thinking. Even if true, it is unimportant; politically, the Asian Indians are colored. The harsh facts of two hundred years of modern history have categorized them as colored; as a result, the vast majority of the peoples of the earth are colored.

This color division of humanity is real and important and will be the determining division in the course of future world reconstruction. The European whites, in their domination and exploitation of other peoples, have been responsible for the creation and application of the term "colored" as a purely political designation and they have always been outnumbered by those whom they so designated.

How did the world's color problem arise? Dr. Charles H. Wesley, a leading African and Negro historian, stated in the 1960 Faculty Lecture Series at Central State College of Ohio that the use of color distinction for purposes of indicating inequality and for discrimination arose with the development of a vast European enterprise of traffic in slaves. He stated Gunnar Myrdal's conclusion, that this supposed inequality was a necessary rationalization of Europeans in order to justify profit-taking in an enterprise which so sharply contradicted the European liberal tradition and its claims of universality.

It was not the slave trade alone, however, which needed a rationalization that would read the colored people out of the human family. Slaves, as property bought and sold, were a special kind of booty of all the aggressive trade practices that we sum up as imperialism. Western imperialism first arose in Europe without color consciousness. It is possible to show from a study of English literature that the first conquests were made of India's markets, customs and counting houses without any special color consciousness, without any sense of ineqality in attitude toward the Asian Indians. Indians were at first considered to be of an advanced civilization, some of whose goods were of a superior order to those of Europe. Yet it is also easy to show, by the same method, that with the development of the doctrine of the "white man's burden," the Indians were driven into the colored camp and every Indian of whatever rank began to be considered by whites as an inferior being.

The whole of the system of imperialism required this rationalization, and it applied wherever the European empires were extended. By 1919 the whole world had been organized into the white man's systems.

It would probably have been impossible for imperialism to continue without color discrimination. Imperialism's purpose was to exploit all the peoples possible, and it chanced that underdeveloped or nonresistant countries were those of colored peoples. The use of color therefore became the main basis for this contrived inequality.

Associated with its use was the West's special doctrine, almost literally its prevailing religion, of the survival of the fittest. This doctrine left man with only one right, that of competing against all others. And so also with nations. In such competitive struggle, the extinction of the "unfit" was regarded as God's way of improving the human species. This doctrine is still deep within our culture.

National imperialism brought about the intertwining of the doctrine of the white people's having a superior culture, religion, etc., with this frank rationale of aggressiveness in the service of God's will. It thus became the "destiny" of white peoples and cultures to make conquest of all the colored peoples, to rule them and exploit them and their resources, toward the end of strengthening and exalting the white peoples and their cultures. This was the Western way "East of Suez" — a bold, bad way from the barracks-room point of view. But this was also confused, among all the higher echelons, as the way of "civilizing" all of Kipling's "lesser breeds without the law."

It can be noted that there is an aspect of imperialism which is more favorable. Many historians emphasize that it was the European imperialists who spread the concept of the nation and aroused nationalistic aspirations and uprisings. It is interesting that Western imperialism faces today the greatest rash of nationalism in imperialist history. Historians of modern India indicate the importance of the introduction of the English language, and through it, the inspiration and insight gained by youthful leaders through their study of John Milton, Oliver Cromwell and others in England's struggle for independence.

This line of interpretation may, in Western zeal, be overdrawn. The Indians and Africans have their own background of history which records their many great philosophers, saviors and liberators. More important, perhaps, is the fact that a few scholars went to the metropolitan countries which dominated their own and saw firsthand the better side of the white man's nature as expressed within his free institutions. They received a vivid impression of the contradiction in the white man's behavior. This impression led to the tragic conclusion that, for purposes of justifying exploitation, the colored peoples had been banished from the human family. This was a fair conclusion, for that was the essential purpose of the color rationalization.[3]

There is another contradiction involved in the fiction of color superiority. On the part of the whites, there seems no desire for pure biological whiteness; the dominating whites of our South have been mainly responsible for a vast mixing of the races. On the part of some colored people, there is a tendency toward a psychological rejection of color and a striving after whiteness that can be called "aspiring whiteness." These points illustrate not only the falseness of the alleged superiority of whiteness, but also the relationship of this contrivance of inequality to the striving and the aggressiveness of any predatory behavior.

Color superiority, or the racial myth, is capable of instilling great fanaticism. All through the course of human history it has been used with resulting serious cultural deterioration. In this country, those states wherein the human groups have been made deliberately caste-ridden through various segregations are also, for that reason, the locale of the greatest soil erosion and of the human poverty and debasement resulting from exploitative philosophies.

Caste in India is believed by some scholars to be simply the result of color superiority on one of the most virile of social structures. One theory of caste origin is that the Brahmanical rigidity of caste, which in its most frightful aspect became untouchability, was also an artful device for keeping millions "in their place." By comparison, the Jim Crow of the Western white man was ill-conceived and crude.

Caste was not essential to the structure of the Hindu *Jajmani,* the village social system, as many have supposed, though stratification may have been essential. Caste is generally believed to have arisen only when the white-skinned Aryan, whose control was spiritualized in the Brahmanical authority out of fear of losing racial identity and purity, turned to deal with the dark-skinned Dravidians in the later stages by whipping up the racial superiority myth. It may even be that the Brahmanical leaders acted out of the fear of losing their Aryan power to the broader-based and more democratic culture of the Dravidian.

The human erosion which this social disintegration brought about led India from its golden age to its age of inner weakness, cultural decay and structural petrifaction. The Brahmans themselves probably represented the only rigidity of caste till near the end of the golden age, and were no doubt largely responsible for India's meeting invasion after invasion with a sadly divided and depleted Hindu culture.

Hitler exploited the racial myth along with the national myth. There is no pure Aryan strain, even in India. But a myth, once accepted, becomes a reality to be reckoned with. Whipped up fanatically in the minds of Germans, Hitler's myth of the master race supported the idea of the supreme nation. Together they became his principal means.

The two myths of racial and national supremacy do not always appear as gross exaggerations or hideous aberrations. They are both characteristic of the cultural texture of the modern world. Stalinist communism frankly exploited the great fiction that the enslavement of man is the way to his freedom. The root of the disease with which the West is sick unto death is this same class-conscious quest for a false freedom — this monstrous self-deception of a "liberty" to maintain domination and industrial injustice. Real liberty always involves equality of legal status and opportunity, even for the one least in innate powers or abilities.

As long as this combination of hallucinations continues to remain characteristic of our society, even our aid and good will, extended to underdeveloped areas, defeat the worthy but contradictory purposes which prompt them. One of England's foremost prophets, Wilfred Wellock, a former labor M.P., has warned:

> Western civilization is like a blind man who has been put on the wrong road. He thinks he is mak-

ing for Arcadia, but is heading for a precipice. . . . The sad truth is that for nearly two centuries the West has been functioning from impulses which it has never seriously challenged or even questioned. Those impulses have been gathering momentum ever since the dawn of the Industrial Revolution, although they had an earlier origin.

The West should remember the extent of its gains from the exploitation of the colored races during the last 150 years and translate them into present obligations. We need not be surprised at the zest with which these races are driving out of their territories the last remnants of Western imperialism. The modern world is in the throes of . . . the turbulent last phase of the Industrial Revolution. Whether Western civilization can survive it is not yet clear.[4]

William Henry Harrison, the ninth president of the United States for a few months before his death, was this country's Indian administrator from 1800 to 1812. As governor, he had under his management the entire Indian Territories, embracing all of the lands west of the original states from Canada to the Gulf of Mexico. A product of colonialism, and a military leader with little in his background of other education or experience, apparently Harrison had none of the sensitivity for people, none of the respect for other cultures, and none of the tact or wisdom of diplomacy which were called for.

Under his administration, the Indian situation rapidly degenerated and he developed Kenya-like conditions within a very few years. This included a Mau-Mau-like, nativistic, blood-letting movement, Harrison's own repression of the native peoples, his settlement and re-settlement of the Indians, and the tearing up of treaties solemnly entered into. Where he was urgently invited to form an alliance of all the peoples of the area in a common purpose, he persisted in producing chaos and unnecessarily created the Indian Wars.

He was, of course, being pushed by many business interests into "getting that land." But the evidence is that the Indians did not really wish to keep their white brothers off the land. What they did want was to know that they too had a place and what that place was.

The history of this period is being continuously revised as more facts become known. It is now clear that the new solidarity that emerged among the Indians was not a result of British intervention. Nor did the British encourage the Indians to make war against the United States. Rather, the British were finally led by the Indians and by the evidence of division, confusion, and weakness which resulted from stupid policies of administration.

What emerges from the later studies is that the United States then had before it a splendid opportunity.[5] Under the leadership of one of the greatest and gentlest of leaders, Tecumseh, the Indians had created their own federation of tribes. Their desire was to be able to negotiate with the white man from the strength of their own unity. They had been inspired to do this because they knew the white man had in turn been inspired to form his own federation by contemplating the ancient Indian federation of the Iroquois nations. This way, they thought, would lead to mutual dignity and self-respect, enabling white and red brothers to live together in the same country in equality and peace under the "Great White Father" in Washington.

An amazing and unparalleled opportunity was thus set before these white colonizers, who could have united these two great federations in a single nation. It was the opportunity of enforcing its own solidarity, with a counterpart of Indian solidarity embracing all of the tribes on the North American Continent. Such a decision would have added the strength which was sorely needed in the continuing rivalries with the European colonial systems. The new and the native Americans could have worked together to make the country good, prosperous and great. But the white man, in typical colonial fashion, wanted the Indians divided and weak to suit his selfish purposes.

Tecumseh, one of the greatest of all American generals and statesmen, was finally lost to the Americans and so was his federation of tribes. But he was in no sense a traitor. To the very last he wished only the greatest and best things for his country, inclusive of the white man and his future.

With such a secure and permanent alliance of the two great federations, the whole course of American history could have been very different. There probably would have been no War of 1812. The incidents at sea would have remained incidents if the newly formed States had not been concerned only with their own solidarity — if they had been able to embrace all peoples of their territories in their newly formulated equality of citizenship. It may be doubted that England would have retained any hold upon the North American continent; the history of Canada would probably have been different. At any rate, a radically different course would have been taken across the continent in ensuing decades, a course very much nearer to the original egalitarian and liberal principles of this nation. This course could have gone far in preparing us for the world leadership responsibilities brought by circumstances upon us — responsibilities we have so far been unable to measure up to economically, socially, or morally.

Finally, and most important, the whole record of our relations with the Indians and our attitudes in our relations with all the peoples of the American hemisphere, both North and South, would have been drastically improved. The Monroe Doctrine would have remained the doctrine of hemispheric solidarity instead of evolving into the present doctrine of hemispheric monopoly. The latter, of course, is more in line with the motives and pursuits of American expansionism as it emerged into the "American Century."

Our course might have been a different course in practical, world-building ways; it might have fulfilled the vague, starry-eyed dream of establishing the democratic freedoms in every part of the world, which Americans as a whole have never yet been able to bring down out of the stratosphere. We, perhaps, would not have been as powerful or wealthy a nation as we are today; but we could have been wiser and truly a democratic people, and an example in democratic living toward which other nations might strive. This is the course we originally charted as a nation; it is not the course we historically pursued.

It is now time to question the impulses which have controlled the functioning of the West. They are not remote and inaccessible to our understanding. The impulses on which the West has acted are in every one of us. Understanding these impulses clearly in their psychological and sociological manifestations is essential to emancipation from them.

An excellent help to such understanding is *Richer by Asia, A Personal History,* by the American war psychologist, Edmond Taylor, who was stationed in India during World War II.[6] He was there when the nerves of the rulers had reached their rawest edge, when fears had mounted until for many, a state bordering on insanity had been reached.

Part II of the book, "The Pathology of Imperialism," analyzes a sickness which can begin in any of us as a fussy concern to manage others, as the desire to be above our fellows, as the drive to get ahead and have things better than others as symbols of our importance. We are all, in this sense, potentially imperialists. In some of us, this tendency is reinforced because we are internally in rebellion against imperialistically inclined parents who love us and mean well but who want to manage all our affairs. This is to emphasize that the imperialism of nations is not something that is remote from us. In Mr. Taylor's book, we see all these human tendencies in the distorted form that is the inevitable result of pushing the aggressive side of our natures at the expense of human qualities in others.

This study reveals also that it is the white man, the "master race," which is most in need of being freed from the chains of his own forging. The West's expressions of the meaning of emancipation in art and literature have been crass and literal, or superficial. The one below is always shown needing emancipation, never the one above. Chains are falling off the slave who is rising to his feet, or he is being lifted by his "superior" who has oppressed him. In India, the European white man was enslaved within the very establishments by which he sought to dominate, enslaved through his fears, through his inverted inferiorities, and through the bewildering uncertainties of his self-imposed marginal status.

The reason for the behavior of *The Ugly American*[7] is precisely the same: we are not going out into the world as free spirits, as genuine Americans. No man is strong enough to bear up under the strain on his character of the desire to be master. The white race needs the independence and equality of status of all the colored peoples at least as much as they need it for themselves.

Human relations, when bad enough, build up popular pressures for their own correction. This may be on a worldwide scale, as in the case of abolition in the nineteenth century and race integration in this century. A crisis emerging under popular pressures indicates a particularly bad cultural self-contradiction. William James explained the violent nature of the antislavery struggle in the United States in terms of such a crisis of "horrible self-contradiction."[8] But this nation has not yet heeded his warning that

> The lesson that our (Civil) war ought most of all to teach us is the lesson that evils must be checked in time before they grow so great. The Almighty cannot love such long-postponed accounts, or such tremendous settlements. And surely He hates all settlements that do such quantities of incidental devil's work. . . . Every war leaves such miserable legacies, fatal seeds of future war and revolution, unless the civic virtues of the people save the State in time.[9]

Even minimum democracy must take seriously our constitutional formula of an equality of status and opportunity which is not restricted by "race, color or previous condition of servitude" (Amendment Fifteen to the United States Constitution). The ending of race distinctions and inequalities, and all imperialisms based upon such distinctions, can be seen as the minimum essential if there is to be a free world.

We are in need of "an American declaration of conscience," wrote Anne O'H. Williamson, referring to the "Declaration of Conscience" of the American Committee on Africa, and especially to John Gunther's apologetic note that accompanied it. That Declaration had condemned the South African government's open, legalized separation of the races called *apartheid.* Gunther had apologized because of the racial tension existing in our own country. He offered "as an ameliorating factor that our founding documents declare liberty, equality and fraternity for all citizens of our republic." But Miss Williamson appropriately commented that

> . . . our constitutional law . . . has not been realized; its spirit has not left the pages of our Constitution to operate effectively. . . . The revered document exists too much as an idealistic theory that we proudly refer to in moments of patriotic zeal. But law has no existence until it is vitalized by action. Perhaps these skeletons in our national and state closets, tacitly acknowledged, need to be brought out into the open. Some truths need vocalization.

Nor, continues Miss Williamson, can we blame an unguided and irresponsible rabble. These groups

> . . . live in a climate of opinion that is favorable to their instinctive and inhuman behavior. They

take their cue from their community, even from certain agents of our government. . . . When these "representatives of the people" flaunt the highest law of the land and lend their mental cleverness to schemes for rendering null and void the fundamental doctrines of our land, they by their example in spirit and action become the "master minds" in the consequent anarchical condition.

Perhaps we need an "American Committee on America," a group consecrated and dedicated to the vital task of creating a constructive climate of opinion . . . that can and will offset and rout the demagogical forces that are disrupting our national life and belittling our national reputation abroad. Perhaps we need an *American Declaration of Conscience* subscribed to by the millions of fairminded Americans who need to stand up and be counted.[10]

This is an accurate picture of the current race issue in the United States. There are those in local and state governments, as well as in Congress, who do not hesitate to use any method, fair or foul, to make impossible any improvement in the nation's civil rights situation. Our democracy is betrayed by our racism before we leave our shores; we have neither moral nor social preparedness for the role of world leadership. Americans must prepare their nation for its task of extending freedoms to all peoples by extending freedoms at home.

The colored peoples of the world have nearly all at some time been victims of an imperialism which still continues and is based largely upon Western "race superiority" and domination. It is this widely held notion of racial and cultural superiority which lies at the heart of the West's inability to act decisively in world leadership.

People cannot choose to treat this merely as a problem of human relations. It is a moral problem and its solution rests in choosing between brotherhood and the subjugation of millions. It will be laid at rest one way or the other; the world will not remain two-thirds slave and one-third free.

Deteriorating United States relationships in many parts of the world are spelling out an important lesson for Americans if they still care about democracy. The lesson is that there is only one basis for continuing good relationships: a combination of good will and equal treatment. Use of force or its moral equivalent, financial pressure, is out. Equal treatment cannot mean immediate equality; equality is slow growing and mainly economic. But treating people equally is possible at once, and it is the only means that will lead toward ultimate equality. Treating people equally means granting them the respect with which we want to be treated. Learning this necessary lesson will have far-reaching implications for all of this country's relations with every part of the world; our future turns upon our mastery of this lesson. Either we will win all peoples through the good will that such equal treatment will engender, or we will lose our own freedom as we lose their support.

The world is watching the United States and the Soviet Union in Cuba and in Africa and around the world, and the stakes are high — the survival of the United Nations and the future peace and security of the world. The competition is not turning upon what will be put into outer space. It is turning on the answer to the question, *Whither go the colored peoples of the world?*

As a nation, we originally charted the course of equality for all people under one law. All our contrary operations have been subversions of government of the people, by the people and for the people. Americans now face a twofold call back to the American dream. The call comes from the world, wherein many peoples now rise, as once we arose, into the dignity and freedom of full human stature; as a world movement, this can never possibly be stopped. The call comes especially from Africans and from the Africans by descent who are our fellow Americans who remind us of the full meaning of the original spirit of the American Revolution: that governments must exist for men, not men for governments.

We must find practical ways to support and strengthen all movements for genuine independence and for the overthrow of tyranny or of economic domination. A movement of people of all nations must be developed to support the establishment of justice for all, under minimum world law which guarantees equality of citizen status to all men and opportunity for the development of all countries.

We must move into the human community, beyond all narrower loyalties. This is the meaning of *The Kingdom Beyond Caste,* Liston Pope's excellent book on this problem.[11] Effort on the local level is the real test; success demands work on such specific issues as open occupancy in housing and inclusive membership in churches. Wherever the economic foundation for resistance is being snatched out by the foes of freedom, a river of financial backing must flow. The struggle must be carried into all those places where people are losing their security because of their stand for human dignity.

We must strive to discover the deep inner meaning of emancipation. This development must work from both directions at once; integration is a two-way street. We can all be completely color-blind if we try. Admittedly, it will be easier for the white race to become unconscious of color than for the long-suppressed colored peoples to disregard whiteness.

Manifestations of color discrimination, like any other disintegrating sectionalism, negate and destroy the community. These characteristics in society, as in all organisms, indicate disease and lead to death. An integrated community is perhaps the profoundest and most significant positive achievement that is possible in human relations.

Increasing numbers of students and others are now moved by conscience and reason to support the nonviolent Freedom Movement against the conspicuous and vastly complicated evil of segregation and discrimination. The Freedom Movement seeks to emancipate all of us from an evil which brings serious degradation to every person involved in it on both sides. No movement in the history of our nation has exhibited a more unflinching devotion, a more joyous readiness to suffer and even give life for the establishment of a fully democratic America. This movement, which began in an isolated fashion in a few locations in the Deep South,[12] now extends organizational strength throughout both South and North. It is a significant instance of the awakening of Americans everywhere to the inequalities which persist in our nation and of the achievements attainable through group solidarity, moral conviction and inspired leadership.

This great human drama now being played against the backdrop of the Stars and Stripes had a previous act performed in the nineteenth century. Echoes of this earlier drama are heard onstage today.

At the beginning of the last century and even later, people of the West, crediting Aristotle, said that domestic slavery was within the nature of man; that God had created men, some to be masters and some to be slaves. Slavery therefore would never end.

Between 1830 and 1844, demands for the abolition of domestic slavery spread throughout the northern United States, largely through a movement of youths determined to end slavery by pressing for what they called "The Immediacy of Repentance." The movement followed upon the heels of "The Great Awakening" of Finney, the revivalist. Leaders were trained in Lane Seminary; at the close of the well-known "Lane Debate" came the famous "Lane Rebellion." An entire student body walked out when told they must swerve from their purpose to free the slaves, and that they must compromise in practical ways with a people not ready to lay down slavery.

At this time there already existed a radical antislavery movement, led by Garrison, which called itself the "Immediatists." They were in favor of abolishing slavery by capturing political power; how, they knew not. A clerical antislavery movement, the "Gradualists," led by Lyman Beecher, fought these Garrisonians. The ministers favored abolition through education. The quarrel over methods split the national antislavery society and rendered it ineffectual.

Later, between these two contending extremes, came "Weld's Seventy." The members of this movement began the work to which they had given their lives, laboring with specific techniques and extraordinary results for their "immediacy of repentance." This powerful spirit-ual-social movement was inspired by and centered around one of the Lane Seminary students, Theodore Dwight Weld, who shunned publicity. He had been the youth worker of Finney's "Holy Band." Weld gathered his youthful force about him, subjecting them to intensive training in institutes where he developed the techniques of conversion into a powerful weapon of social reform.

These young "Anti-Slavery Association Agents," beginning in Ohio, spread through the churches their gospel of release for all men from the tyranny of slavery and called for repentance. They left behind them little bands of the dedicated which became the Abolition Societies of the North. These young men were buffeted and abused, and there was violence, but their cause was won.

The full story of this spread of *The Antislavery Impulse* illustrates the power of the American's own weapon — the "all-sided sword."[13] The great social revolution that ended slavery was a spiritual one; it was waged by men with strong spiritual convictions. If the social revolution of our day is to be democratic and peaceful, it must be won by a similar spiritual movement.

Among the records of the meetings of the abolition societies there is evidence of a great deal of impatience at their having been confronted with antislavery alone. The country bristled with problems that had already been proposed for solution; it was one of the greatest of reform periods on both continents. Some felt that they ought to put aside the slavery question and get on with the other great issues which needed attention, just as many now complain that our nation is giving too much attention to the segregation issue. But in any movement to purge and purify, the axe must be applied to the roots of the tree; little else could be done, even in the North, until slavery was abolished.

Today, little else can be done in the world until discrimination based on color is abolished. As our earth becomes smaller through modern internationalizing processes, inevitable and inexorable as they are, the problem of human integration becomes more and more obviously the ultimate basis for the solution of all other world problems, in economics, politics, organization and defense.

FOOTNOTES CHAPTER EIGHT

1. W. E. Burgardt DuBois, *The Souls of Black Folk* (24th ed.; New York: Blue Heron Press, 1953), p. 13. (First published 1903.)

2. George Adam Smith, *The Book of the Twelve Prophets,* Vol. I (London: Hodder & Stoughton, undated), pp. 143-144.

3. A personal experience of the author illustrates this point well. In India, my wife and I were confronted with the practical necessities of the rationalism of superior status when we went there as missionaries in 1925. Immediately, by the appointment to our jobs, by the way we were expected to live, by the social distance we were asked to maintain, we were placed in the strange world of a favored race. I now marvel that the suddenness of that plunge rendered us unable to question what was happening, unable to question that I had been elevated, but one year out of the university and without educational experience, to the combined role of principal and manager of a large boarding school, over a capable Indian leader with long experience and special fitness for the job. I know now that I had the magic skin color and the Western credentials.

I was suddenly faced with two separate categories of thought which had developed within missions as a whole, being as they are, partially a copy of the ways of the ruling group. One category of thought operated in relation to one's own race and the other, in a different sphere, applied to the race with which the missionaries were associated in labor. This dualism worked out into a thousand details, from the house one lived in to the hat one wore and the title "sahib" by which one was known. This taking for granted of the white prerogative, without question of qualification, this subtle temptation for even the missionary to forget Christian truth, convinced me that color prejudice had become inherent in the white man's psychology. He carried this feeling of superiority and its rationalization with him unconsciously.

4. Wilford Wellock, "New Horizons" (privately published pamphlet, 1955), from the Introduction.

5. Glen Tucker, *Tecumseh Vision of Glory* (New York: Bobbs-Merrill Co., 1956).

6. Edmond Taylor, *Richer by Asia* (Boston: Houghton Mifflin Co., 1947), especially Part II, "The Pathology of Imperialism," pp. 29-104.

7. William J. Lederer and Eugene Burdick, *The Ugly American* (New York: Norton, 1958).

8. Horace M. Kallen, *The Philosophy of William James,* pp. 312-315.

9. *Ibid.,* p. 314.

10. Anne O'H. Williamson, "The Editor's Postscript," *Journal of Human Relations,* VI, No. 2 (Winter 1958), 159.

11. Liston Pope, *The Kingdom Beyond Caste* (New York: Friendship Press, 1957).

12. Ralph Templin, "Human Frontiers," *Journal of Human Relations,* Autumn 1956, Autumn 1957, Summer 1957. For a summary of the beginning of this upsurge of conscientious assertion on the side of Negroes in Montgomery, Alabama, and on the side of whites in Koinonia Community in Americus, Georgia.

13. Gilbert H. Barnes, *The Antislavery Impulse* (New York: D. Appleton-Century Co., American Historical Assoc. Pub., 1933).

CHAPTER 9

CONSCIENCE: THE CITADEL
OF DEMOCRACY

Facing the loss of those liberties that have been the very source of our greatest blessings, we citizens of the Western world are keeping our eyes steadfastly turned from the handwriting on the wall. We are heartily sorry that our superior way of life is getting out of hand; we would like to have things more as they were. But we would rather pursue business as usual than think too much.

We are sorry about the most recent scientific arrangements for self-destruction, of course. We are sorry for the helpless recipients of our new methods in our distant battlegrounds and proving places for our frightful experimentations, which we keep as far as possible from our own homes. We are sorry that our Negroes find it necessary to fight the status quo. We are sorry about the crushing tax burden. Sorry that our Western social system creaks on its ancient skids; that it periodically stalls when left to itself; that it increasingly needs wars (or massive reconstruction of the devastated areas) to keep it going.

Yes, we are sorry; these things disturb our complacency. We would like to be our old Western selves — "East of Suez," and enjoying our peaceful and prosperous business. We would like to get back again to our serious and comfortable exploitations, our familiar wars; not too often, with the deaths of only a few, and mostly others' sons. Oh, yes, we are sorry! We want a better world, of course. But not too much better.

People cannot improve society without changing themselves, because constructive development of institutions is dependent upon the mental and spiritual growth of persons. It is equally true that human beings cannot change permanently unless their institutions also change.

Does this explain what happened to the West's war to make the world safe for democracy, its war to end war, its Four Freedoms? Does it explain why we now live in a world where democracy was never more threatened, where the human race lives in constant fear of devastating and suicidal war, where our remaining freedoms may be sacrificed at any moment for other preferred interests, and where nations have never been so divided or so concerned about national survival?

Nor can the West claim that these threats have come upon it from outside. The Western world is still very young; it can scarcely yet claim that it has ever made an important reform stick. We can call no man names. We ourselves are both inheritors and propagators of the basic nature of our society, a nature older than either capitalism or democracy. The plain fact is that we who accept and shape Western culture are also shaped by it, and as we spread it throughout the world we are threatened by a world of our own making.

The West has riveted its chains securely upon itself. In South Africa, in East Africa, in the Deep South and other parts of the United States, the white man can apparently no longer live with himself even if left strictly alone with his ways. Perhaps he does not know what has happened; somehow all his greatest sentiments have turned sour, rending him internally asunder.

The world's predicament is a situation so complex that those most alert and concerned are perplexed as to where to take hold. Can all concerned people find a common core in their struggle for freedom and justice, in which all the ramifications of our modern bondage will be dealt with at the source?

We have one hope. All the storms, all our national hysteria, all the continuing whirlwinds of antidemocratic passions and fevered nationalism have not yet destroyed for our use our basic way of life or our original ideals of democracy. We do not have to look outside ourselves for the key which will unlock this prison house of Western society, and we share it with all citizens of this society.

It is responsible democratic man who must take the initial step for the world's new birth of freedom. That initial step, the immediate vehicle for the human spirit's mastery over itself, is individual repentance.

Repentance means turning away from a past; it means turning toward and actively seeking a new and different future. Masses and societies do not themselves repent, but repentance must determine the actions of an adequate number of the members of society. Repentance may be made social both in depth and in extent by a sufficiently concerned minority.

Although the matter of numbers is initially of minor importance, the West as a whole will have to be led into this necessary attitude. This is the work of the new pioneer on the frontier of the human community. He must begin this long trek both for himself and for all the world's peoples.

Responsible man must repent his loss of sovereignty wherever entrenched institutionalism — ecclesiastical, racial, political or economic — has sought to advance special interests at the expense of human values. He must repent his failure to share in equity with his fellow human beings, his failure to sacrifice actively to oppose and put down by nonviolent means every form of man's inhumanity to man. This means that a personal inner revolution must first occur — the spiritual upheaval that is basic to all genuine revolution.

Repentance in even the simplest matter is a most radical and revolutionary act. The word "radical" literally sums up "laid to the roots." The first place of "roots" is in men's motives. The second place, requiring simultaneous action, is in the motive-forming institutions of education, religion, communication and the like. Ours is an age that must begin deep within itself to rediscover the spiritual and cultural ground that can support a human society.

There is no way to make good or right prevail except by committing our lives to the good and the right. Religious leaders, educators, parents — all those who are responsible for moral training and leadership — must themselves recover lost spiritual ground. If they do not deliver themselves, how can they speak the word for this hour? Institutional and personal bondage to materialism must go. All those aspects of their own organizations and practices which suppress the human spirit — such as servile dependence on moneyed interests, support of aggressive or violent enterprises, overemphasis on ostentatious equipment, competitive struggle for bigness, lust for power and position — must be repudiated. The sword of the spirit, keen-cutting and effective, can never flash bright in the hands of persons seeking prestige or wealth or power or notoriety.

The struggle of freedom for humanity is a classless struggle for a way of life in which each will prosper because all prosper. Such a society can be sought and won only by this struggle which begins in men's hearts and effects its first revolution there.

And this means total revolution! No man wants a ruling elite, or its power, or its privilege, if he wants human beings to be in charge of their own lives and institutions and the works of their hands. Then the greatest and the least are equally worthy of consideration. The elite will then be the elite no longer, though they may be the elect.

The will to resist all that renders man less than he can be at his best is the only power we can trust. It is the power of people still slumbering or just coming to consciousness, the power of millions of our troubled but aspiring fellow men.

Joseph Mazzini, the great Italian liberator, opened vistas still on distant horizons of modern man's range of vision:

> High above every country, high above humanity, is the country of the spirit, the city of the soul, in which dwell all our brethren who believe in the inviolability of thought and in the dignity of our immortal soul, and the baptism of this fraternity is martyrdom. . . . Beyond the Alps, beyond the sea, are other peoples now fighting or preparing to fight the holy fight of independence, of nationality, of liberty; other peoples striving by different routes to reach the same goal — improvement of association,

and the foundation of an authority which shall put an end to moral anarchy and relink earth to heaven; an authority which mankind may love and obey without remorse or shame. Unite with them; they will unite with you.[1]

The world is struggling on fronts far from this front.

So the democratic job, keeping the human spirit in control, means a revolution within each life. It means freeing economics from our lusts which bind it. It means freeing others of our arrogance and aggressiveness. It means abandoning our preoccupation with violence in dealing with conscience, that solitary citadel of democratic hope and place of integrity of each human spirit.

This does not imply a mere escape within ourselves for the satisfaction of private salvation. It rather proposes social repentance personally experienced, for the guilt is ours, not that of someone vaguely called capitalist or warmonger or fascist or communist. It is ours, as is our share in representing the most widespread culture of our time. That culture will not change by any class conquest of the same old power-over-people which has brought the West to its extremity. Our culture will have to discard the self-contradiction in which it was conceived. Only the people, repentant and free, can help Western society to that achievement.

We have had ample recent demonstration that the man who is without fear can still be sovereign and can stand up against all the powers of the superstate. If he fails to win out over those powers, he nevertheless wins his own humanity. And he wins the support of others. It will require only a minority of such persons to turn the tide of affairs in the United States and in the whole world toward world law and peace.

The realization of such a seemingly utopian order may be years ahead, but it has already begun in human breasts fired with liberty and freedom for all men. This is the power and importance of conscience: no one can afford to wait for others to act or for masses to move, and one man of conscience inspires others. The Freedom Movement, like every movement of people with conscience, returns us in this land to the original American spirit, the spirit that is as universal as humanity. The ruggedness of unshakable conscience is the beginning, end, and eternal ground of human sovereignty and the source of human destiny.

The functioning of conscience thus represents the basic and determining principle in all democratic development at whatever levels of achievement. But its functioning has meant far more than this for the total evolution of the human species and the society which sustains and preserves man at a special level of life. The basic positive human reality, conscientious assertion, is that which has always extended the frontiers of man's mind and spirit outward into a vast and shrouded unknown. Conscientious assertion is thus that functioning of man which is responsible for the quests of science and philosophy and religion, for man in pursuit of truth and man living by truth.

It is conscientious assertion that declares, "The time is past for talk; I must act with my life." Though its spirit and essence have been illustrated by all the world's truly great, it has also been practiced quietly and calmly by thousands of unknown. It has never played a power game or snatched power from class to class. Its goal is universal; its faith is in the worth of humanity. It is the source of all just law and all government by consent of those governed.

Josiah Royce gave an excellent exposition of conscience and its meaning and importance in *The Philosophy of Loyalty*.[2] The supreme human achievement, which he terms "loyalty to loyalty," means living for the universal human qualities. People, he says, have always sought "the city out of sight." No man can ever rise above the sum of his "ideal of life which constitutes . . . his moral philosophy."

The modern psychologist says the same thing: man is at every point his own self-conception, what he has drawn out of his environment and integrated or not integrated at the core of his being. If there is in this total human equipment that mysterious something which leads him decisively to devote himself to the highest that he knows at a given time, however mistakenly, he is a man of conscience. As Royce puts it,

> . . . my conscience is the spirit of the self, first moving on the face of the waters of natural desire, and then gradually creating the heavens and the earth of this life of the individual man. This spirit informs all of my true self, yet is nowhere fully expressed in any deed.[3]

In summing up his definition of conscience, Royce says that this highest functioning is always compounded of two inseparable characteristics of conduct, decisiveness and fidelity.

> Decide, knowingly if you can, ignorantly if you must, but in any case decide, and have no fear. . . .

> With all your heart, in the name of universal loy-
> alty, choose. And then be faithful to the choice.
> . . . If one persists, *But you and I may be wrong,*
> the last word of conscience is, We are fallible, but
> we can be decisive and faithful; and this is loyalty.[4]

Such loyalty is the opposite of conformity. It is at
the same time the most individual and the most socially
constructive of human functioning; but it is always of
the individual, not of the masses. It is personal experience of the social community. Historically, it has been
the way of responsible men. The way of the state, mass
conformity, is its opposite.

It is conscientious assertion that has led man toward
his democratic realization.

Today, the individual's relation to the state under
democracy is a question coming steadily to the fore and
pressing with increasing insistence for clarification.
Every citizen concerned with the survival of democracy
must face and settle this problem. On its solution depends the existence of a free world, for democracy can
be realized or destroyed only by its defense or its betrayal in its place of inner integrity: the conscience of man.

Western culture has generally evaded this problem
of the individual conscience versus the state in two ways.
The most superficial way has been to assume what has
never been true, that the state and democracy are the
same. This statist evasion of democracy considers the
democratic state as a collective conscience. This view-
point overlooks the fact that throughout democratic history, the people have struggled against the exploitative
and autocratic state. This struggle has been democracy's
fundamental reason for being.

The idea that collectivity, coupled with the great superstate of the present, could lead toward the realization of democracy has been a serious mistake. Instead it has everywhere led toward increasing regimentation and diminishing freedoms. The present competition for a "place in the sun" forces the Western nation or its prototype to try to be at once the war state, the production state and the social welfare state; such pressures have put citizens under greater and greater demands with less and less regard for individual liberties. The modern state at its best merely tends toward modern forms of the very evils which democracy first set itself against. Totalitarianism is the end result of the superstate and its essential nature, competitive aggressiveness. Democracy can differ today from its original nature of struggle against the state only by being a greater struggle.

This statist evasion of democracy reveals a further contradiction. For purposes of military dominance, it is claimed that within the enemy state, democracy's way is to rise up and overthrow the state. This the people are urged to do; it has become the principal psychological aim of modern war. The statist is thus basically hypocritical: for him, on whichever side of the cold war struggle, his state is "democracy"; but, of course, the enemy state is not democracy. The statist reserves the right of conscience for the enemy citizen, and he encourages the exercise of conscience only for the citizen of the enemy state. In his own state, "democracy" is the regimented "collective conscience."

The other Western way of evading the problem of the individual conscience versus the state is that of the rationalist. The rationalist is more consistent than the statist, and he is more sophisticated, though he arrives at essentially the same conclusion. He tries to evade conscience altogether by assuming the reality of a modern never-never world within whose complexity any functioning of the highest mental equipment has no place. Conscience, like all the rest of what he calls "supernaturalism," has been exploded as a myth of an old order. For him, the possibility of the original democracy, popular sovereignty, has also been exploded. Since a pragmatic age can put no finger upon conscience nor examine it with a dissector, an effort is being made by the rationalist to define out of existence that part of man which makes him human.

The rationalist thus presents a psychologically and sociologically impossible concept of man: that man is either by nature one among the statistical many, or in special instances so favored that he is among the few who use the statistical many. Man, in either case, is not in this view a creature of conscience. The rationalist, if consistent enough, and he usually is, adds that man might as well forget democracy in its original, impossible meaning and get on with the business of making the state supreme in the matter of dealing out "general welfare."

The Soviet Union today uses the term democracy in this way. It can, under benevolent auspices, be a government for the people; but it is not by or of the people; and however concerned with its citizens, it cannot be democracy. If not sovereign, people are not free, no matter how benevolently treated.

These two methods of Western evasion of the problem of conscience versus the state, that of the statist and that of the rationalist, have much in common. Both refuse to recognize as essential to democracy the responsibility and the integrity of the individual. Both give totalitarianism of either left or right a rationale; advocates of both statism and rationalism try to blind all eyes to this basic issue. And the exponents of both these evasions are leaving the people of the world in chaos and on the brink of destruction, with nothing left to them but their consciences. Neither of these two evasions of the basic meaning of democracy — individual responsibility — can continue if democratic man is himself to survive.

Gandhi was a lawyer scarcely excelled in understanding of democratic legal processes. He once said that every proper democratic law carries with it the alternative to obedience which is available to every citizen. When the citizen believes a particular law to be immoral and enforcement a menace to his nation's welfare, it then becomes the citizen's duty to choose the alternative and openly and nonviolently to accept the full penalty of his act. This is an act of the highest obedience, according to Gandhi, and is open only to the law-abiding; those who violate law do not seek to face the consequences or to face openly the issue which the law involves. This is the summarized essence of the Gandhian position of the issue of the individual conscience versus the state.

It is difficult for a mind schooled in the current concept that a majority is a democracy, to grasp the Gandhian teaching. Yet it is Western and it is basic to democracy. Democratic progress throughout history has consisted in the acceptance, albeit partial, of three intermingled strands of basic principle. The three are

(1) The law is above authority.

(2) The people are above the law.

(3) The individual conscience is above people taken in the mass.

Democratic political achievement can be measured by the extent to which the first two of these basic principles have been enshrined in law. The first goes back at least to the Magna Charta. To it we owe all our civil rights and even the idea of rights beyond the reach of governments. The second upholds the reality of human consent, personal and popular — all sovereignty and representation. Although the third has been less accepted and implemented than the others, history shows that it has been the means to whatever other democratic achievement there has been.

The Gandhian position thus can be historically arrived at as the basis of all democracy; conscience, a name for man's highest functioning, is democracy's final irreducible minimum, its only ground, its ultimate hope. If this citadel is battered down, democracy is lost.

This is not the first time democratic peoples have been called by their times to act with conscience for democracy and against their states. Indeed, there has been little else to the story of democratic development; the limited democracy that has been politically realized is simply the result of such a struggle against the state and against the power elite which the state always tends to represent.[5]

The crucial and timely nature of this struggle between the conscience and the state in this country and throughout the world is being pointed up in a series of events and movements in which both individuals and groups are standing with conviction and courage against states and provincial governments. This has become a worldwide phenomenon. It means that people are again stirred to fight for their liberty as they were in the Revolution which brought democracy to the New World.

There is now a basic difference, however, which may have special significance for the future of democracy. By definition, democracy must be committed to its own method by which alone it can exist, the development of moral and social sentiment and will by persuasion only. Therefore it is highly significant that the present surge of conscience seems bent upon taking the way of nonviolence instead of violence. The existence of democracy in the future may well depend on the continuance of this nonviolence in the struggle of responsible democratic man.

FOOTNOTES CHAPTER NINE

1. Joseph Mazzini, Louis J. Rosenberg, *Mazzini: The Prophet of the Religion of Humanity* (Chicago: Charles H. Kerr and Co., 1903), pp. 78-79.

2. Josiah Royce, *The Philosophy of Loyalty* (New York: Macmillan Co., 1916).

3. *Ibid.*, p. 176.

4. *Ibid.*, pp. 189, 194, 196.

5. For an authentic record of the power within and behind the American state, see C. Wright Mills, *op. cit.*

CHAPTER 10

THE SEARCH FOR TRUTH

Democracy is the ideal of man who, through his organization of mutual aid, achieves sovereign control over his political, economic, social and spiritual destiny.

Democracy also involves a moral commitment of a religious sort. Indeed, a religion divorced from the political, economic and social fulfillment of common man is a religion divorced from morals, for it is in these spheres that questions of social morality arise.

The resolution of the world's present dilemma will require a revision of accepted moral, religious and social perspectives. A new morality and sense of purpose must be devised which will return peoples to the realities of their world of nature, of human nature and of man's innate creative capacity. The perpetuated fictions of the past have become malignant. We must seek new truths for a new age.

Religion in the West can be characterized as a blind eye. Because the eye is blind, the whole body stumbles in darkness. The secular world is crying out for some deep synthetic principle that can unify it. At the heart of the Judeo-Christian tradition is the concept that the familyhood of the human race is of great significance.

Church unity cannot fulfill this universal need. It will take more than ecumenicalism to restore light to the blind eye, to establish a foundation upon which a dis-

tracted world can build a structure for peace, reconciliation and cooperation. The crisis of this age is passing
judgment on the religion of the West, every church of
whatever name and sign.

In the United States and in most of the West there
is on the one hand a return to religion and a trend to
church union, and on the other hand a secularization of
religion. The return to religion is characterized by increases in church membership rather than by the quality
or effects of faithfulness and by the substitution of psychology for religious conviction. The trend to church
union is a tendency toward a diluted ecumenicalism based
on a desire for solidarity.

Religious beliefs are tending toward a nominalism
that accepts complacency instead of social concern, class
instead of brotherhood, and tolerance instead of moral
convictions. The corrosion of religion has been assisted
by a hedonistic concept of success, the impersonal nature
of organizational contacts with human beings, and the
secularization of church life.

One team of sociologists has concluded that worship
in the West is not centered in religion, since the greatest
unifying forces focusing the devotions of peoples are
nationalism and communism. (But is not communism
today also a form of nationalism?) This team, Ogburn
and Nimkoff, draw a historic parallel:

> Once before nationalism rose to great heights, as-
> sumed the proportions of a religion, and opposed
> the constituted religious authorities. This was dur-
> ing and following the French Revolution. It was
> proposed that the new religion of nationalism be
> called La Patrie. . . . The church lost much of its

power and influence because of this burst of nationalistic religion.[1]

The aspect of modern absolutism characterized by "thus saith the State," through its power over communication, builds its own mythology. Western nations are increasingly exemplifying this statism. Absolutistic nationalism pervades both the collective and the unilateral conduct of nations; it thus approaches the old theological absolutisms by substituting its own myth for the search for truth, and by seeking to control society and the individual. Its morality is a vassal's morality.

No absolutism, ancient or modern, religious or secular, can meet the needs of the free spirits of the earth. By definition, an unquestioned authority kills all desire to seek truth. An accepted absolutism with its quality of omniscience destroys man's urge to pioneer and renders the scientific quest impossible. Does it not also destroy the religious quest?

Absolutism's insistence on conformity replaces faith with fear, the light of knowledge with the darkness of ignorance, and the search for truth with an overworked fragment of discovery. Ancient absolutisms usually tried to dominate all aspects of life. Modern absolutisms frequently add to the whiplash of conformity the paralyzing effects of a specialized focusing of man's senses to a constantly diminishing aspect of reality.

Only vigilant human beings seeking truth from every possible source can free themselves from such absolutisms. Historically, man's freedom has involved his reaching beyond his orthodoxies in his searching for truth. In this quest, absolutisms have invariably been left behind. To escape the statist orthodoxies of the modern civilization is especially important for all the world's peoples; the West which once nourished the liberal tradition still remains its reluctant guardian.

The Protestant Reformation was not merely incidental to the awakening of liberalism in modern Europe; it was the new atmosphere which made men liberal. It not only combined the personal and social in a new dynamic experiencing of religion, it tied the new concept of direct personal access to God to practical applications of that concept in everyday life. The movement was nonconformist and, later, nonsectarian. At the outset, it was not nonreligious; secularism was a more recent development. Persecuted nonconformist religious groups became the custodians of almost all the democracy which remained in Europe after the great Napoleonic counterrevolution.

On its positive side, Protestantism stresses that true religion can be found only in the immediate experience, that true religion is a quest in which all stand as equals at every stage of the quest. An example is the Quaker emphasis upon the individual and group experience of the "Inner Light," and the expressions of its influence in all aspects of their daily life. "The just shall live by faith" was a watchword of the Protestant Reformation, but the faith was that of a dynamic experiencing of religion.

The religious emphasis that permeated and supported the whole of the Enlightenment started modern man in pursuit of truth. Truth, being universal, is impatient with the narrow loyalties of creed, caste, race or nation, condition of birth, or geography. It is equally impatient with all barriers to its discovery, whether of ignorance, superstition, authority, materialism, false pride, or bigotry. The religious fervor of the great awakening applied itself in a new sense to all people, all nations, all areas of life.

When the West exorcised the binding traditionalisms of an earlier age, it left its house in order but unoccupied. It was unwilling to take its new outlook seriously; the individual conscience as the final source of truth, as the ultimate arbiter, was abandoned. When the West became conscious of its destiny as the champion of freedom, it also became restricted by the narrowness and barbarity of its drive for conformity to its own special orthodoxies. It could not spread democracy as the experimentalism of the people and at the same time spread it as conformity to a preferred set of absolutistic economic and social principles.

In this context, the present need to revive the pursuit of truth and give it worldwide application becomes clear. Even in today's scientific search for truth, scientists themselves are alarmed about the failure of American scientists to continue the search for truth wherever it may lead. Much of the nation's scientific manpower is diverted into high-paying areas of industrial research which are designed to increase mass production, managerial control and profit but are nonproductive in a truly scientific or cultural sense. The products of this sort of research have frequently proved detrimental to human life and health. Much governmental research is devoted to military ends. There are scientists who can be persuaded that overtaking Russia is paramount.

Other scientists, however, are doing two things which are in sharp contrast. First, they are refusing to participate in socially wasteful and destructive uses of scientific knowledge. Second, they are pointing out the serious dangers inherent in the distortion of the search for truth.

Scientists who pursue truth wherever it leads are, of course, paying the price for their refusal to be diverted in their search.

The West once hoped that the common people, through the new insights of democracy and science, would master their world and create a brotherhood of man. But this age has not reached that goal; common man has never controlled science. We surrendered our own great idea and became a mob without a soul.

We cannot say that science has fashioned our world. We cannot say that what we call technology has yet become an instrument for achieving man's highest goals, physical, social, mental or moral. Though man has acquired amazing understanding of nature's laws, processes and forces, he is farther and farther from the real conquest of nature. Having suddenly lurched forward into an understanding of heaven's secrets, he is as suddenly flung back in his fears to the first mudsill in the slime of the misty flat.

A one-sided obsession with science, developing throughout the West from the rise of secular science, has now been tragically carried over into the social sciences. A complete science must be envisioned as an extension of man's spirit. The social factor should appear in all scientific equations, for it is man who is the knower, the discoverer and the user. Feats of science have been performed only in limited segments, often in disregard of man, the knower. The laboratory of man the knower has been nature; he has not made himself his first laboratory.

Thus has developed a dangerous and deadly dichotomy. The science of man-in-control tended to give way to a science of some men in control of other men. As science has become an instrument of power over people, for millions it has become an instrument of a new subjugation.

If one thinks of the search for truth as a total search, having as the criterion of its validity maximum human growth, one may then well ask, "When will we enter the age of science?" The truths of science are only a measure of momentary grasp or understanding: "This I know," or "This is how it seems to me"; included in all conclusions must also be the question which gives them true meaning, "What will we do with it?" This is as true for dynamic religion (a religion concerned with the problems of life rather than the absurdities of doctrine) as it is for science. Both are eternally revolutionary in casting aside the impediments of static dogma or outmoded theory in their quest for fuller knowledge and truth.

What we call the scientific spirit has many of the elements of the profoundest religious search. There is the hunger to know which led John Dewey to say that children were in attitude close to the true scientist. There is humility about knowledge which is also characteristic of unspoiled children. There is the experimental attitude, the spirit to try and try again. There is the spirit to revise, without which free inquiry is not possible. Through all, there is the persistence in the search and the true liberality which cannot rest in dogma, not even in a "scientific conclusion." There is the attempt to establish general principles, on the basis of recognized partial and tentative understanding, while living and acting, with due humility, according to the light of new knowledge. There is the hunch or faith which beckons the searcher onward toward what he neither sees nor knows, and the gamble which leads him to risk all for what he feels will prove true.

In all these elements, dynamic religion and science are alike in spirit; the religion-against-science controversy or dichotomy exists only where scientific inquiry has been stymied by religious dogma. Truth is undisturbed by this or any other controversy. Unaffected by mental wrenchings or furious arguments, truth is impossible to possess dogmatically. Nothing is true because some particular religion or authority sets it forth. All truths are set forth as they have been formulated and founded in human experience.

In our concern to control nature's forces, we have harnessed many natural sources of power; we have also managed to unleash forces over which we have little, if any, control, such as the atom. We have, however, throughout the course of recent history, neglected to socialize and control the most potent force in our world, the human mentality or the soul-force. The real age of science, if life and civilization are to survive, will be one in which the human spirit will hold sway over all natural forces, beginning with the humanization of its own mentality. Without learning to control this inner force, how can we hope to control and make use of the physical environment?

> The ancients . . . wishing to order well their states . . . first cultivated their persons . . . they extended to the utmost their knowledge. Such extension of knowledge lay in the investigation of things . . . all must consider the cultivation of the person the root of everything.[2]

This is a teaching of Confucius called "The Root of Everything," written about 500 B.C.

The ancient saying is remarkable for its identification

of the cultivation of our persons with what the West now calls science: the investigation of things. This cultivation of our persons, it points out, is the root of everything else.

This gives to science a deep and culturally encompassing connotation which is not found in the West. It is in this deeper meaning that Gandhi was extraordinarily scientific in his personal approach to religion, to life and to social and political problems.

The name of Mahatma Gandhi is irrevocably linked to "experiments with truth." It was one of his favorite phrases, and he used it to describe the quest of the life in which one's utmost awareness of truth can be lived. The nearest Gandhi came to expressing a formula for his own faith is his title of a series of personal episodes printed in his magazine *Young India* and called "The Story of My Experiments with Truth." (In this country it became *Gandhi's Autobiography*,[3] though it was not intended as such.) In these episodes, Gandhi reveals himself as the weakest of men with much frailty, but possessed of a unique inner and outer sensitivity and a vast devotion to his slender grasp of truth. Through his writing he invites us to witness his deepest struggles and his choice of steps, moving steadily in the chosen way.

Although experiments with truth might be merely the formula for science, it defines even better this religion of transformation which is unique for its simultaneous conquest of human nature and social environmental factors. The search for and experimentation with truth can be best described as the act by which one seizes upon all available knowledge and penetratingly examines all such fragments in the light of a human community and the probable consequences for human thought and social action. Such an act serves to clarify and concretize previously vague and fragmented ideas and notions and readies them for realization as actual truths to be initiated and acted out within the framework of society. This philosophy is nothing particularly new or modern. At its best, however, it probably is capable of a modern application which could embrace all that we mean by science, technology, democracy and a religion of life.

"I mean by religion," Gandhi said, "that which transcends Hinduism, which changes one's very nature, which binds one indissolubly to the truth within, and which ever purifies. It is the permanent element in human nature which counts no cost too great in order to find full expression, and which leaves the soul utterly restless until it has found itself, known its Maker, and appreciated its true correspondence between the Maker and itself."[4] This is far more than religion as usually conceived; it is more than life as generally lived. It is not a set of dogmatic beliefs, it is a method of living and dealing with life's problems.

This conception of religion comes close to science. Both in their fullest sense can be described as the search for and experimentation with truth. Actually very few persons have recklessly devoted themselves to searching for and experimenting with truth without concern for consequences or personal danger.

John Dewey, one of the greatest interpreters of science, made the classroom his laboratory. In his writings he conceived of the laboratory of democracy and of education in universal terms and as twofold: the inner volitional life of man and the external world of all environmental affairs of man. The philosophy of "interactionism" thus derived and applied to science, technology, education and the "religion of the community" left Western science far behind this man, its chief mentor. (In this connection, a study of what is regarded as a valid application of scientific methods in the social sciences is enlightening.)

Religion as revealed in varying degrees by reformers such as Jesus, Gandhi, and Kagawa carries with it the search for and experimentation with truth in the same intensity of devotion as we find among our greatest scientists.

A high degree of devotion to the pursuit of truth, the spirit to risk all, is distinctly a superior religious quality but does not belong exclusively to what we call religion. The purification of desire in terms of what any discipline means — laying aside every weight which may impede the quest — is dynamic religion's essential method, generally summed up under the term discipline or its equivalent (such as yoga). The surrender of the desire for reward is regarded by Hinduism as the highest religious attainment, "detachment." But these highest religious qualities also apply to the superior scientific attitude; the science of the Curies (Marie and Pierre), for example, approaches this religion and may even be identified with it.

A way in which religion goes beyond the legitimate scope of scientific inquiry is in its special propensity to integrate new knowledge into the mainstream of life. The scientific approach has tended to view reality in fragments. A dynamic religion views reality and life in its wholeness. To a particular science, the efficiency of a remarkable invention may indicate progress. To a religion of life, this increased efficiency has no intrinsic value whatsoever except as it serves to benefit "the last and the least of these my brothers." For dynamic religion the welfare and happiness of the least person is as central as that of the greatest person. Values born from this sense of completeness are, in their very nature, universally applicable. It is only in this manner that social and scientific truths should be evaluated and applied.

For example, are we really concerned for that part of the social science of democracy which we call civil liberties? Secularism in its segmental approach might say, "In this time of stress, limits have to be set on civil liberties for some people." But religion will say that to have civil liberties at all means that they must be preserved for the most irritating or obnoxious or threatening sect or minority. To withhold them from even one person is to invalidate them for all.

Another illustration is the Western machine called technology which works, as we say, with an efficiency of its own. It produces great material prosperity, of course. But one must ask, does it really work? Does it work for every man? Does it work for the sharecropper, the migrant worker, the Puerto Rican immigrant in East Harlem, the displaced person, the dispossessed American Indian? Does it work for the Vieques Island Puerto Rican population, who were expelled from their ancestral lands after fifteen day's notice to make room for America's most eastern military outpost in the Western hemisphere? Does it work for the people of debased and ravaged and jeopardized Okinawa?

Even the most fragmental glimpse of truth in any area must accept as the criterion of its reality human living in its universal totality. Religion must not rest with a truth in a limited frame of reference. Neither could a complete science.

In the West, to experiment with truth is now practically unheard of or, at any rate, not regarded as scientific. It is this lack in Western science that has given the phenomenon of Gandhi's life, movement, experiments and death their special significance against the Western background. Future historians may regard Gandhi as the most consistent pursuer of his age of the truth which makes men free, and the most valiant experimenter with truth in the greatest of all laboratories, the human community.

A constructive course in line with Western culture's soundest aspirations must be to return the West to the comprehensive all-life search for and experimentation with truth which was the original genius of its liberalized approach to all human problems. It can set this way of experimenting with truth over against any and every known way whether of the right, the left, or middle-of-the-road; against every absolutism, ancient or modern, whether of "thus saith the Lord" or "thus saith the State." This way of total experimentation with truth, which the modern Western genius originated, is the way of constructive solution also and, indeed, the way that involves the greatest apparent risk and demands the greatest moral courage.

FOOTNOTES CHAPTER TEN

1. Ogburn & Nimkoff, *Sociology* (Boston: Houghton Mifflin Co., 1958).

2. Robert O. Ballou (ed.), *World Bible* (New York: Viking Press, 1944), p. 509.

3. M. K. Gandhi, *Gandhi's Autobiography* (Navajivan — 1941).

4. Marc Edmund Jones, *Gandhi Lives* (Philadelphia: David McKay Co., 1948), pp. 59-60.

CHAPTER 11

EXPERIMENTALISM: ITS MEANING FOR DISCIPLINE AND TRADITION

In the search for truth, the mind cannot be closed to truth from any source; truth has no regard for name or date of discovery. To the experimental mind, truth can speak; through the experimental mind, truth becomes preeminent and dynamic. Truths arrived at by the facile, experimenting human intelligence are opposite in spirit to the sterile truths of dogmatic religion.

There can be no pride in the possession of final truth, because the achievement of truth is an ongoing process and our knowledge of the whole can be only fragmentary at any given time. There is always the possibility that one may be mistaken in one's conviction: this possibility is an appropriate basis for a significant humility. But it is not a basis for doubt or hesitation. An experimenter with truth must yield devotion to the inner prompting at a given moment. It may be a small measure of truth or even a mistaken hint, but the mind's devotion to the pursuit sets it right in time.

Thus he is a dependable instrument of truth who regards the truth he has grasped at any moment with humility and devotion. If the searcher believes he has arrived, he cannot be used further by truth; yet if he does not base his actions upon his limited grasp or understanding, there can be no further progress toward an awareness of what is actually sought. For it is devotion to truth which leads to the discovery of further truth.

"Understand and live in the significance of each thought as it arises," urges Krishnamurti, one of the modern masters of the meditative method.[1] He advises against the attempt to crowd ideas out of the mind or to whip the being into any line. One must always strive for growth where one is at a given time. The inner life is one's altar; let thought lie there until it is understood. We need no magic, no strain, no act of will to put ourselves in the care of the supreme spirit of life. The supreme gift, the gift of life, is already ours. We grow by becoming acquainted with ourselves. The maximum function of God's spirit is to introduce us to our real selves.

The struggle of the human spirit to achieve maximum fulfillment is limited to no sect nor section. Sectarian religion, in its striving for unity, may be likened to a pyramid, the broad base of which is the warring, disputing plane of earth-bound consciousness. This plane is divided by men's differences as each religion is itself fractioned into innumerable subdivisions. But unity and truth, which constitute the apex, tower above and out of reach of the warring factions below. This higher truth, as it is reflected to some extent in all religions, is the motive within each faith capable of lifting it toward the oneness and indivisibility of the universal. The founder of each of the great religions was himself first moved by an experience of universal, cosmic consciousness. But the disciples and followers of these religions became sectarians, the jealous, competitive contenders for orthodoxies which they themselves fashioned.

As the searcher is lifted within his own faith by this cosmic experience, his nature begins to take on the attributes of the apex of the pyramid: its drawing of all into its oneness, its indifference to boundaries fixed at lower levels, and its identity with and responsibility for the form of the whole of its being. It is thus that any shift across boundaries of religions at lower levels loses its relevance for the searcher after truth.

It is thus, also, that a perfect fellowship in faith cuts across religious boundaries, as did the life long fellowship of the English priest, C. F. Andrews, and the Hindu reformer, Gandhi. Neither shifted to the other's religion. Such a shift could have resulted in great loss: loss to them personally, loss in the richness of their fellowship, and loss to their people.

And so a dynamic faith is experimental and unfolding in life. It is not of any absolutism, dogma, system, or method, nor the absence of any of these. It is the inner mind searching for the best light upon each new step. It is a continuing quest for certainty.

What place does discipline have in this religious view? Discipline is the concentration of available energy. Who knows how much energy of various kinds is available to the human being? Energy is a unity; the laws governing its use are universally applicable.

The problem of human discipline may be seen as the problem of concentrating the energy available to us and directing it into the accomplishment of what we earnestly seek. "Strait is the gate, and narrow is the way which leadeth unto life, and few there be that find it."[2] Here is a principle so general that it applies to every great purpose that people set before themselves. If the kingdoms of medicine, of athletics, of any art or science are unavailable except by such concentration of all the accessible powers of mind and body, is it not also true that the kingdom of the inner spirit is inaccessible to those who neglect to concentrate their energies in their quest?

The Hindu ideal of *bramacharia only for those who desire to make the search for "realization" their aim, and who therefore turn from the role of "householder,"* contains this scientific meaning of concentration of the energies of life. Hinduism includes evil, suffering, destruction and death in its sense of unity in the supreme reality. Bramacharia rests upon this basic concept of unity. The search sets before the life the goal of identification with the eternal creativity lying at the heart of all being and form of being. For the masses, in whom this sense of the unity of all things is also the basic concept, the search is one which stretches through the eternities of many births. For the adherent to bramacharia, access to realization within the space of a lifetime is thought to be possible — full realization resulting from the concentration of all available energies, those known and those unknown.

This quest for understanding, covered by the general term yoga, finds its purpose and its functioning within each life at the highest possible level of its own being. The West has falsely if naturally regarded its meaning simply as that of strict sexual chastity, whereas chastity is merely one of its elements. Sex, a creative urge at a physical level, is hallowed by the Hindu religion for the masses who never get beyond the "householder" stage of development. The practitioner of bramacharia leaves this level, but does not spurn it or regard it as unclean. He rather seeks co-creativity in his identity with the supreme reality which is inclusive of all levels of creation and functions in all being. This is the Hindu meaning of bramacharia.

Whatever we of the West may think about this ideal, we cannot justly class it with the religious concepts which, by emphasizing the conflict of good and evil in human life, develop the sense of sin that attaches itself to carnal experiences. Even the utmost opposition to the bramacharia ideal does not warrant this attack; these arguments are specious. Bramacharia is not abnegation of human urges. It simply seeks to transform and channel these powers through sublimation. It is a discipline aimed at the concentration and focus of diffuse energies toward higher pursuits.

Some believe that it is part of the search for truth to free men from all the old restraints. The disciplines of the old discarded "Superstitions," as they were called, did not require replacement, and for the most part they were not replaced. If license did not result, it was generally because of other motives for seeking a "strait gate." But it was diffcult for modern man, upon being delivered from his sense of sin, to see any reason for religious discipline.

Modern pedagogy has been more scientific. It has taught that the only effective discipline is to arouse interest in the pupil in the etymological sense of what is between the learner and his goal. To overcome obstacles requires persistence. The effectiveness of any discipline, whether from within or without, is measured by "the depth of hold the foreseen outcome has upon the person."[3] Progressive education, therefore, if it is worthy of the name, provides not less but more and stronger discipline, in the true meaning of the term.

If achievement requires surrender of the pupil to his goal, then the pupil's surrender to each step leading him to his goal is his discipline. He cannot actually choose his goal except by choice of step after step, each of which is, in its own character, directed toward the goal.

The end cannot justify the means either in education or in life. On the contrary, we can actively choose a goal only as we choose some means in which we see a definite likeness and appropriateness to the goal. This is why the use of physical force as a way to peace is impossible of success. This is why religious experience as a way to material success is sheerest hypocrisy. This is why whatever gets our attention gets us. This theme runs through eighty-two verses of the Sermon on the Mount (Matthew 5 and 6). Most of the Sermon is saying that men get whatever they seek. In various ways they have their reward.

The climax of the passage turns the meaning around: What men seek gets them. Moffatt translates it, "Where your treasure lies, your heart will lie there too." What has our attention commands our faith; people give themselves to material security in terms of gain and savings because that is where they put their trust.

If one's trust is in the search for truth, one is not apart from life in the world. Quite the contrary; being more *in* the world can come by being less *of* the world. Electricity in its raw form is an illustrative analogy. When electricity is not insulated from earth, it wastes away futilely or is a danger. In order to be useful, electricity has to be held within bounds and focused in concentrated measure through fitting mechanisms — the bulb, the motor. Such concentration and focus are also basic to the life that is lived in seeking and experimenting with truth. In this respect the deepest meaning of spirituality is an all-embracing practicality which cannot allow life to be parcelled out into fragments. It renders impossible a science which is "pure" because amoral, a business which is accepted because practical or efficient, a physical draining of life with its inevitable toll of the spirit, or a spiritual side of life which ignores actual human behavior.

Such compartmentalized living and thinking is inconceivable to the person searching for and experimenting with truth. One must seek to perform his everyday duty according to the light within at each moment, and with utter disregard for the consequences to himself personally. There can be no quest for popular support or other personal rewards. No specious rationalization of conduct, no high-flown apologetic for a faith of accommodation, can meet the test of this pure water of life.

What is the place of the religious traditions of any faith in a religion of dynamic experience? What is the role of the traditions of the past in the devotionalism of the continuing and living present?

When courageous persons pursue truth to make its discoveries their way of life, they become not only sensitive to and aware of what is available within, but also increasingly reverent toward all that is external and all that is in the past of the whole human race. It is humbling to become aware of the unfolding of truth within human experience.

Even the greatest saint in his moment of ecstasy cannot but "wear the chain he forged in life," to use Dickens' classical phrase. His sainthood is a series of luminous moments, but each moment is influenced by those that went before. Every life must be built not only upon its own small past, but upon that greater past, that flow of history from which each life arises. There is no "pure and virgin moment," as Aurobindo said.

This is why there is no contradiction between putting roots deeper in one's own faith and becoming more open at the same time to every other religion and source of truth. Religious traditionalism takes on a significance in the search for truth which it could not otherwise possess. If we cut ourselves off from tradition in order to be modern, we are as much as saying that there is no importance in what has come before us, that history and culture are "bunk." It is in our traditions that we must seek out the records of past experiments with truth, insofar as these records have been preserved. Like the prospector, we can trace the slender vein of valuable ore. Prospecting the religious traditions for precious stuff results in a transmutation of traditionalism which greatly broadens its scope, yet purifies it as gold ore is panned and refined.

The assertion might be made that such a search for truth from all sources could but result in a broad, watered-down eclecticism. It is rather the traditional orthodoxies of all existing religions, in their popularly accepted forms, which are the watered-down eclecticisms. No one of them exists in the purity of its origin. Century after century, each has gathered the bag and baggage of traditions from various cultures and other religions, adding them in the name of the original teacher of the religion. (To be possessively defensive of all that our religion has passed on to us and of all that goes under its name is not wise; who tries to defend all may try to defend the indefensible.)

There are three reasons why it is important, in searching for truth, to put our roots down deeper into our own religious traditions while at the same time being open to truth from all other sources. First, we have to begin the search where we are. We cannot by any personal act, magic or religious formula be transported out of our own beginnings.

Second, careful study reveals that our own religion is not what we had superficially thought it to be. We find ourselves stripping away incrustations of long outmoded institutionalism when we look critically into the development of any faith. Recognizing the accretion of centuries is an important exercise because it helps us to understand the human weakness in which we share. Scarcely any religion known to man began other than as revolt against religious traditionalism: Jesus revolted against Hebrew servility to Mosaic law, Buddha against Hindu religious rigidity, Laotze against Chinese punctiliousness. The greatest prophets of all ages and places rebelled against excessive formalism.

A third and most important reason for exploring our own faith is that the religion of our background is usually the religion of the society and of the people about us. To find a deepening of life within that tradition is to find a deepening for all our own people. When we care more for religious traditions or systems or exercises than we do for people, we betray the true purpose behind all religions, the amelioration of human anxiety and suffering.

One who takes the Christian tradition seriously enough to trace it back to its roots will find that it is a fusion of other great religions still existing in our time. Jesus, who lived and died a faithful Jew, was not a Christian; he never tried to found a new religion; his first followers were Jews, not Christians; they wished to improve Judaism, but they had no desire to leave it.

Jesus found Judaism particularly compromised in his time and did not represent it as a whole. What he did represent and fulfill was a fresh outbreak within ancient Judaism. Such outbreaks can be traced throughout Judaic history. The constituted rivulets of dissatisfaction which set themselves over and against the mainstream of tradition and had their origins in the teachings of the earlier prophets.

Whence came this radical shift in thought away from prevailing theocratic nationalistic Judaism? Why did God now begin to say even of the Jewish Dispersion, "I am the Eternal, your God, training you for your good, leading you by the right way. . . . It is too slight a service to set the clans of Jacob up again . . . I now appoint you to bring light to the nations, that my salvation may reach the world's end"?[4]

Many modern scholars agree that this remarkable shift away from a God only for Israel to the Father of all the nations of earth came out of the Persian Zoroastrian influence. So the study of Zoroastrianism as well as Judaism is necessary to trace the roots of the Christian tradition. Ahura Mazda of the Persians was never regarded as god of a particular people. He was the Sky Father, the Father-God of all upon the earth, whose will is that "love shall support justice through deeds" of those who "commune with Health and Immortality."

Doctrinal insurrection can be traced all through Christian history up to the present moment. It is the manifestation of what Francis Peabody called the Church of the Spirit in contrast to the church of authority: the authentic stream of truth flowing like a subterranean river beneath accretions of creedalism and formalism, "a stream of spiritual vitality . . . always testifying to its source and transmitting the water of life."[5]

This minority stream is not confined to the Judeo-Christian history. Other existing religions, particularly Hinduism, have similarly become vehicles of this same flow of truth to the ends of the earth. It cannot be identified with the institutionalism of any religion, including Christianity. At intervals it has burst forth through centuries of incrustations from its pure, unsullied source.

How, then, can we know what to believe? Can we say what our faith is? The discovery of a faith lies in the constant questioning and reformulating of one's position. Each of us has to work out his own salvation with fear and trembling. The most that others can do is help. We may examine the world's greatest teachings as possible building blocks of a new understanding and devotion which is our own, but no borrowed or inherited faith can be personally vital. For understanding, we may turn for some revelation of truth to two great gospels of grace, the New Testament account of Jesus and the Hindu Bhagavad-Gita. Both these gospels support the concept of an inner religion which is to be expressed in life's work. Both set forth a religion of searching for and experimenting with truth. The Gita is a post-Buddhistic writing of near the time of Jesus, according to the scholarly critics who have analyzed its text. The inability of some Western writers to interpret the Gita as a nonviolent treatise is due to their literalism; the application of scientific criticism, either historical or textual, to the book, reveals it in a different light.

Jesus, in his teachings of the "Kingdom," concerned himself with a motivation capable of laying hold of and transforming everything in the environment. The institution, he said, was made for man; spiritual realization involves man's supremacy over all he creates. Nothing in man's culture can be omitted from spiritual consideration. From this view of religion, the extension of man's spirit and moral ascendency in the affairs of his society is actually the means of whatever spirituality man can ever know. Jesus lived and met his death according to this view. In deliberately turning away from an amazingly useful service in villages to go to Jerusalem, he brought to a focus the political crisis of his day and concentrated all the force of his "kingdom not of this earth" against its violence.

So with the community which gathered around his memory and became the Christian Church. It took shape as a brotherhood solving its social and economic problems in harmony with the spirit within its members which had made them "of one heart and one soul." They were called the people who "have turned the world upside down."[6]

These brotherhoods, later called Nazarenes and finally Christians, in their long and historically famous nonviolent struggle against the old Roman social order, finally won out through love and self-sacrifice. The story of the beginning of that early Christian movement, long before it became a church or a religion, is a record of the effect of one of the great gospels.

The other great gospel of grace, the Bhagavad-Gita, supports and sets forth this concept of an inner spirituality laying hold of all of life's activities to command obedience to the highest human principle. As in the Book of Job, the dialogue form is used to set forth the conversational wrestling of God with man and man with God.

Also as in Job, allegory is used as the literary vehicle.

From the great ancient epic, the *Mahabharata,* the writer of the Gita presents a scene in which two armies are poised and ready for battle. Between the armies waiting to strike stands the chariot of Arjuna, the warrior, who represents man confronted with the external requirements of life in a violent world. With Krishna, his chariot driver, representing God in human form, he wrestles in heart, mind and spirit over the agonizing problem of the absolute life confronting a relativistic world.

This struggle has to be seen against the background of the religion of Hinduism for an understanding of its message. Renunciation, through abnegation of the demands of earthly living, had been popularly set forth as the way of spirituality. But Arjuna is a man of action, though of deep spiritual desire and insight. The struggle is not an easy one for him. Gandhi interpreted the Gita as an allegory of the life of all devout people who desire to fulfill God's purpose for bringing them into the world.

The problem in the Gita is that of the active man who devotes himself to good — to love and truth — in a world characterized by a violence that thwarts and crucifies love and truth. The conclusion is characteristically Hindu: man can find his higher path of action through yoga, the Hindu methods for practicing the presence of God.

But before that conclusion, the groundwork for the solution of the problem has been laid in terms of a different kind of reunuciation: it is to be renunciation not of life nor of action in the external field, but renunciation of the reward for the action. One is to be detached from the results of what one does when moved to fulfill God's purpose and will. As a key verse expresses it, "Action is thy duty, reward is not thy concern" or, with Kipling "treat those two imposters (triumph and disaster) just the same."

Gains Glen Atkins used for the apt title of his study of comparative religions, *The Procession of the Gods.* Of course it is really the story not of a procession of gods, but of the procession of humanity. We ourselves become part of that procession as it emerges in our generation. As we enter this procession of man toward truth, every part of the struggle to achieve it becomes equally precious to us, because mingled with our reverence for absolute truth is our reverence for the race of which we are a part, the human race in all places and ages. There is, therefore, a double universality which is inescapable: the universality of truth which is unchanging, timeless and unaffected by our conquest of its fragments, and the universality of the human race. Both are precious beyond possible recording.

To experiment with truth is to purify one's motives and loyalties until devotion can be single and steadfast toward truth and only truth, the universal character of both cosmic reality and the human race. This linking of cosmic reality with humanity returns us to the originally authentic genius of the Enlightenment, from which sprang the ideals of democracy.

FOOTNOTES CHAPTER ELEVEN

1. A formula which sums up Krishnamurti's teachings about meditation. Source unknown.

2. Matthew 7:14 (King James).

3. John Dewey, *Democracy and Education* (New York: Macmillan Co., 1932), p. 150.

4. Isaiah 48:17 and 49:6 (Moffatt).

5. Francis Peabody, *The Church of the Spirit* (New York: Macmillan Co., 1925), p. 55.

6. Acts of the Apostles 2:44-47, 4:32-37 and 17:6 (King James).

CHAPTER 12

SOCIAL EXPERIMENTATION:
SAFER THAN A KNOWN WAY

Man's struggle to dominate, debase and exploit his fellow man has in every age been the cause of vaunted ambition, of insane dreams, of rage. It is a struggle which has been intensified among the larger social units, especially among mass aggregations dominated by centralized dictatorial leadership. It has led to the destruction of tribes, peoples, empires and even whole civilizations. Memorials of man's failure to understand himself are strewn about this earth, the permanent markers of human self-demolition.

In the West, social development as a continuing struggle of the individual against others, especially in its prevalent form of competition, has been rationalized by an inaccurate interpretation of Darwinism. This concept of survival and improvement through the struggle of man against man is not the conclusion of Darwin, nor is it supported by study of man's evolution. There never has been any guarantee that good and excellent qualities would endure in a struggle for survival. Arthur Morgan called attention to this fact:

> Survival of the fittest means no more than survival of the power to survive. In human affairs, as elsewhere in the world of life, power may survive at the expense of that which would make life worth living. It is the essence of ethics and religion that we live so as to increase the prospect for the survival of ex-

cellence, that is, of quality which makes life worth living for the whole of life, even at the expense of personal interest. . . .

What survives is not necessarily excellence, but power to survive, and sometimes in case of human affairs that statement can be shortened to: what survives is power. About the chief unfinished business of humanity is the control, discipline and taming of power, so that "the survival of the fittest" will be in fact the survival of excellence.

As to democracy, the degree of its suppression was not evidence of its lack of value, but only of its lack of power.[1]

Cultural history and anthropology reveal that human freedoms have been secured by steady though slow elimination of the struggle of man against man through the development of the "we" concept or social bonds in ever-widening circles. The record clearly shows that man is a social being and that his survival depends upon his unique power to form communities with his fellows. Village communities were the determining factor throughout millenniums of the nurturing of the culture of men and their societies. Man's struggle against other men has never advanced the human community.

Western man has not only forfeited the community way of life, but has also developed considerable technical facility for self-destruction. Yet he has developed facilities within the same technology which tend to promote social survival.

Consciously sought social progress has been a phenomenon greater than any one man's idea, any one nation's struggle, or any one period's historical emergence.

It is an age-old concept of dynamic living faith and practice which has had gradual but widespread emergence in human history. Although its major possibilities are still unrealized, it is already as susceptible to scientific study as any human phenomenon.

The practice of a dynamic living faith is another expression of the search for and experimentation with truth, because to seek and experiment results in growth not only in personal perception but also in social application. When a person experiments with truth, he makes of his own and other lives a laboratory for research into what life can be and what man can do to promote his improvement, both in personal and in social matters. The personal commitment to an attitude of search and experimentation in the quest for truth may be thought of as the highest expression of any faith.

In history, many approaches have been made to this total-life concept of religion. Outstanding among them have been Tao (seventh century B.C. in China), Jesus' Spirit of Truth, St. John's Logos, Charles Wesley's Inner Principle, John Wesley's Witness of the Spirit, George Fox and the Quakers' Inner Light, Emerson's Over-soul, Gandhi's Satyagraha, and Kagawa's concept of the role of conscience as "the sword point of evolution."

A pursuit of truth exemplified in social operations is superior to religion as commonly practiced. Sri Ramakrishna, great Hindu saint and author of the modern comparative religions approach to religion, said that "common men talk bagfuls of religion but act not a grain of it; while the wise man speaks little, but his whole life is religion acted out. What you wish others to do, do yourself."[2] The reality of religious truth expressed in external affairs is demonstrated by the strange phenomenon of the power of a noble and dynamic inner faith to transmute every detail of human existence. Pursuit and application of knowledge is the way of true science, of religion, and of the democratic spirit and method.

Searching for and experimenting with truth does not divide life between a spiritual search and everyday action. Nor does it lead to action which, though not spiritual in itself, may some day rest upon a newly discovered spiritual foundation. Such a division of the human personality would be dishonest and unspiritual. It is characteristic, however, of secularized life in the West, where the church and the social order heap together human individuals like grains of sand, hoping the total will come out in some desired pattern.

Personal experience unrelated to its external expression, and personal experiences unrelated to one another, result in the individual's being lost within the mass. Social experience begins and continues as passion and experience within the life of persons; external human relations are rooted in internal attitudes. Spirituality is, in essence, community realization of individual dignity and significance. There is no genuine place for human spirituality outside of life here and now, even though there may be a quality of "good life" which endures eternally.

To know and love others is human; lonely life is less than human. A lonely man in meditation is an inconsistency, because true meditation leads not to a stratosphere of purely personal enjoyment but to identity with others. It is through one act of identification that one realizes his own worth as an individual and his responsibilities to other men.

> The individual as spirit or being is not confined within his humanity; he has been less than human, he can become more than human. The universe finds itself through him. . . . The individual is the key of the evolutionary movement. . . . The individual does not owe his ultimate allegiance either to the state which is a machine or to the community which is a part of life and not the whole life; his allegiance must be to the Truth, the Self, the Spirit, the Divine which is in him and in us all. . . . to find and express that truth of being in himself and help the community in its seeking for its own truth and fullness of being must be the real object of existence.[3]

These words of Aurobindo Ghose present a spirituality that actually unfolds by means of a profound and superb practicality and lays hold simultaneously upon everything in the external field. A religion which stresses inner experience is thus at the same time applicable to the whole of life.

The gospel of Jesus gives a further clarification and illustration of the significance of man's outward expression of his inner truth in the story of the temptations of Jesus. Told in the characteristic language of an Oriental, it portrays symbolically a long inner struggle that was a point upon which the man's future turned. He had spent a long period in retreat. We may call the conclusion of this wrestling with his problem his enlightenment; and was not his problem that of how the religious person relates his inner volition to his action in the physical world?

Jesus revealed in his life and in his death the coming together of man's quest for God and God's quest for man in man's discovery that God had designed him to be a temple of the living God, and had sought to realize divine destiny within humanity. "The kingdom of God is within you" is the spiritual basis for the hope that, within the community of God, His will may "be done in earth, as it is in heaven."

How different has been the experience of the modern West with Christianity! Jesus' social message has been little more than preached. Walter Rauschenbusch, a theologian of Rochester and Princeton seminaries, was influential in developing the social emphasis within Protestantism in this country with his teaching and his principal work, *Christianity and the Social Crisis.*[4] Christianity failed to embrace the teachings of this prophet of the social gospel, however, and developed social and political action programs that were characteristically Western.

The reaction against his programs was never against a "gospel" or against an experience; neither was the opposition any more wholesome or constructive than the programs. The truth was not to be found at either extreme. Koestler's *The Yogi and the Commissar* and John Dewey's *Human Nature and Conduct*[6] point out the result of this tendency of Western people to gravitate to one or the other of the extremes of reform, personal or social. It is easy to say, "The day of the social gospel is past," when the truth is that we have never had a social gospel, and its day is not yet at dawn.

The life of Aurobindo Ghose provides an interesting illustration of the effect of this swing from one extreme to the other. Ghose was very near to leading India's revolutionary resistance movement before Gandhi was known. Today, however, he is remembered only as the great saint, Aurobindo, who spent forty years in lonely hermitage at Pondicherry, which, through his influence, became one of the greatest religious communities of the world. Out of his lonely search after God came his great devotional poems and the philosophical-religious writings which year after year have steadily turned thousands in every part of the world to the same search.

Time after time he refused the presidency of the nationalist Congress Party. In reply to such an invitation of the nationalists to take leadership, Aurobindo said that his was the search for a new spiritual foundation, for "work in the external field." He was still seeking and formulating this foundation for himself and his disciples at his death in 1950. Their actual work in the external field, formerly Ghose's consuming concern, lies in the indefinite future. How did this remarkable change in one man's life come about?

Aurobindo Ghose was educated in England and remained in Europe until his return to India, where he became Professor of English in the University of Baroda. He became known as a Bengali poet, writer and thinker who stirred the nation deeply. While still in Baroda he became the leader and great inspirer of the resistance movement, the first revolutionary nationalism in India, which centered in his own Bengal. The movement, which included violent underground insurrection, aroused the whole of India, especially the student world, and first gave rise to the hope and impulse which later was to support the nonviolent resistance which Gandhi led.

Ghose left Baroda for Bengal, where for a year he edited the first revolutionary nationalist paper, *Bande Matarem,* named after the national hymn which was then banned. He was twice arrested by the British; he was released the second time, after a year in prison without trial, in 1910. That same year he established his retreat at Pondicherry, where he remained until his death in 1950.

The difference in Ghose and Gandhi, two remarkable leaders of the Indian resistance, was that Ghose was wholly unable to conceive of a resistance which was itself spiritual, or a reform which was in its essence religious. He had drunk too deeply at the fountain of Western learning and was therefore unable to conclude that religious love itself can best resist.

Attempts have been made to describe the inner experience called experimentation with truth. They indicate that its growth has occurred mainly through love for people, and that the laboratory of these experiments is at the same time the mind within and the social environment without. Even the most meager grasp of truth (itself relative always) points to something greater than and beyond the individual. Truth in this comprehensive sense is valid only in universal intercultural and interreligious application. The smallest and most culturally distant sects cannot be omitted from its operation.

The Hindus use the term *Self* (capitalized) to express the personal experience of universal identification — the ultimate of shimsa and the goal of yoga or meditation. It is a term that significantly embraces the human community and its environment. Despite an unfortunate popular interpretive trend toward abnegation or renunciation of life itself, this faith coincides with present scientific understanding of human nature as that part of the personality drawn from the total social environment shared with all others within the limited range of the group's comprehension. This is contrasted with the "individualism" by which the individual stands out slightly, if at all, as unique. Therefore, it should not appear strange if Hinduism, among the existing religions, should more readily than others unite the personal and the social in the integration of human experiences.

Such a concept takes the devotee out of himself and into a ministry of love wherever there is human need. The whole of life becomes the devotion, since it is laid upon the altar within in one's identification with others and in one's capacity to sacrifice.

No religious writing better expresses how the experience of truth preeminent in life brings the social and personal together in a single awareness than a book called *Love, the Law of Life,* by Kagawa of Japan.[7] What the book sets forth is not merely a synthesis of what Christianity has called "the Social Gospel" and "the Personal Gospel"; it is an attempt to reveal all-embracing inner experience. It reveals Kagawa's dynamic faith and remarkable devotion throughout his long and useful life.

It would be a mistake to conclude that Kagawa's thought represents no departure from orthodox Christian thought, although he has written mostly from within orthodox Christian circles, using characteristic terminology. He also uses terminology from the sciences, especially psychology. For the experience we are describing, he uses the term "the Holy Spirit" — the familiar expression for God in human experience. Kagawa's concept of love unfolding within life at the point of conscience indicates the all-inclusive nature of the experience in its embracing of all humanity.

To Kagawa, the Holy Spirit was expressive simply of the operation of divine love within the conscience of man. "By the Holy Spirit," he writes, "I mean absolute consciousness of God. Jesus lived God, He lived redemptive love."[8] Without strain, Kagawa appropriates much of the teaching of science. Evolution is to him simply God's continuing creation. The message of evolution is that "the world is still in bud." Belief in it becomes "Faith in the progressive entrance into an ever-expanding freedom — from seed to shoot, bud to flower, from anthropoid to human, from man to son of God. What a courageous faith!"[9]

But so far as an individual is concerned, the "idea of progress must be acquired experimentally" and "originates from an inner conviction of the power of growth . . . The ego is the treasure vault of evolution. . . . Conscience is the sword point of evolution." It is here, within man, that Kagawa finds God thrusting upward into the new consciousness of His "New Creation" — through the operation of the laws which govern the universe, at the point of individual conscience. "Conscience," Kagawa continues, "is simply the individual's equipment functioning" and "the sole process leading men to God." Religionists call this process conversion, but Kagawa tries to avoid the use of this word. In this he was like Gandhi, who felt that conversion was a badly misused and misunderstood term.

But all the laws rest, for him, upon one basic to them all and to all being and life — "Love the Law of Life." Kagawa's religious thought, which he characterized as his "system of Love," presenting as its foundation the concept that if God be creator, then — as evolution in the universe is God's Nature unfolding — religious experience in human life is God's Nature unfolding within the human community.

This "system" led Kagawa to an inner identity with the processes of God's love in all life which is unique both in theory and in result.

I become aware that the good seeks its outlet for evolution within me. The good is my God . . . The Love is within me more than conqueror of suffering. . . . Love that tramples on death. . . . Love alone is absolute. . . . I know that Love and the good which seek in me an outlet will give me victory over all these.[10]

This Love Kagawa does not hope to understand. But it is available and "it is the secret of the Absolute."

This leads to faith as action. "The structure of Love is an unparalleled mystery. It is not we who love, but first God loved us. (I John 4:10). Our love is the mainspring that God has wound up."[11]

This is faith in a God intimate within the experiencer and within all being. It engenders a power of the Love within.

Kagawa believed, and others with him, that his own life was a daily miracle of God's love and power. (It is reported that American doctors who examined him found within his small frail body enough incurable disease to destroy any ordinary person.) He called this miracle of inner power the hidden significance of the incarnation.[12]

Kagawa is a mystic, great among the modern mystics. Much of the prose in *Love the Law of Life,* even in the English translation, is poetry worthy to stand with the best devotional poetry of all scripture. In Kagawa's mysticism there is no indication that life was ever abnegated. Life for him is rich and full, made so by the unfolding of God's Nature within the life of men.

Japan's contribution to Christian interpretation through Kagawa, her Christian prophet, is strikingly similar to Gandhi's contribution. It rises above any particular religion's gift, however, because it results from the basic but neglected fact that it is a blend of the mystical and the natural which can speak to all human needs.

Understanding of Kagawa's thought is furthered by knowledge of the influences of three great religions on an extremely sensitive, artistic soul. Buddhism was the first. A lonely boy, Kagawa was driven to books and to communion with nature. He came of a family high in political circles and like all respectable sons was drilled in the elaborate and colorful theology of Buddhism. A sense of mystic unity with all being, characteristic of Buddhism, deeply colors all his devotional writings. The mysticism of Buddhism contrasts strikingly with Kagawa's mysticism, however, since the former is characteristically other-worldly — the mysticism of the cloister.

A second great influence on the boy was an opposite extreme. Society steeped his sensitive spirit in the prevailing Shinto culture, characterized by naturalistic worldliness. The religious thought of the Japanese masses has been traditionally worldly, in contrast to the other-world emphasis of India's religion. In Shinto, gods mingle freely with men. The emperor is a god-father and his subjects are sons of the gods. Japan's modernism was an inevitable outgrowth of her prevailing beliefs; her leap to science was as natural to her as it was unnatural to India. Shinto was, indeed, the ideal religion to support the modern state without strain or substantial change in basic culture.

The third influence in Kagawa's life was Christianity. For Kagawa, the Cross of Jesus was at the same time as other-worldly as the divine reality and as this-worldly as the human community. God loved the world enough to come into it and identify Himself with men in the redemptive purposes of His kingdom on earth.[13] Since the Cross measures God's identification with all that is human, fellowship could mean for the earnest follower only the same identification. Nothing could be more social and at the same time more deeply and inwardly spiritual. Japan thus may have furnished a more natural setting for the all-inclusive application of the Christian gospel than could be found in India or in the West.

Given up by doctors to die of tuberculosis, Kagawa left college for a retreat where he devoted himself to meditation and to the creation of the work that became his first best seller, *Across the Death Line,* an autobiographical novel. Later he completed college, then spent five years in Kobe's worst slum, Shinkawa.

Next he appeared at Princeton University for two years. Walter Rauschenbusch's teachings of the social gospel had a deep effect upon him. When he returned to Japan, he sought to apply the social gospel to his immediate environment — the same horrible slum where he had lived previously.

Years later at a meeting of the Kagawa Fellowship at a country inn in Japan, the writer heard him expounding Japan's Kingdom of God Movement. No phase of life is outside his concern; his gospel, more lived than preached, seemed more social by being personal and more personal by being social.[14]

This profound concept of the unity of the personal and the social in religion recommends itself today as perhaps never before in human history. It is easy for us of the West to see that whatever is personal to us is within personal experience. It is not so easy for us to see that whatever is social, insofar as it affects us, is equally personally experienced. We see so much we think is outside ourselves — that government, those officials, the capitalists, a collective order, a world order for peace. A truly efficacious brotherhood of mankind cannot exist unless it embraces the personal and the social at the same time. It is more difficult for us to grasp the fact that complexity, distance or any other factors in human relationships do not alter this principle.

This social-within-personal experience is a matter of the psychological and sociological understanding of man's nature. The potential to experience socially is responsible for cultures and societies; it is equally the basis of Hitler's *Herrenvolk* and of democracy. Benjamin Franklin, discussing the possibility that the new government of the United States might pass into the hands of tyrants, said that in the long run the people would get the government they deserved. Gandhi said the same thing: that freedom can have existence only within men, and that it can never be so vast or extensive in its application that it does not retain its ground and vitality within personal experience.

> If they (the rulers) are dominated by their environment they do not surely deserve to be killed, but should be changed by a change of the environment. But the environment are we — the people who make the rulers what they are. Moreover, violence may destroy one or more bad rulers, but like Ravana's head, others will pop up in their places, for the root lies in us. If we reform ourselves, the rulers will automatically do so.[15]

The profound spiritual teachings of the Quakers are an authentic interpretation and application of the Christain social gospel. These teachings give Christianity the same significance in life and lead it into the same results for human character and social reform as the teachings and works of Gandhi did for his nation and era. The Quaker concept of the Inner Light expresses especially well the religious experience of experimenting with truth. The fresh and fervent use of this concept by George Fox and the early Quakers in England stripped religion of its almost fatal formalism in that period. More important, it restored Christianity to its original purity of action: "acts" of the early Christians were but acts of the inner spirit. The Quakers did not regard as separate the personal and social functioning of the Inner Light. This led to an unusual community fulfillment and a strong worldly sense. The worldly sense led in turn to significant social and political reform movements. The Society of Friends thus brought first-century Christianity into a seventeenth-century English setting and continued a tradition of nonviolence in action against every life-thwarting formalism and institutionalism of its time.

Today the Society of Friends stands Christlike in the midst of the more compromised Christianity of the West. Among them are a multiplying host who are as moved by the inner spirit as were George Fox and his followers. They understand the present world's "mount of anguish," as James Russell Lowell called it, and determine to do something about it. They are being joined by an increasing number of youths from all denominations and faiths in a movement strikingly resembling the Acts of the Apostles and the satyagraha movement. Their activities take many forms — in this country's Freedom Movement and Peace Corps, in the land reform and other movements in India, in South Africa's struggle, and in many other movements and places throughout the world.

Free spirits alone can make a conquest of an abiding order. Beings that "nourish a blind life within the brain," as Shakespeare aptly characterized the fundamental irreligion, can pursue only predetermined tracks. Pioneers do not emerge from among them. The fundamental irreligion is not atheism, which is only another one-track dogmatism; it is pursuit of any track without vision, without the inner struggle for truth to unfold and without the devotion to be faithful to whatever knowledge is apprehended.

Keeping the spirit free is a continuous process, a growth of knowledge and of life which is without end. As truth is discovered, both life and society are fully committed to its discoveries one by one. Experimenting with truth goes on first within man's inner spirit, then inevitably within the community of man.

It is by this process that democracy began; it is by this process that all free spirits live. To the reverently experimental mind truth can speak; in the reverently experimental life truth becomes preeminent in action. The reverently experimental community is democracy in its fullest sense. Devotion to the pursuit of truth, dedication to the ultimate discovery of truth, however partial, and living in the degree of the universality of its tentative grasp — this is the way of science, of living religion and of the democratic spirit.

The supremacy of the human spirit is possible only through this extension of itself. Man's culture must be permeated by this genuine personal sovereignty, the mastery by the spirit and intellect of every aspect of his external world. Economics, therefore, becomes the extension of man's spirit in his conquest of the material universe, and science the application of man's special genius for the conquest. Both are conditioned by and dependent upon democracy — the people's experiments with truth in freeing themselves and keeping themselves free from all environmental enslavement, physical or social.

Within each of these areas, the economic, the political, and the religious, there must develop profound revolution. Each such revolution must issue from the free spirit of man in the nature of genuine religious self-fulfillment. For out of the heart, for good or ill, arise all of the issues of life. Whatever has been created by man in his external life, even the greatest technology, is but the extension of his spirit. Our world is beyond human control only if we enslave ourselves.

On Christmas Day, 1939, in a radio broadcast to the Empire, George VI quoted some famous lines:

> And I said to the man who stood at the gate of the year, "Give me a light that I may tread safely into the unknown." And he replied: "Go out into the darkness and put your hand into the Hand of God. That shall be to you better than light and safer than a known way." So I went forth, and finding the Hand of God, trod gladly into the night. And he led me toward the hills and the breaking of day. . . .[16]

Religion, defined as the quest for truth expressed in the whole community of man, is not only safer than a known way. It is a way that can lead with more certainty than any absolutism, ancient or modern, toward the comprehensive security, peace and world order under law which the present age is urgently demanding. It is the way of the all-life revolution for this age of rebellions, the rebellions which our Western self-contradictions have bequeathed the present generation.

FOOTNOTES CHAPTER TWELVE

1. Arthur Morgan, *The Community of the Future* (Yellow Springs, O.: Community Service, Inc., 1957), p. 156.

2. Robert O. Ballou, (ed.), *World Bible* (New York: Viking Press, 1944), p. 84.

3. Sri Aurobindo Ghose, *The Divine Life* (Pondicherry, India: Sri Aurobindo Ashram, 1949), pp. 929-930.

4. Walter Rauschenbusch, *Christianity and the Social Crisis* (New York: Macmillan Co., 1907).

5. Arthur Koestler, *The Yogi and the Commisar* (New York: Macmillan Co., 1945).

6. John Dewey, *Human Nature and Conduct* (New York: The Modern Library, 1930).

7. Toyohiko Kagawa, *Love the Law of Life* (Chicago: John C. Winston Co., 1929), p. 298. All quotations not otherwise indicated have been taken from this book, which Kagawa regards as his system.

8. Toyohiko Kagawa, From "Meditations of Kagawa," distributed periodically in Japan and India; specific source unknown.

9. Kagawa, op. cit., p. 298.

10. *Ibid.*, pp. 307-308.

11. *Ibid.*, p. 125.

12. A summarization of the idea expressed by Kagawa in his first biographical novel, *Before the Dawn*, pp. 257 ff., and elsewhere, as quoted in Jessie M. Trout, *Kagawa, Japanese Prophet* (New York: Association Press, Second Series, 1959), "Incarnate Within the Personal," pp. 45-46.

13. Kagawa's interpretation of John 3:16.

14. Like Gandhi, Kagawa impressed one with his simplicity and directness. He was a guest in the writer's home while visiting in India. In meeting with the teachers of the two schools, he did not lecture; rather he drew them out about the folklore and tales of their own people. When he took leave from our Fellowship the last day, several hundred students started in lines from various points for the farewell. They could not be held; they broke ranks and came running, thronging about him and shouting their farewells. He was so overwhelmed he could scarcely speak, but he counselled them to devote their lives to helping "those in the villages who are poor and need your help."

15. Nirmal Kumar Bose, *Studies in Gandhism* (Ahmedabad, India: Navajivan Pub. Co., 1947), p. 12.

16. Minnie Louise Haskins, *God Knows,* 1908.

CHAPTER 13

GANDHI: A MAN OF THE FUTURE

Personal greatness may occur when the impact of an age upon a man results in an impact of the man upon the age. During life, his greatness may be recognized, if not embraced; the West, which gave little heed to the teachings and example of Mohandas Gandhi during his life, bowed in homage at his death. Western people paused as though before a revelation of soul-force which they sensed within themselves. During that pause they beheld what that man revealed: a glimpse of their own spirituality.

This era has been one of political power; it has produced its materialistic man as a natural counterpart of its acquisitive outlook. It has seen the West set aside its own highest moral purpose, the full emancipation of human beings. Gandhi came just as a climax of arrogance and futility was being reached; he was one of the forces instrumental in striking the death blow at colonial imperialism.

Though not recognized as the man of his age in any crudely accepted sense, Gandhi's impact is still gathering momentum. His voice was not stilled by death. Mohandas Gandhi is the man of the coming age.

Born in 1869 of conservative merchant parentage, Gandhi grew up in the village of Porbander in Kathiawar, India. At nineteen he was sent to London to study law; he once said it was there, through reading about the movement for the abolition of slavery in the United States, that he first conceived the idea of the mass use of civil resistance against injustice.

Soon after his return to India at the age of twenty-four, the enterprising young lawyer was called to take an important legal case in South Africa. Gandhi won the case by reconciliation, a success which he claimed greatly influenced the course of his life. He said he learned that the true practice of law is "to find out the better side of human nature and enter men's hearts."[1] This South African experience was important in the molding of a remarkable life and career.

Gandhi sent for his family and remained in South Africa, because his countrymen were suffering oppression there; his people needed to be led out of African bondage, like another great alien race which suffered Egyptian bondage and escaped by the Red Sea route. This new Moses led his people by an even stranger route. He taught them to stand on their own feet by the power of pure and fearless hearts. To enter their new freedom in the midst of their former enemies simply by entering into friendship with them, they laid siege to the kingdom that was within themselves. They were amazed to discover that to "fear not them that destroy the body" meant that no power on earth could debase or enslave them while they pursued in love for all men the truth that makes men free. While they followed that light, they remained free.

During this same period in South Africa, Gandhi taught himself and others the ways of a new life, foreshadowing a new kind of community. This was the beginning of his *ashrams,* which were continued throughout his long life. The first of these agricultural colonies he established at Phoenix, South Africa. Still a youth himself, Gandhi gathered about him a faithful band of young people. Among them was the priest from England and India, destined for fame as Gandhi's greatest Western friend and interpreter, C. F. Andrews.

It was here, living in this brotherhood of loving identification with the poor, that Gandhi began the development of his thought on revolution through active love. But struggle, as well as brotherhood, had its part in that development. The positive assertion of the new life required its negative side in resistance; the ashram was the center of a struggle for freedom. Organizations and institutions that were thwarting life had to be overcome.

With remarkable skill, Gandhi drilled untrained laborers in the art of a basic dignity: noncooperation with the arrangements which were denying them the status of men. They were trained to offer civil disobedience (or civil resistance) in nonviolence, suffering injury without flinching, anger or retaliation. At the same time, these people nursed throngs of the sick during a great plague; later, on the battlefields of the Boer War, they cared for the wounded and buried the dead of their persecutors.

Out of this positive way of cooperative and constructive living and its inevitable resistance to evil, Gandhi was beginning to shape his thought and his life. Two streams of religious devotion, the Hindu Bhagavad-Gita and the gospel of Jesus of Nazareth, were also influencing Gandhi. The Gita and the gospels are alike concerned with the inner spiritual grace by which active men, while living in a violent world, can devote themselves to good. For Gandhi, truth was to be apprehended and obeyed, whatever its source; he never compared the best of his own religion with the worst of others — that greatest possible barrier against good will.

Though he remained Hindu, Gandhi became one of the most astute and accurate interpreters of the teachings of Jesus. Beginning with the reading, in South Africa, of Tolstoi's *The Kingdom of God is Within You* and soon after with Ruskin's *Unto These Last,* Gandhi's absorption in the gospels grew and inculcated in him the determination to apply their basic teachings.

At a later time at the College of Colombo, to an audience mainly Hindu, Gandhi spoke on "The Place of Jesus." The sermon, widely published in India, included the following remarks:

> Your lives will also be incomplete unless you reverently study the teachings of Jesus. . . . By all means drink deeply of the fountains given you in Jesus' Sermon on the Mount. . . . But then, you will have to take up sackcloth and ashes with reference to your failure to perform the things taught you in Christ's sermon. . . . If then I had to face only the Sermon on the Mount and my own interpretation of it, I should not hesitate to say, "Oh yes, I am a Christian" . . . But negatively I can tell you that much of what passes as Christianity is a negation of the Sermon on the Mount.

This passage suggests how sensitive was this spirit which entered so deeply into the study of a faith not his own with a thirst after righteousness which led to every fountain whence flows the pure water of life.

Concerning himself with the way the inner spirit can organize its manifestation in the forms and techniques of a divine commonwealth, a community of God,

Gandhi presented a message distinctively social. *Satyagraha* (the outreach of the devotion of love in pursuit of truth), which Gandhi called "the all-sided sword," was his offering to an age which was calling itself social at the very time that society was becoming increasingly fragmented. Gandhi, in evoking the best of religious consciousness, was leading man to a profound experience that would express itself in politics, economics and sociology in a period when most of the world was turning to power politics for its salvation.

At the outbreak of World War I, Gandhi, then forty-five years old, returned to India. In the West, a superficial familiarity with India's freedom struggle resulted from excessively political and sensational reports of the press, with the good stamping out the best. For example, few realize how many times Gandhi risked his political leadership and even his life to offer loyal service to the British Government of India. He was always the citizen of his country first, law-abiding in spirit and actions. It was only when true patriotism was forced underground in India that civil disobedience became his way of bringing it again into the open in the form of the highest citizenship.

The nonviolent civil disobedience of India was democratic and highly patriotic, because it worked toward the goal of ending tyranny, of inducing those resistant to reform to yield to democracy's method of peaceful persuasion. Against arbitrary laws, procedures or officials, democracy brings civil disobedience into the role of highest loyalty and truest patriotism. The oppression that India opposed was the same arbitrary government which brought about the American struggle for independence from the same tyrannical foreign yoke long before. The only difference was in the method of struggling for freedom. The persistent perfidy of promises of freedom, made only to be broken, the fanfare about new "formulas" intended to make the rest of the world forget the struggle, and the thousand and one repressive acts and measures, led to a series of mass nonviolent civil disobedience campaigns.

Contrary to the impressions given by the Western press, Gandhi's practical teaching and program were mainly a positive nation-building program, not the negative political and separatist action which struck off the British yoke. The whole of life and India's entire social organization absorbed his interest. The many-sided nation-building program was carried out through local units which Gandhi called village republics; these activities are known in English as "constructive work."

Four main areas of the program had nation-wide suborganizations, each as separate as possible from the political actionist program: (1) agriculture, the peasant, and land problems; (2) village industries, including spinning and weaving; (3) village education, which developed into the now well-known Basic Education; and (4) social reforms, later concentrated on the removal of "untouchability."

This comprehensive program gave practical meaning to freedom for the people in 700,000 villages, where nine-tenths of all Indians were living. Basic to their deliverance from a bondage largely economic was their nationwide production in home, village and factory, and their organization of an exchange in which men, women and children could all take an immediate part. Thus, a broad economic foundation was laid for the Indian resistance movement which was to follow.

Gandhi advanced simultaneously three profound changes: a revolution in economics, a revolution in politics and a social revolution. The social revolution was made possible by a transformation in the attitudes of his countrymen and was basic to the other changes.

Few in the West have recognized the importance of the first of these revolutionary achievements, Gandhi's revolution in economics. Gandhi began with a people who believed that for them resistance was utterly futile because they knew of no resistance that was not political and violent, and they were totally unarmed. A fatalistic apathy that was universal among Indians had been produced by the Mutiny failure in 1857. Therefore Gandhi's first aim was to turn the masses away from the political to the economic instrument which he insisted was not only the most direct route to their freedom, but within their grasp.

Before the overall struggle ended in victory for the Nationalists, this economic revolution led to nationwide development by Indians of production for their own consumption. This resulted in control of the new economy's extension and exchange through several all-India economic, research, training and exchange organizations. In their nationalist movement, the Asian Indians built "a nation within a nation." This was the great slogan of their struggle for national independence. The greater portion of their movement of nonviolence consisted of this vast and complicated nationwide social-economic program which left scarcely any aspect of life or any Indian village outside its range.

Nor did the Nationalists fail to plan for their future time of independence. An economic planning board was set up with Jawaharlal Nehru as its head; for many years this board charted the course that the new India's economic development would take, through a series of plans ranging in length from five to twenty-five years. India is today reaping the benefit of efforts to prepare for the responsibilities faced when Britain quit India.

Here, little known outside India, yet most powerful in its effect, was one of the profoundest revolutions ever developed. It did not merely scratch the surface of the political power scramble in the familiar revolutionary way. Rather it cut the economic ground of profit and secure investment out from under one of the mightiest establishments of imperial dominance in history.

This aspect of Gandhi's all-life revolution is illustrated by its application to a single item of British exploitation — the exchange of raw cotton for Lancashire mill-made cotton goods. India was thrice exploited: in the production. It is this part of Gandhi's program, most to slave labor; in the processing of the cotton far from India's shores; and in the deliberate development of a preference, even among peasants, for the supposedly finer (more expensive) materials from the English mills. This exploitation destroyed the production of some of the finest handmade fabrics in the world. It was, therefore, more than symbolic that the spinning wheel and the wearing of the homespun became the most important discipline and insignia of the liberation movement.

Some in the West considered this part of Gandhi's movement as a turning back of the clock; they regarded it as a repudiation of the use of machines. To such a charge Gandhi said, "To say that is to caricature my views. I am not against machinery as such, but I am totally opposed to it when it masters us." Again, "Machinery has its place; it has come to stay." Again, "I would prize every invention of science made for the benefit of all. There is a difference between invention and invention. Scientific truths and discoveries should first of all cease to be mere instruments of greed."[2]

If the clock was turned back for India, it was from the hour of imperialistic dominance and exploitation to an earlier hour of sturdy independence through the people's regaining control of the materials and means of production. It is this part of Gandhi's program, most criticized by westerners, which may prove most significant for western reform. Gandhi demonstrated the principle by which man can grasp his economic instrument and turn it to his own ends, regaining control over his life.

> I believe myself to be a nonviolent revolutionary. My means are noncooperation. No person can amass wealth without the cooperation, willing or forced, of the people concerned . . . I do not teach the masses to regard the capitalists as their enemies, but I teach them that they are their own enemies. The system must be destroyed and not the individual.[3]

The struggle for control of India's economy meant revolution on a second front — a revolution in politics. When the people began their struggle for self-rule, political parties faded from the scene. No longer a scramble for governmental power over the people, politics became a single-minded drive by all to obtain the power necessary to cast out the forces which had frustrated them in fulfillment of national hopes and well-being. In keeping with a forward-looking approach, long before they were a free people the Nationalists wrote a constitution for the new India.

When the 1919-1922 Satygraha Campaign was over, the British had succeeded in rounding up and imprisoning all of India's nationalist leaders. India then became very quiet. The British, however, were deceived, and their violent methods of suppression were conspicuous in apparent victory. At this point, the Indians, exhibiting a complete loss of control, answered violence with violence. This clearly demonstrated to the British that Gandhi had not lost his influence even though his doctrine of nonviolence had been perverted. The Tory government, holding power in England, deliberately confronted the previously nonviolent peoples of India, whose leaders were in prison, with brutal armed might, under the direction of Birkenhead. Britain's military answer to the democratic uprising cast the die leading to an increase in Gandhi's influence and the eventual collapse of British imperialism in India.

In the West, the success of the Indian people in their nonviolent struggle for independence was attributed by some to a mysterious and inimitable blend of a singularly prepared people, an extraordinary leader, and favorable circumstances. The Indian people, in their early twentieth-century apathy and complete loss of faith in themselves, appeared unlikely revolutionists; they were certainly no superrace. There was nothing magical about what transpired, not even the magic of an impossibly "saintly" leader. India's freedom movement took place under the familiar and widely prevailing circumstances of the oppression of one people by another. The strength of this movement inhered not in the leader, great as he undeniably was, nor in the temper of the Indian masses, nor in any uniqueness of occasion.

The strength of the economic and political revolutions lay rather in the third revolution, most profound of all, and the solid foundation upon which the movement rested: the revolution in the attitudes and motives of men. This transformation was far-reaching in its social consequences; the change in cultural outlook and behavior was such that it was called the "Indian Renaissance."

It is possible, as some Americans seem fondly to hope, that India furnished a specially favorable setting for this change in outlook and behavior when it adopted as its leading theme the philosophy of nonviolent resistance. There is a tendency in this hemisphere toward rationalization of the principle of violent action in matters requiring drastic change: the East could rely on nonviolence as an instrument for social change but the West cannot.

India did provide a favorable setting for this historical development. But that setting had been congealing — culturally, morally, intellectually and spiritually — for well over a hundred years. Much of this new attitude was drawn from Christian teachings introduced by Westerners. To attribute to the esoteric fatalism of the Oriental mind the entire intellectual and social revolution to which Aurobindo Ghose originally contributed, and which was built up by such men as Ram Mohan Roy (1774-1833), Dayananda (1825-1888), Ramakrishna (1836-1886), and Vivekananda (1863-1902), is nonsense. These men were more than a little tinged with the traditional mysticism of India. But they were also the spiritual leaders most influenced by the impact of Christianity and the West upon India and upon her religious life and temper.

The poet Swami Vivekananda had prepared the ground for the awakening of his people. His cry, "My God, the suffering people!" embraced the afflicted and oppressed of all the earth. To his own countrymen he proclaimed:

> Come up, Oh Lions!
> And shake off the delusion that you are sheep!
> You are souls immortal, spirits free, blest and eternal;
> You are not bodies.
> Matter is your servant, not you the servant of matter.

Jawaharlal Nehru pointed out that through Vivekananda and others there was aroused "a measure of self-respect" and "dormant pride in our past."[4]

Vivekananda established the Ramakrishna Mission to spread the gospel of that great teacher, to organize a service of love to the poor, and to labor for India's rebirth. Vivekananda's early death was attributed to his wearing himself out as he "thundered from Cape Comorin on the tip of India to the Himalayas," affirming his "constant refrain . . . be fearless, be strong. . . . What our country now wants are muscles of iron and nerves of steel, gigantic wills which nothing can resist, which can penetrate into the mysteries and secrets of the universe, and will accomplish their purpose in any fashion, even if it means going down to the bottom of the ocean and meeting death face to face."[5]

It is to this call to religious awakening that India traces her renaissance. Gopal Krishna Gokhale, regarded as the father of the Indian National Congress, established the Servants of India Society, a semimonastic, simple-living truth-seeking group still influential in India. This Society set the example of what "service" (a prostituted concept in English-dominated India) could mean in an awakened India.

But it remained for Gandhi to give form and direction to this revolution in the spirit and will of the people. Gandhi was able to awaken in others what he had personally experienced in South Africa — a radical break from the reward consciousness and quest (approximately the Western success motivation) and a turning toward the way of sacrifice in brotherhood and the giving of one's self to higher causes. This, his greatest achievement in revolution, was profoundly religious and was built upon the great awakening that had preceded him, the roots of which ran back a hundred years and involved the interactions of several of the world's greatest living faiths.

The Congress Volunteers, Gandhi's inner circle of "servants," became the tried and true who later were to go to prison by thousands again and again. They first sought the discipline of simplicity and even austerity. They spun their own thread and made their garments of white homespun cotton as a sacrament; they wore the garment of the village and the white Gandhi cap as symbols of their dedication and identification. They then went out into the villages of India to serve the needy.

Who were these white-clad servants of the poor? They were mainly young intellectuals from the Western-type colleges that had been designed to turn out a different kind of servant — civil, military, railway, governmental, church and mission. These young men had formerly responded to the command, "Eyes West," and had sought characteristic Western success in terms of Western man's salary, his way of life and dress, his standards of living and his habits and actions, including late afternoon tennis and tea. At the top of this striving pyramid of youthful intellectuals were the hundreds who, like Gandhi himself, had returned from European universities with their graduate degrees and specializations. It was the achievement of this revolution that these self-seeking intellectuals became the self-giving servants of their society in India's new age.

Later, the Congress Party of Gandhi's nationalism elected eight provincial governments in a general election under the "Provincial Autonomy Constitution" of 1935. Such was the preparation of the Congress Volunteers in service and austerity that their first act of governing was to strike off the last zero in the figure of their own salaries in all the government positions they inherited from the British. These young men had pursued truth and experimented with it regardless of self or of power over people or of concern for what others might think or do.

Against the dark background of violence, arrogance and futility, Gandhi had socially implemented the insight of another great religious leader, the Nazarene, who said we could become masters only by becoming servants. Gandhi's life gives interpretive significance to Jesus' "Spirit of Truth."

Gandhi's applications of truth-force may well be regarded by future historians as the most practical performance of the age which has called him impractical. Before nuclear threats had demonstrated the necessity of men's controlling their own destiny, he proved that men can learn to master their destiny. He taught, lived by and led others to live by integrity of the human spirit and by active love in operation.

Gandhi corresponded with two of America's great scientists, Albert Einstein and George Washington Carver. He once said to the writer, "Dr. Carver has been doing in the world of nature what I have tried to do in the realm of the spirit: conserve the materials and forces formerly wasted and bring them into use."

On Gandhi's death Einstein said, "Gandhi demonstrated that a powerful human following can be assembled not only through the cunning game of the usual political maneuvers and trickeries but through the cogent example of a morally superior conduct of life. In our time of utter moral decadence he was the only statesman to stand for a higher human relationship in the political sphere. . . . Generations to come, it may be, will scarcely believe that such a one as this ever in flesh and blood walked upon this earth."

"Mahatma Gandhi was the spokesman for the conscience of the world," wrote General George Marshall as United States Secretary of State. And said General Douglas MacArthur, then supreme Allied Military Commander in Japan, "In the evolution of civilization, if it is to survive, all men cannot fail eventually to adopt his belief that the process of mass application of force to resolve contentious issues is fundamentally not only wrong but contains within itself the germs of self-destruction."

Gandhi met his death as he had spent his life. In a world of violence, Gandhi directed unto himself the arrows of dissension, hatred, prejudice, cruelty and superiority of attitude. He who gave his life to unite India against her tyrant fell victim to the hatred engendered as the specific means to a common enslavement.

The violence which resulted in Gandhi's death was the inevitable aftermath of the imperialist principle of "divide and rule." In India's vast wine press, those grapes of wrath had been stored up for well over two centuries. Fratricidal carnage points up the lesson of modern imperialism: if people can be divided and led against each other, they can be exploited even without political domination.

Gandhi's death not only pointed up the tragedy of organized economic imperialism, but at the same time proved that it is inner violence which has to be surrendered to brotherhood if any degree of security, freedom or peace is to be attained, for our greatest enemy is within ourselves. Thus did Gandhi's death reinforce the revelation of his life; this is the essence of his message to mankind.

FOOTNOTES CHAPTER THIRTEEN

1. Gandhi's *Satyagraha in South Africa,* trans. from V. G. Desai, Gujarati (Ahmedabad: Navajivan Trust).

2. Gandhi in *Harijan,* February 27, 1937, p. 18; *Young India,* November 5, 1925, p. 377; and *Harijan,* June 22, 1935, p. 146; quoted by Nirmal Kumar Bose, *op. cit.,* pp. 34 and 48.

3. Gandhi, *Young India,* Nov. 26, 1931, p. 369; Bose, *op. cit.,* pp. 92-93.

4. Jawaharlal Nehru, *Toward Freedom,* New York: The John Day Co. (English, Bodley Head Edition, *An Autobiography,* 1936), p. 426.

5. Nehru, *The Discovery of India* (New York: John Day Co., 1946), pp. 340-341.

CHAPTER 14

THE POWER OF ACTIVE LOVE

The approaches of Jesus and Gandhi particularly illustrate the concept and the practice of nonviolence. This profound concept can be formulated and emulated; to do so is the beginning of the nonviolent society. By its nature, nonviolence can be neither blocked nor defeated by any barriers in its surroundings. Gandhi said,

> While violence is successful only when it is stronger than that of the opponent, nonviolent action can be taken in respect of an opponent, however powerfully organized for violence. Violence per se of the weak has never been known to succeed against the stronger in violence. Success of nonviolent action of the weak is a daily occurrence.[1]

The implications and applications of organized nonviolence have not been recognized in the West, even by most of its staunchest peace advocates, as a truly religious profession and implementation. Earnest consideration needs to be given to this concept of a faith dynamic in all the external fields of human action. Such a faith is even more applicable to the needs of the West than to any part of the Orient, for the West has specialized in spectacular inner psychological probing and social scientific outreach, yet has been unable to unite these inner and outer excursions of the explorative scientific mind. Wholeness of concept and awareness has been difficult for Western minds, steeped in a fragmented secularism, to understand.

The West once thought it had taken unto itself the original demonstration of such an all-embracing and vigorous faith. Except for rare outbreaks of this original insight and application at intervals throughout its history, however, what it had taken over was a religion that set apart an exclusive "spiritual" sphere, marked off for special operations. Christianity developed into a kind of devotion and practice of religion quite opposite from its original intent.

Jesus taught: The kingdom of God is not only within you, but also in the way you live with your neighbor and in the way you treat "the least of these my brethren." The Christians of the first century demonstrated that active love had become real among men. Some New Testament historians say that the evidences of their reorganization of Mediterranean society around "brotherhood economics," to use Kagawa's apt term, can be traced through three full centuries of Christian history — a greater endurance than any modern Western ideology has shown.

It was the early Christians' patient suffering of the inhuman cruelty of a pagan world, in a love great enough to embrace its enemies, which led Gandhi to acclaim this as the first satyagraha — the first application of active love throughout a whole society — in history. Nero's carnival of blood was only the beginning, "as it were the fiery portal, through which the Christians entered the arena in which they were now called to strive, to bleed, to die for their faith during two and a half centuries. . . . In patient silence they endured all. The Heroic

Age of the Christian Church had begun, a heroism not of action but of a suffering mightier than all deeds."[2]

The nonviolence of the first Christians which led to their suffering was, on its positive side, an activity which reorganized the whole of society. At that time in the Roman Empire, when the gulf between the rich and poor had never been so great, the Christians in their community of all classes and creeds found a common plateau of devotedness and mutual endeavor which commanded the admiration of increasing thousands. Out of the rapid growth of this new revolutionary brotherhood and its irreconcilability with the prevailing laxity and corruption of the older order came the resentment and jealousy which led to the persecutions.

The old order struck hard at its rival for ascendency, as old orders always do. The old order, however, was already in its death throes — still another reason for the attractiveness and strange drawing power of a faith which meant certain persecution and threat of death. It was in loving supremely that the first Christians so lived as to court danger and so died as to win even their adversaries to their way of life.

Since this time the use of active love has written other pages of history. One of the most remarkable stories of its use comes out of Brazil. General Candido Rondon, one of the world's most successful exponents and users of active love, was also one of the West's greatest anthropologists and ethnographers of the past generation. He conceived the idea of dealing through love with "underdeveloped" and fanatically resistant aboriginal tribes, the Brazilian Chavantes. He concluded that this meant their protection from the ravages of the stronger culture. His story is one of service to some of the fiercest Indian tribes in the Western Hemisphere through the Brazilian Indian Protective Service. Rondon, using nonviolence, was able to pack more success into this Service's brief forty years than the United States has been able to achieve in all her history of Indian Service.

Rondon had served in Brazil's western outposts where he became seasoned to the rigors of many storms; from these experiences he developed a new and gentle firmness. It led him to the conviction that the Indians could be won over only through nonviolence. An Indian Protective Service was created whose policy was specifically that firearms might not be used against Indians, even in self-defense. Indians turned from marauding to helping, from chopping down telegraph poles to reporting damage to lines from fallen trees. The story, which can be read in Hernane Taveres de Sá's *The Brazilians, People of Tomorrow*[3] or John Collier's *The Indians of the Americas,*[4] is worthy to be classed with the greatest sagas of conquest in history by any method. In rapid and permanent results, it ranks with such specific campaigns as those of Bardoli and Champaran under Gandhi in India.

Collier, America's leading Indian authority, writes of Rondon, "The task was gigantic; but the task was entrusted to a giant. . . . a man of greatness, intellectual, emotional and moral. He was a man of achievement even before 1910 (when the Central Brazilian Foundation and its Indian Protective Society were formed by him) as a soldier, a civil engineer, a geographer and an ethnographer."[5] He was a man of extraordinary courage, hardihood, persistence and discrimination, coupled with humane and universal insights rare even in those known as saints — a combination of frontiersman and apostle. He was a companion to Theodore Roosevelt during that

President's famous trip to the Amazonian jungle in 1913. From 1910 to 1930 he developed the greatest Indian Service in all the Americas on the standing principle for action, "Die if you need to; but kill, never."[6] In the beginning some devoted members gave their lives. But in the long run, blood did not flow, as it did in Brazil's great northern neighbor.

John Collier has this to say about the practicality of the method of active love: ". . . the Brazilian Indian service is the best equipped and most thoroughly committed of any of the Indian services; and taken as a whole, it is both the most inspired and down-to-earth, and probably the most economically operated."[7]

The Brazilians, a Western people, repudiated violence as a means of dealing with the fiercest and most fanatical of American tribes by the process of first eradicating violent or exploitive motives and purposes in themselves. Exploitation of people, their resources, their societal organization, their culture, is impossible in this kind of conquest.

Brazil now has a historical background of reforms, political and social, effected without violence. The facts have been briefly and strikingly summarized by one of the best interpreters of cultural development in Brazil, Gilberty Freyre:

Brazil is famous for its "white," or peaceful, revolutions. Its independence was the result of one of these. Though it remained an empire when all the other Latin American countries were republics, a peaceful revolution transformed it into a republic. A peaceful revolution transformed it from a slave-holding country into one where everybody is born free. A peaceful revolution separated Church from State, solving a problem that has been the source of much friction in other Latin countries. An almost peaceful revolution — that of 1930 — has favoured Brazilian town labourers with a social legislation that is, in theory if not always in practice, one of the most advanced of our day. Brazil will therefore probably be able to revolutionize immigration policies without violence either to immigrants or to old residents.[8]

From first-century Christianity to today's Freedom Movement, active love has proved itself as a means to nonviolent victory. By combining civil disobedience and nonviolence, Indians brought their struggle for independence to a successful climax. In Montgomery, Alabama, 50,000 persons faced the burnings and bombings of their churches and homes and the imprisonment of their leaders in order to "walk with God." In Koinonia, not only Southern white citizens, but the merchants who dealt with that community and the families who showed friendship or sympathy, braved bullets, bombings and burnings. Those struggling on three significant moral fronts — race equality, world peace, and the stemming of an encroaching wave of state and corporate suppression of individual freedoms — are suffering expulsions, imprisonment, beatings and extreme treatment without expressing hate or bitterness or revenge in an attempt to build for themselves and for all peoples a world in which man can survive.

Love in lesser forms of expression certainly existed long before active love appeared among men, but human love is a universal unfolding of only a few thousand years, of the millions of years of probable human existence. It has been limited to no particular people or area; it has characterized all the significant elements of later social evolution.

Kagawa in his *Love the Law of Life* likened love to a mainspring existing within human life from its very beginning. The unwinding of this mainspring of love is what is meant by social evolution. Kagawa pointed out that higher human love came with a development which was from within but was expressed creatively as the initiative of love.

This proceeding of active love from within has been traced empirically by a leading social anthropologist, Pitirim Sorokin of Harvard, in *The Ways and Powers of Love*. He confirms this unfolding experience of active love as relatively recent in human history. He concludes that

> For contemporary man, ravaged by moral atomisms and egotisms, an emergence of great genius of love is particularly needed. One or a few such heroes of unselfish love can morally ennoble the demoralized humanity more than most of the ordinary agencies. Only the human incarnations of unbounded love can accomplish this task.[9]

But Sorokin is not under any illusion as to the effect of this love in our world or of the significance of that effect; love of this kind has inevitably taken its Cross. He declares it has always run into violent resistance and hatred.

> Hence the tragic martyrdom of the apostles of universal love, who have been condemned to death, im-

prisoned, banished, tortured and variously persecuted by the partisans of tribal loyalty. Socrates,
Jesus, St. Peter, St. Paul, Al Hallaj, Gandhi, and
some thirty-seven per cent of the saintly Christian
Altruists are eminent examples of its victims. . . . Almost any universal altruist is bound to become a
"subversive enemy" to be persecuted by the "patriotic" tribal altruist. In this sense the eternal tragedy
of the *agnus dei qui tollis peccata mundi* continues
in human history unabated. . . . Most of the political
groups have been guilty in persecution of their "disloyal" members whose "disloyalty" consisted exactly
in extension of their love far beyond the boundaries
of the respective organization. And so this drama is
continued up to this day when a multitude of "patriotic governments" and "crusading communities" relentlessly persecute many a "disloyal" altruist in the
name of Communist, Socialist, Liberal, Conservative, Fascist, Democratic, Capitalist, Labor, Atheist,
Religious and other tribal solidarities and lilliputian
in-group patriotisms. And so far, no end of this
tragedy is visible.

But what is more practical and courageous than defense or invasion or conquest by active love? "Tribal
solidarities," when stirred by their highest patriotisms
cannot match the courage, the nobility or the practical
accomplishment of a Jesus, a Socrates, a Gandhi or a
General Rondon; "in-group patriotisms" are no match
for the active love of a nonviolent army.

Throughout man's eons of development he has slowly discovered this way to organize his oppositions and
tensions so as to further his social organization and accom-

plish his survival and human fulfillment. Long after the glory of the Roman Empire, Christianity lives; the British lion's tail was successfully tweaked by unarmed soldiers in homespun uniforms; and if the Freedom Movement in this country grows in active love rather than giving way to violence, it, too, will go down in history as a triumph of the highest human values.

We do not yet know what active love can do when even a considerable minority of any people learn how to apply it. The idea of its use in varied ways to attain success in areas where failure has been most frequent is growing upon peoples in both East and West. Active love, unfolding in the life of humanity, is man's hope for achieving a human community secure in its self-mastery. It is a power available to every person at all times. Patience with the moral forces that react from one individual to another is the way of the new community.

We do not live in that kind of world, but this does not mean that we must wait for a favorable environment. Each can possess and employ this power to change society without waiting for any external change. Active love, beginning its revolution within each life, immediately takes hold in any environment; it does not hold back from politics, from economics or from any of the other of life's affairs. This extension of man's spirit into the mundane is the path to man's full humanity. It is truly democratic social action.

FOOTNOTES CHAPTER FOURTEEN

1. *Gandhi's Correspondence, 1942-44,* pub. data, 1945, p. 179.

2. Gerhard Uhlhorn, *The Conflict of Christianity with Heathenism* (New York: Charles Scribner's Sons, 1912), p. 248.

3. Hermane Tavers de Sa, *The Brazilians: People of Tomorrow* (New York: John Day Co., 1947).

4. John Collier, *The Indians of the Americas* (New York: W. W. Norton & Co., 1947).

5. *Ibid.,* p. 298.

6. *Ibid.,* p. 300.

7. *Ibid.,* p. 301.

8. Gilberto Freyre, *Brazil, An Interpretation* (New York: Alfred Knopf, 1951), pp. 120-121. (The Patten Foundation Lecture at Indiana University, Autumn 1944.)

9. Pitirim Sarokin, *The Ways and Powers of Love* (Boston: Beacon Press), p. 460.

10. *Ibid.,* p. 460.

CHAPTER 15

REVOLUTIONARY NONVIOLENCE: AN INSTRUMENT OF SOCIAL CHANGE

Nonviolence has been criticized as being negative, and has thus met opposition from those who believe in being positive. The cry "Be positive" is not always sound. It is never sound if it is an urge to turn away from the problem at hand. Nonviolence is not merely *anti-anything,* nor in essence negative.

In *The Power of Nonviolence,* Richard Gregg calls attention to the fact that every living organism exists by a rejection of that in its environment which it cannot use. In many cases, "much of its action is then a refusal. Yet the essence of its action is positive, although in quantity, most of it seems to be a negative rejection." His position can be traced in higher human, psychological and esthetic processes and finally in political and economic action. He concludes,

Hence all creation has its negative aspect, but that does not entitle us to call the creative process negative in essence. Nonviolent resistance or soul-force is in essence positive and creative.

It may be said, "All this sounds beautiful, but it is based on nothing but an intangible idea, an assumption of a spiritual unity among mankind."

. . . tangible things, too, grew out of nothing but intangible ideas.[1]

Positive values always create tensions. It is impossible to confront falsehood with truth, hate with love, injustice with justice, evil with goodness, without causing tension, conflict, even violence. As those qualities upon which better human relations must be based — good will, confidence, fair play, justice, and the like — advance into the setting of their opposites, they must set up tensions against themselves and make overt the divisions among humans. Such tensions and divisons are inescapable but need not be permanent. They need not be allowed to reign over affairs. In bettering human relations, sound counsel will never urge absence of conflict, but will urge nonviolent solution.

There is an important difference between violent and nonviolent social action. Nonviolence does not overlook evil for the sake of peace; it is a faith for those who understand that when people are violent against evil, it is practically impossible for them not to become brutalized by the violence they practice. Nonviolence embraces freedom from enmity and rancor and strives for a real inner change in its opponents. It cannot by definition fall victim to a mentality of violence through practicing violence.

The negative role of nonvolence is always an incident of its positive assertion and activity. It is not passive, but takes an active position to alter existing conditions in order to bring about a more fully human society. For example, the Gandhians said they were building "a nation within a nation"; to that constructive enterprise they devoted perhaps two-thirds of their organizing efforts and energies.

There is a tendency for the novice in nonviolence, fired with the fresh idealism of this faith, to tend toward perfectionism rather than toward virile, dynamic personality growth as a lifelong process. The exponent may perhaps become devoted to an inner search, sincerely hoping to perfect himself in order to become adequate for appropriate action in the world.

But nonviolence that strives only for inner perfection is incomplete, because true nonviolence is *active* love. It develops such precise personality factors as love for the last and least of the human race, social insight, social passion, universal awareness, self-giving, and a capacity to suffer; these can be developed only within society and in action. In addition, a faith that is not externalized withholds from society the very catalytic qualities which any vital transformation requires.

By a reasoning similar to that of perfectionists, pacifists sometimes assert that only the truly nonviolent who have reached a certain state of awareness and refinement of personality should participate in a campaign of nonviolence. Or they may insist that some applications of nonviolence in a reform movement are not real nonviolence, or that the reforms are unworthy of the genuine conscientious objector to violence. From such beliefs a kind of purism of nonviolence may develop and paralyze most reform.

Nonviolence of this type is like a fruit shriveling as its vine withers for lack of the sap which alone can give life to both. Not only are such puristic exponents of nonviolence of little constructive influence; they also inhibit the spread of this doctrine to those who are not presently advocates of nonviolence but who might otherwise become active practitioners. Their concept is far from the Gandhian concept of nonviolence.

Nonviolence is not yet commonly understood in the West. There are many fallacies regarding its nature and function, among them that it is the cloak of those too cowardly to "fight like a man," that its adherents are encouraged to be lawless, that it is a method of desperation undertaken by the oppressed who would be violent if the means were available, and that it is a cover for those who want to pursue selfish ends without running the risk of getting hurt.

The facts are entirely to the contrary. Nonviolence is not for those who would be perfect, but for those with the honesty to admit their humanity. Nonviolence is not for the weak who will come to terms with the oppressor, but for the strong who will not cooperate in their own oppression. Nonviolence is not for the undisciplined, but for those who can learn control over themselves and obedience to moral direction. Nonviolence is not for those lacking in self-respect, but for those who refuse to accept any prescribed status for themselves. Nonviolence is not for those without conscience, but for those who will not obey an immoral law. Nonviolence is not for the unfeeling who seek greatness through arrogance and cannot love, but for the compassionate who serve others and can face bitterness without resentment. Nonviolence is not for the ambitious who seek personal success at any cost, but for the moral who will not consent to the exploitation of themselves or any other human being. Nonviolence is not for the complacent who, having lost their humanity, are busy maintaining their comfort; nonviolence is for the dauntless who will face danger without flinching and blows without retaliation. Nonviolence is not for those who would be safe, but for those who will obey conscience at the cost of suffering and even death.

Above all, nonviolence is not a way for the uncommitted. Commitment cannot be forced, and without genuine commitment there is no will either to resist violence or to do the constructive work of nonviolence. The way of nonviolence calls for the same devotion to liberty as that which consecrated Bunker Hill and Valley Forge. It calls for the same ardor that fired Patrick Henry:

> Is life so dear, or peace so sweet, as to be purchased at the price of chains and slavery? Forbid it, Almighty God! I know not what course others may take, but as for me, give me liberty, or give me death!

This auspicious human determination not to yield to tyranny at any cost requires passion, but it does not call for violence.

Gandhi's nonviolent revolution wins the future as it triumphs; his slogan, "Die, but do not kill," points the way for those who would struggle against dehumanization without losing their own humanity. Gandhi always emphasized as basic that one person could, if true, stand utterly alone, and that individual reason could effect social and political change. Satyagraha was the reform technique he developed.

Gandhi apparently never tried to define satyagraha in words. He lived by it and brought into India's liberation movement what he considered its appropriate social applications. In 1939 he wrote, "I have no set theory to go by. I have not worked out the scheme of Satyagraha in its entirety. You can join me in my quest if it appeals to you and you feel the call."[2]

Gandhi coined the term *satyagraha* when it became necessary to make clear, especially to the West, that passive resistance or any kind of passivity, or resistance by itself, could not possibly express his concept. *Satya* means the goal of truth toward which man must ever aim his search and life experimentation. *Agraha* means force, in the sense of engendering rather than in the abstract. Soul-force is not an adequate translation of satyagraha. Truth, burning hot within, in process of realization through love, might come near to the meaning if we think of this as both inner personal experimentation and external social experimentation at the same time in the same person.

Satyagraha has three elements: nonviolence, truth and self-suffering. In *Conquest of Violence: The Gandhian Philosophy of Conflict,* Joan V. Bondurant says:

> Satyagraha . . . seeks to effect change and it operates within a conflict situation. As do all techniques of action for effecting change, it employs force. The character and the result of the force of satyagraha are essentially different from those of conventional — violent — techniques of action during conflict.[3]

The concept of satyagraha arose and developed in Gandhi's thought and use beginning with the concept of one of its elements, nonviolence or *ahimsa*. This is an ancient term made up originally in exactly the same way as the Western anarchy was made up in ancient Greek philosophical thought. The *a* and *an* carry the same meaning of negation. *Himsa* and *archy* have the same value in etymological development. They are terms that resulted from looking at that redness in "tooth and claw" of all nature (including human nature) which led early thinkers to the impression that all of nature reveals violence — the original meaning of the Greek *archos* and the Sanskrit *himsa.*

Gradually these concepts, influenced by the development of the cultures in which they were used, diverged in meaning. The West, under the statist political obsession, ran off, so to speak, with the negative political application of the term and gave it an emphasis in line with Western political development. Anarchy acquired the connotation of absence of coercive organization and developed a derogative implication, which can be found even in the writings of Plato.

The Hindus remained much more absorbed in the philosophy of ahimsa. In orthodox concepts, especially through the Jain and Buddhist influences, this philosophy was developed further into the Hindu understanding of ahimsa. Ahimsa, which remained philosophical in Vedic development, meant nontaking of life — when consistent, inclusive of the lowest forms of life. Today, however, ahimsa means more than this even for the orthodox; it means nonaggression toward others and results from an identity with all of life.

Violence, which may be within the inscrutable providence of God, is not to be indulged in by His creatures who are able to be worshipers; nor is violence ever to be regarded as the basic reality. For the devout Hindu, nonviolence or ahimsa is the ultimate divine reality and is to be sought by all as the only way of enlightenment. For the philosophical Hindu, ahimsa is the goal to be sought — the "city out of sight."

Gandhi's study of the Bhagavad-Gita led him to repudiate the abnegation of life that resulted from this philosophy. Taking as his keynote the verse, "Action is thy duty, reward not thy concern," he breathed new life into the sacred scriptures. Man is to be active in life while making himself pure as God is pure. Desirelessness is not to become total, but is to be a lack of interest in personal gratification, self-aggrandizement or acclaim. Detachment is not to be from the senses, from life or from the world, but from concern for whatever may result from acting under conviction. This Gandhian interpretation of ahimsa therefore makes the philosophical nonviolence an inseparable continuum of means and end.

Much of that called faith in the Western tradition remains pinned upon its distant goal, impotent to go beyond a worshipful reverence. Gandhi's interpretation of faithfulness offers a course of action. Faith must be lived out. He saw the Gita as essentially a gospel of action, not of contemplation or abnegation of human experience. Yoga in the Gita is yoga as the practice or devotion within action. It is in this reform spirit and method that ahimsa coincides most closely with the teachings of Jesus in the Sermon on the Mount and with the Judeo-Christian elements in the original idealistic democracy.

It is at this point that Gandhian nonviolence is most difficult for Western thought. Whatever else nonviolence was to Gandhi, *it had to be social reform action in process.* It had to be at work in the world, dealing with all humanity.

Life of himsa or violence begins not with any overt evidence of its nature, but with the person's separation of himself from the last or least fellow creature. This is the initial, responsible violence. Ahimsa or nonviolence also begins not in a superficial but in a profound union of oneself with all creatures. This is the initial, responsible nonviolence. Ahimsa in practical application means identification with creation in contradistinction to separation from it.

This identification motivation was predominant in Gandhi's development as well as in the development of his movement. He recognized the inevitability of and necessity for revolution in a violent world. He addressed himself to the question, What kind of revolution? Against the background of the West's contradictory presentation of democracy, he set forth an alternative revolution to the violent revolution spreading across the world.

The use of nonviolence, involving identity with and action throughout all of human life, means that the work has to be done exactly where one finds oneself, in an attempt to move society one step closer to the goal of the idealized and perfect kingdom to which nonviolence, as faith, remains always attached. An illustration of Gandhi's reform method, presented as an alternative to violent change, was the transformation of India's middle-class Congress Party (founded by a British Viceroy as a debating society through which the top echelon civil servants could "let off steam") into a powerful party of the Indian masses.

This reform was achieved through demonstrations of local success (employment of the outward expressions and methods of nonviolence), application to the broad economic base of the society (brotherhood economics), and identification with the poor and outcaste (personal psychological embracing of one's fellows). The last factor appears to be foremost in initiation, in efficiency and in importance; this is available equally to everyone and makes nonviolence available to everyone. Second in importance seem to be the social aspects of brotherhood, economics and politics, etc. The outward expressions and methods of nonviolence, far from being the whole of nonviolence as some suppose, are but the issuing forth of overt forms appropriate to an inner commitment, and thus less primary than the doctrine itself and the goal toward which the doctrine is pointed.

The same order of initiation and development are true of violence. The real violence is in psychological separation from one's fellows; in that inner attitude and the goal of personal or narrow "tribal" satisfactions, not in the outward expressions and methods of violence, is to be found the primary causative violence.

The truth that stands with nonviolence as an element of satyagraha refers to all the facts relevant to the situation. These must not only be searched out carefully and thoroughly as a basis for the satyagraha campaign and direction, but must also be reassessed continuously. Any change in the position of the opposition or in other circumstances must be considered in terms of its effect on the campaign. At no time must the participants fail to give adequate regard to any fact or truth that becomes known, or fail to change their own position if that is indicated. The campaign is waged for the triumph of truth and must never degenerate into a static posturing or struggle of one "side" against another.

Besides pursuit of truth and nonviolence, satyagraha also requires an element of self-suffering, necessitated by the tensions and conflicts created when a principle is steadfastly adhered to. Self-suffering is accepted in connection with the moral persuasion of those because of whom the satyagraha is undertaken, as an alternative to the suffering of others which violence causes. Because of this decision to suffer rather than cause suffering, courage is required of the truly nonviolent. The training of the satyagrahis in India was directed in part to the overcoming of fear by discipline and to the development of courage. Gandhi referred to satyagraha as the nonviolence of the strong — a reply to those who misunderstood satyagraha as mere passive resistance, which has been called a weapon of the weak.[4]

The Western mind is quick to misinterpret self-suffering and slow to accept the necessity for it. Gandhi did not countenance meek submission, cowardice, or asceticism for its own sake. The dignity of the individual is paramount; suffering of the physical self, even death, is more desirable than humiliation. The courage required of satyagrahis is that which makes free men and women of them and prevents the kind of demoralization that comes from submission, passivity or cowardice. The beginning of freedom is in being without fear and without price.

Bondurant's *Conquest of Violence* lists the nine fundamental rules governing a satyagraha campaign. They indicate how much more extensive satyagraha is than mere nonviolent resistance or noncooperation of any kind.

(1) *Self-reliance at all times.* Outside aid may, in the proper circumstances, be accepted, but should never be counted upon.

(2) *Initiative in the hands of the satyagrahis.* Through continuous assessment of the conflict situation satyagrahis should, by means of constructive efforts where possible, by positive resistance where indicated,

or by the tactics of persuasion and adjustment, press the movement ever forward.

(3) *Propagation of the objectives, strategy and tactics of the campaign.* Propaganda must be made an integral part of the movement. Education of the opponent, the public and the participants must continue apace.

(4) *Reduction of demands to a minimum consistent with truth.* Continuing reassessment of the situation and the objectives with a view to possible adjustment of demands is essential.

(5) *Progressive advancement of the movement* through steps and stages determined to be appropriate within the given situation. Decision as to when to proceed to a further phase of the satyagraha must be carefully weighed in the light of the ever-changing circumstance, but a static condition must be avoided. However, direct action is to be launched only after all other efforts to achieve an honorable settlement have been exhausted.

(6) *Examination of weaknesses* within the satyagraha group. The morale and discipline of the satyagrahis must be maintained through active awareness (by members and leaders alike) of any development of impatience, discouragement, or breakdown of nonviolent attitude.

(7) *Persistent search for avenues of cooperation with the adversary on honorable terms.* Every effort should be made to win over the opponent by helping him (where this is consistent with the satyagrahi's true objectives) thereby demonstrating sincerity to achieve an agreement with, rather than a triumph over, the adversary.

(8) *Refusal to surrender essentials in negotiation.*
Satyagraha excludes all compromise which affects basic
principles or essential portions of valid objectives. Care
must be exercised not to engage in bargaining or barter.

(9) *Insistence upon full agreement* on fundamen-
tals before accepting a settlement.[5]

It is clear that satyagraha involves more than nonviolent action of any kind. Genuine success can be
achieved by nonviolent means — boycotts, strikes, demonstrations and so on — but such victories are limited to
the immediate issues. Larger goals require the greater
scope of satyagraha. Within the satyagraha campaigns
of the Nationalists of India, noncooperation and civil disobedience were most commonly used. It must never be
forgotten that "Constructive program is a positive aspect
of satyagraha in action, and is the concomitant of re-
sistance-action."[6]

India's development and advancement of satygraha
made a unique and threefold contribution to democracy.
First, democracy's own method of survival and extension,
the use of mass persuasion by peaceful means, was repeatedly successful and is still achieving victories. Second, civil disobedience and nonviolence were joined for a
people's resistance to tyranny; the fundamental right of
nonviolent civil disobedience is enshrined in India's constitution. Third, the establishment of a broad base of
brotherhood economics was begun by Gandhi and is still
being carried forward.

The mass use of persuasion by peaceful means was
strikingly illustrated in India when, probably for the first
time in history, the right of nonviolent resistance as a
democratic procedure was upheld. A decree of the Alla-

habad High Court stated this right as being within the provisions of the Constitution of India.

The case upon which this decree was based was one in which a socialist leader, Rammanchar Lohia, had been arrested with seventeen hundred volunteers during the four months April through July of 1954. They had conducted a "no tax" campaign in the state of Uttar Pradash in India. The civil resistance was nonviolent and against the impossibility of paying heavy irrigation taxes.

The decision, one which will rank with the great documental milestones of democratic development, released the satyagrahis from prison and, in the words of Justice Agrawala, stated: ". . . our Constitution safeguards to every citizen of India the freedom to preach nonviolent disobedience to civil laws, not being laws mentioned in clause (2) of article 19." The exceptions, seven in number, are (1) security of state, (2) friendly relations with foreign states, (3) public order, (4) decency and morality, (5) contempt of court, (6) defamation, and (7) incitement to an offense.

Democracy has always posited the necessity for people to resist injustices or tyranny when legal avenues are closed to them, but it had never before found a means for that resistance in harmony with its essential genius of persuasion by peaceful means — a way which in the taking can and does breed the good will out of which democracy is fashioned.

The most extensive nonviolence now in operation all over India carries forward the extension of brotherhood economics. The Bhoodan Movement (Land Gift Mission — in the West most often called "the Constructive Work Program"), led by Vinoba Bhave, is a land reform program. Tenant farmers, evicted for joining the Movement, were imprisoned for moving back onto their land. By act of the Court in 1961, they were freed with full restitution of rights and property.

One of the most important aspects of satyagraha is its peculiar effectiveness in winning not only the cause, but the opponent — it does not win the battle and lose the peace. India's victory in expelling the strongest Western imperial power took time. But victory by any other method could not have brought India into her present place by now, either in her relationships with England and the British Commonwealth — the freest of all the international associations — or to the degree of democracy achieved in India.

Because India's struggle for independence excluded violence, at least officially, it forged a new and bright bond of the free people with the former oppressor and enemy. India's place as the first nation of colored peoples in the British Commonwealth of Nations, a place chosen by a free people, will stand historically as a revolutionary and statesman-like achievement of the first magnitude. This revolution also illustrates the principle that there can be no evil of class consciousness or class struggle in a truly democratic resistance. Democracy cannot divide its community.

India is today, despite notable setbacks in her nonviolence, perhaps the most favorable setting in the world for the further development of democracy. Her examples of citizen alertness and responsibility are certainly commendable to all the world.

Gandhi's all-life revolution was his alternative to Western futility and despair. His voice, rather than silenced by death, is now beginning to speak to the West in a thousand tongues. Like Gandhi, we are beginning to understand that total reliance upon material and physical strength is the way of confusion and death. The message of Gandhi speaks directly to the fatal Western dualism which separates the spiritual from the secular; it is beginning to be understood by the pilgrims of the new age. As reactivated and responsible citizens of a world community, we are beginning to be challenged by what Gandhi was, and to question our economic, social and political institutions.

Gandhi has turned growing minorities of peoples in an increasing number of countries with great hopefulness toward nonviolence as the appropriate instrument of democracy, through every phase of its development from the revolutionary struggle for independence through the throwing off of every shackle of inequality to the final organization of the world for the interdependence which modern life demands of the world's people.

The power of the people is what some sociologists call social dynamism. As a direct result of the inordinate growth of accumulative technological knowledge with all its ramifications, this timeless and universal social quality — the power of the masses — is now enhanced to an extraordinary degree in the West. This characteristic of vast populations, when somnolent, can make possible totalitarian power in its essence; when in action, it can create revolutionary upheaval in its overt struggle.

"Anything that millions can do together," said Gandhi, "becomes charged with a unique power."[7] This power can be for good or ill; it can be expressed in action, in resisting action, or in being indifferent to either evil or reform. Whatever power a Gandhi or a Hitler may develop, whatever power democracy or any other way of life achieves, exists in this power of people in the mass.

There is ultimately no power of parliaments or manipulators, dictatorships, or cartels, except that of the popular will, whether slumbering or wakeful. Gandhi trained his people to use this power in the dignity, fearlessness and forbearance of personal conscience, and in so doing he challenged the whole contradictory structure of Western society.

While India was still a colony of Great Britain, early in the Second World War, Krishnalal Shridarani wrote,

> Democracy's first victory in India must be won, and the ground is prepared. India's dynamic present is devoted to endowing Western democracy with the spiritual serenity of the East. The noble experiment of Gandhi can be summarized in his own belief: "In true democracy is found the very essence and spirit of the divine principle. True democracy allows the people to govern themselves and decide for themselves; it grants them liberty of thought and liberty to express that thought. In so doing they may often fall into error and perhaps commit crimes that cause untold suffering; but so long as they have liberty, they will detect the error and finally overcome it at its roots. The gain may be slowly won, but it will be lasting because it was achieved by their own will and effort. No gain is worth the winning, save that you win it yourself."[8]

A social structure exhibiting closely knit patterns of interpersonal relationships has an infinitely greater capacity for effecting social reform.

If the individuals of a society have lost out in primary behavior patterns (those factors involving the sense of belonging, the intimacy of face to face contacts, neighborliness and personal responsibility for others), they may be incapable of fulfilling the purposes of their society or civilization without the whiplash of compulsion. The culture of the West is tending to produce more and more individuals without common purposes or ideals and consequently without the sense of responsibility required for intelligent democratic social action.

Democratic institutions are dependent upon an individual sense of responsibility. Those who wait for any injustice or expanding monstrous evil such as impending war or encroaching fascism to lay its hand on them before taking a position are not living democratically. Democracy cannot be maintained by those whose private positions against evil render them immune until accosted by the evil.

For example, war cannot be resisted even by pacifists if pacifism is merely a private position regarding what one proposes to do when tapped on the shoulder. Hitlerism was not successfully resisted in Germany by those waiting for the menace to lay its hands on them individually. Pastor Martin Niemoeller, the First World War U-boat captain who became the most famous of all the Second World War resisters, recognized this fatal defect in the personal piety of many devoted people. In repentant mood he told American audiences,

> When communists were jailed — I was not a communist.
> When Jews were hounded — I was not a Jew.
> When union leaders were jailed — I was not a union member.
> When Catholics were jailed — I was not a Catholic.
> When I was jailed it was too late to do anything.

The necessity of the individual's resistance to the state under certain circumstances is assumed. The reverse logic is that one who resists his government for any reason is subversive. Such logic would refute the idea that our revolutionary forefathers were true patriots. It would also assume that the whole of the North was subversive in the pre-Civil War years, when escaped slaves were not surrendered as required by federal law.

Historically, democratic movements for freedom, equality and justice have been followed by establishment of the people's own way of peaceful and continuous change, the method by which democracy has always maintained itself as a political establishment. But special privilege does not like change, no matter how secured. This brings into being democracy's continual struggle for reform, its necessity for eternal vigilance against privilege and abuse.

Only as people have remained alert, active, intelligent and in opposition to every formal tyranny have measures of democratic substance or method been realized. Democracies have been legally constituted in a manner guaranteeing to the people their right to oppose their government and to overthrow it by peaceful and legal means, in accordance with the popular will and without the necessity of waiting until the end of any term of years. Those in power must never close the door of access to power upon the least of their opposition forces; the minority must never short-circuit the peaceful-persuasion way to power; patience is required on both sides. Experiments for the best methods must be continuous — only limited democracy has thus far been achieved. The town meeting is not perfect, nor can the use of only consensus guarantee the elimination of tyranny.

Democracy is a never-ending experiment — a search for ways to discover and implement the human community from neighborhoods to provinces, to countries, to continents, ultimately to the world. Its essential nature is a great affirmation, a positive or constructive action movement; its resistance is a necessary negation of those forces that impede the attainment of democracy's goal: a universal community of all men.

This community can never be advanced by violence. The use of violence deteriorates the spirit of man and can never be equated with democracy, which gives new life to the spirit of man. Only nonviolent social action is capable of resolving conflicts without violating and destroying democracy itself.

Gandhi's message and work were a great gift to the West, where violence has caused democracy to falter. He wrote,

> Fundamentally the disease is the same in Europe as it is in India. . . . No mere transference of political power . . . will satisfy . . . The people . . . are being exploited by the ruling class or caste under the sacred name of democracy . . . The same remedy is, therefore, likely to be applicable. Shorn of all camouflage, the exploitation of the masses of Europe is sustained by violence.
>
> Violence on the part of the masses will never remove the disease. . . . I do not believe that the spiritual law works in a field of its own. On the contrary, it expresses itself only through the ordinary activities of life. It thus affects the economic, the social and the political fields. . . . Violence will be wholly unnecessary.

True democracy . . . can never come through un-
truthful and violent means, for the simple reason
that the natural corollary to their use would be to
remove all opposition through suppression or exter-
mination of the antagonist. That does not make
for individual freedom.[9]

Gandhi made practical mass nonviolent action, which
begins by stripping away from each true satyagrahi or
nonviolent volunteer all such divisive and disorganizing
elements as the desire to exploit, to regiment and to have
power over people, and all violent attitudes, superiorities
and methods. He demonstrated the practicality and power
of nonviolent brotherhood economics — the mutual application of labor to natural resources in the production
and equitable distribution of all that is needed by the
human family. He demonstrated that the people's search
for and experimentation with truth engage them actively
in the mastery of their destiny through the conquest of
power and through the establishment of the human community. He demonstrated that such a revolution does not
have to wait for any group or any institution, but begins
in the heart and in the daily life of every man.

Gandhi demonstrated that nonviolence is democracy's own essential method of resistance to tyranny. As a
method of social change it spreads good will and extends
democracy's own application; it is educative and recrea-
tive of the human material. It is the method of social
action least in keeping with that which seeks to capture
the power of the state and then to assert control over
people through the application of such power.

Taking nonviolence and democracy as ideals, leaving aside for the purpose of definition all their specific

and limited uses and partial applications, they are very close in meaning. They are both rational popular reforms alike in motivation, application and results. Both are dependent upon peaceful inducement only and are determined by a persuaded consensus. Being unavailable through either class consciousness or class struggle, both avoid — in struggle and in realized structure — the dividing of class from class or race from race. Both are universal principles; they have no nationalistic or other sectional outlook in determining their ultimate goal, which for both is the realization of the total good of all the people.

Democracy as a political arrangement requires nonviolent social action as its instrument of continuous reform. Nonviolence, however, goes beyond democracy in the degree of faith in and devotion to the power of rational processes in common man. It also answers more directly than democracy the need for revolution that is periodically inescapable.

The preservation and extension of democracy that will further the social advancement of man require that the people resist all violence, psychological or institutionalized, beginning with that which is within their own natures. They cannot wait to take their stand against violence until it becomes overt or comes their way. The real violence goes on continuously wherever people arrogate superiority for purposes of any personal advantages whatsoever. Such continuous aggression is responsible for all other violence; it must be resisted now and all of the time. It must be resisted by setting against tyranny and exploitation a human community of all classes, races and nations — the people's community of the world. This, the people's nonviolent resistance, is also their constructive program. Man's identity with his fellow beings, essential to nonviolence, is democracy's hope in the resolution of the present world crisis, and in the development of man himself as he proceeds toward his goal of a universal community.

> I troop forth replenish'd with supreme power, one
>   of an average unending procession,
> Inland and sea-coast we go, and pass all
>   boundary lines,
> Our swift ordinances on their way over
>   the whole earth,
> The blossoms we wear in our hats the growth of
>   thousands of years.
> Do you see O my brothers and sisters?
> It is not chaos or death — it is form, union, plan . . .[10]

FOOTNOTES CHAPTER FIFTEEN

1.   Richard B. Gregg, *The Power of Non-Violence* (Ahmedabad: Navajivan Press, 1938), p. 239.

2.   *Harijan,* May 27, 1939, p. 136.

3.   Joan V. Bondurant, *Conquest of Violence: The Gandhian Philosophy of Conflict* (Princeton, New Jersey: Princeton University Press, 1958), p. 36.

4.   *Ibid.,* p. 27.

5.   *Ibid.,* pp. 38-39. For Code of Discipline (pp. 39-40), Steps in a Satyagraha Campaign (pp. 40-41), see Appendix II.

6.   *Ibid.,* p. 36.

7.   *Harijan,* Sept. 3, 1940.

8.   Krishnalal Shridarani, *My India, My America* (New York: Duell, Sloan & Pearce, 1941), pp. 603-604.

9.   *Young India,* March 9, 1925, p. 304.

10.   Walt Whitman, "Song of Myself," *Leaves of Grass* (New York: Random House, The Modern Library, 1950), pp. 61 and 74.

CHAPTER 16

THE EMERGENCE OF A NEW TRADITION OF CIVIL DISOBEDIENCE AND NONVIOLENCE

In many parts of the world, the use of nonviolence is a rapidly extending frontier of human relations. Its applicability is made the more valid and urgent by the rapid development of its opposite: the modern means of violence which are coming to be regarded by man as less and less useful or even sane.

Inspired by the success of Gandhi and his followers, national groups have used nonviolent revolution to accelerate release from imperialistic power. Successes such as the organization of the Ahmedabad Textile Workers into one of the best organized and most effective labor organizations in labor history[1] are being continued in India and experienced elsewhere. In many cases the most remarkable local successes of nonviolence have taken place where violence had failed repeatedly. This too, was demonstrated in India; for example, in Champaram in about six months of nonviolence, the Gandhian leaders won success for the village peasants from repressive measures that sixty years of struggle with violence had not been able to eradicate.[2]

Such uses of nonviolence to gain social reform or national autonomy have been further encouraged by its successes in quarters where a minimum of struggle has been necessary, as in Burma, Ceylon, Ghana and Malaya. Western critics who do not grasp the real significance of nonviolence have inclined toward the view that these successes were achieved because it was the British who were resisted rather than the Dutch, the French, the Portuguese, the Nazis or the Russians. Although the British development of democracy has without question been a favorable factor in these struggles, there is probably no page in the history of brutality, torture and repression which cannot be matched in the records of British imperialism. The Amritsar massacre is one of the most infamous of such events.

Nonviolence has sometimes been employed in national resistance movements because of the contagion of its revealed success where the use of violence had repeatedly revealed its ineffectiveness. India is the supreme illustration of such success after long failure. In Madagascar, the French steadily yielded ground under a nonviolent resistance movement; after a long and futile struggle with violence on the part of that island people, nonviolence gained them their freedom.

Nonviolence has also been employed by nationalist groups to eliminate the possible and fearful totalitarian consequences which lie dormant in any selectional use of violence in a struggle for freedom. This was a lesson learned from the Russian Revolution; the violent struggle of the Russian Workers for their rights resulted not in freedom for the Workers, but in the retention of power by an elite who set aside the ideals of visionary men.

One of the most significant and relatively recent uses of nonviolence, as exemplified in India, is seen in the reoccupation of land by the dispossessed. It is also widespread in Latin America where it is known as the squatters movement. The basic assumption that all land must be held in trust for all the people clashes with the prevalent Western militarist view that a government is sovereign in the matter of eminent domain. In a real democracy, it is the people's power which is eminent over governmental power; that is the meaning of democracy. But when we in the United States spread military bases throughout the world, we deal only with governments; in Puerto Rico we act without permitting any popular representation whatsoever. In our military fever we conveniently forget to be democratic.

In Japan and Okinawa, the people massed nonviolently to prevent extension of certain military bases in areas already greatly overcrowded. The Japanese gathered by thousands and remained for many days. Fed by food that was brought to them, they remained resistant to repeated brutal treatment by police who attempted to remove them. Without violence, in silence and in sorrow, they waited until finally the governments of the United States and Japan were forced to abandon their purpose to extend that base.

Probably a great portion of the land of the world has been taken from the people in ways and for reasons which would justify their use of land revolution to take it back; the continuing plunder of the American Indian lands is a notorious case in point. Policies of this kind are a great weakness in Western diplomacy; communism's most effective drive is its radical land revolution.

An alternative land revolution is in the making in the voluntary surrender of land under the Land Gift Mission of Vinoba Bhave in India, and elsewhere in the nonviolent struggle to keep land in the people's control or to return it to the people's control when it has been taken from them wrongfully. This may prove to be one of the most significant developments of this century.

Nonviolence is becoming a familiar phenomenon in the struggle for social reform. Over the last decade Americans have witnessed a sporadic but growing adherence on the part of individuals and groups to the principles of nonviolent and noncooperationist social action. Consistent with fundamental democratic values, these episodes have arisen in many areas of government policy and social practice. Many of them have had or are expected to have a significant effect upon government policy and social organization. Some, which seem to be particularly important for the development of a new tradition of nonviolence, are enumerated in this chapter. These events can be looked upon as beachheads from which a new ethical awareness radiates over the nation, stimulating and conditioning people to act in accordance with their consciences and in a democratic and nonviolent way.

The great possibilities of nonviolence in social reform have hardly begun to be explored, but the use of nonviolence to end racial discrimination has had a long development. World attention focuses at present upon this use because of the Freedom Movement in the United States. Desegregation of every kind has become magnified in the West's awakening consciousness now that America's spirit and mission are being spoiled by this greatest of all subversions of democratic principles.

Such freedom as the American Negro has attained since the Civil War has resulted from the conquest of nonviolence over the violence in human hearts of both North and South. The most unyielding foe this nonviolence has had to face has been the bitter spirit fed by defeat in war and a towering desire for revenge, so intense it put Lincoln to death because he sought the way of reconciliation.

A national movement of nonviolence is not something that leaders can choose or not choose at will. It is produced by the special needs of the times and met initially by special leadership locally. When students first used the "sit-in" to open a lunch counter, they had no idea that their action would catch on and spread as a student movement in the South. They probably knew that CORE (Congress on Racial Equality) had used this and other strategies for eighteen years without such results; prior action had remained local. But now the time was ripe; something was in the wind. It was the same in the twenties and thirties in India.

In June 1957, there began a boycott of white shops and businesses by the Negroes of Tuskegee, Alabama, where the race supremacists had brought about the redrawing of the city's boundaries in order to shut out the Negroes (who were in the majority in the city) and thus insure white supremacy. In addition to sit-ins and boycotts, freedom rides became widespread.

In 1961, the Reverend James Lawson called in the press for a "non-violent army" of from two to eight thousand for "mass nonviolent action in the Deep South." The nonviolent army, he said, was needed because the movement in the country was tending toward "real revolution."

> We must recognize that we are merely in the prelude to revolution. . . . I do not wish to minimize the gains we have made thus far. But it would be well to recognize that we have been receiving concessions, not real changes.

We rarely blame this on the system and the structure of our institutions. Most of us work simply for concessions from the system, not for transforming the system.

The Reverend Martin Luther King of the Southern Christian Leadership Conference took up the call for this nonviolent army and toured Mississippi to recruit volunteers for it and for the voter registration campaign.

Of the millions who have responded in the years since to Lawson, King and other leaders, many are not committed to nonviolence as a philosophy and many do not understand its full implications. Nevertheless they have been able to be nonviolent in their common cause; it was the same in India. Gandhi wrote:

> I adhere to the opinion that I did well to present to the Congressmen nonviolence as an expedient. I could not have done otherwise, if I were to introduce it into politics. In South Africa, too, I introduced it as an expedient. It was successful there because resisters were a small number in a compact area and therefore easily controlled. Here we had numberless men scattered over a huge country. The result was that they could not be easily controlled or trained. And yet it is a marvel the way they have responded. They might have responded much better and shown far better results. But I have no sense of disappointment in me over the results obtained. If I had started only with men who accepted nonviolence as a creed, I might have ended with myself. Imperfect as I am, I started with imperfect men and women and sailed on an uncharted ocean. Thank

God that though the boat has not reached its haven, it has proved fairly stormproof.[3]

On the question, "Should satyagrahis be perfect people?" Gandhi said:

I admit at once that there is a doubtful proportion of full believers in my theory of nonviolence. But it should not be forgotten that I have also said that for my movement I do not at all need believers in the theory of nonviolence, full or imperfect. It is enough if people carry out the rules of nonviolent action.[4]

And again,

Let no one understand that a nonviolent army is open only to those who strictly enforce in their lives all the implications of nonviolence. It is open to all those who accept the implications and make an ever-increasing endeavor to observe them. There never will be an army of perfectly nonviolent people. It will be formed of those who will honestly endeavor to observe nonviolence.[5]

If the Freedom Movement is held strictly to nonviolence in thought and deed it cannot fail. The Negroes and those who join with them in their struggle, however, need to continue developing economic independence and social reforms as the Gandhians did through their famous "nation within a nation" program. Education, changes in legislation, open housing, job training, selective buying, boycotts, publicity, demonstrations and other means are revealing to those on both sides of the struggle the power inherent in unity of purpose and action, carried out nonviolently to further the human community.

The resisters have clearly demonstrated the superior effectiveness of their method: (a) in holding steadfastly to moral principles; (b) in freeing men and women from their own hate or fear; (c) in winning friends for their cause; (d) in the contagion of their faith and method; and (e) in creating a solidarity of humanity capable of leaping the very barrier especially resisted.

This solidarity is deeper and more significant than any cooperation that could develop out of interest, sympathy, legal participation, or mere benevolence; in it is the essence of nonviolence. It has arisen because the Negroes began to realize that they alone could pronounce their own freedom and dignity, and because thousands of whites — both South and North — began to experience repentance and repudiation concerning the inequality of the races, with its implicit denial of the humanity of both oppressors and oppressed. This repentance and repudiation must spread throughout North and South and become universal in Western culture.

The importance of the nonviolent Freedom Movement to our nation cannot be overestimated and is clearly expressed in the following words of Noel Day, a young Negro leader of his people:

A fire is sweeping the country today. Twenty million Negroes are beginning to burn with a new dedication to the cause of immediate equality in all phases of the nation's life. . . . A sense of the depth to which the fire has burned in the Negro and the persistent ache it has caused while it worked its withering effect can most readily be gained by seeing how relatively easy it has been to arouse these millions.

The fire that flared so infrequently in the past has been blown from dark and dusky embers deep in the Negro's heart into a major conflagration that may consume the soul of America.

Based on a new spirituality uniquely geared to the condition of the Negro, the revolutionary character of the Freedom Movement found its emotional roots in the yesterdays of Negro history, borrowed liberally from Gandhi's methodology, and is applying itself to the problems of Twentieth-Century America. . . . If we can face reality it may still be possible to save America. If we cannot or will not, we almost inescapably face national death — not in the sense of nuclear destruction, but rather in that peculiar dry-rotting and noisome way in which a nation kills itself, losing influence, prestige and power, and finding that it has become surrounded by unfriendly people who hear only the hollow ring of its ethical statements.

America must plainly decide either to love or to perish. A continued adherence to such outdated traditions of our national life as racism, or an inability to develop and utilize a sincere vision of the future of mankind, can lead only to a creeping necrosis. . .

. . . the final purpose of nonviolence is to save man from himself. . . . Unless white America can confront itself very quickly and realize that it is not in fact white and cannot afford to be, it is easy to imagine the great concentrations of Negroes in New York, Chicago, Washington, D.C., Detroit, Cleveland and many other cities rising up like a sword in the hand of God to cut through everything before

them. They could be suppressed, but only with time
and with such savagery that the moral fiber of the
nation would be withered beyond repair . . . the
dominion of the world would heap coals upon
America into eternity.[6]

Every man must decide whether he stands for the
violence of separatism or the nonviolence of identity
with his fellows. Every man must realize that in making
his decision — whether for destruction or for an emerging new world, whether to be alerted for action or to be
another somnolent ghost-walker of a relentless transition period — he is writing the history of this hour. How
much better to live one's life, even give one's life, for the
human community, than to be a negative force or a cipher,
or even a mere statistic in the possible downfall of our
civilization!

It is the determination not to be a statistic in a
world holocaust which has turned men to active nonviolence in the area of nuclear testing and armament.
Such active exponents of nonviolence have made recent
history in several countries of the West for the conquest
of conscience over the arbitrary, irresponsible and self-
willed state. One of the most unbelievable (for a democracy) of these stories is that of the fishing ketch, The
Golden Rule.[7]

Bert Biglow, a former Naval captain and navigator,
now a prominent and well-to-do Pennsylvania Quaker,
had no idea to what it would lead when he took the as-
signment of presenting to the President of the United
States a Quaker petition with 21,511 signatures asking
the banning of nuclear testing. After a full day of "run
around" in which he got no closer to the President than
the guard in front of the White House (following sev-

eral days of equally futile efforts by the American Friends Service Committee itself in the same matter), Biglow left Washington a sadder but wiser man; Americans, if they were to save themselves and restore democracy, would have to stop signing names, as Milton Mayer fittingly expressed it, and put themselves on the dotted line. So Bert Biglow followed his decision with action.

Thousands came to the support of his crew of four, Quakers but for one; purchased for them the 30-foot ketch, the Golden Rule; and sent them out across the seas to Honolulu. They openly proposed to sail into the ocean area which the United States had arbitrarily and autocratically marked out for the testing of its atom and hydrogen bombs.

The crew was arrested on May 1, 1958, having merely made the attempt to sail out of the Honolulu harbor; an Administrative Decree of the Atomic Energy Commission had been hastily promulgated for that express purpose. On June 4, Bert Biglow was arrested and held in prison on a charge of conspiracy against the court. The crew, out on suspended sentence, had again openly proposed to sail.

A new captain, William Huntington, took over on behalf of the American Committee on Nonviolent Action Against Nuclear Weapons, which had organized the project. Being less communicative about the crew's purposes, as was appropriate for the situation, the Golden Rule succeeded in sailing several miles outside the Honolulu harbor. The crew was again arrested; this time all were given six-month sentences.

But the Golden Rule had not failed. It had focused American attention as had not been done in this generation upon the important matter of individual conscience and responsibility as the true meaning of citizenship in a democracy. It also focused attention upon the callous disregard of the United States for the sentiments and wishes of people, including its own people; and especially the callousness regarding the security, safety, health and welfare of the peoples of the area where it illegally carried out the act of testing its bombs. The Golden Rule reminded all of us, as a thousand petitions could not, of the meaning of democratic government. It reminded us that the American idea has always been that government exists as the servant of its people, and that the people must serve their own consciences. Just so were we born as a nation; only so can we survive as a democracy or as a nation of democratic people.

One direct result of the Golden Rule was the actual sailing of the Phoenix into the testing area.[8] The captain of the Phoenix, Dr. Earle L. Reynolds, former professor of anthropology at Antioch College and neither a Quaker nor a pacifist, made clear that the Phoenix sailed because of the example of the Golden Rule. He, his family, and one additional crew member and friend, a Japanese named Mikami, were in the court at the trial and sentencing of the Golden Rule crew members. Dr. Reynolds had gone to Hiroshima to carry on a three-year program of research on the effects of the bomb for the Atomic Bomb Casualty Commission of the American Academy of Sciences. After that experience, the family made a four-year trip around the world and were on their way back to Hiroshima at the time the events transpired in Honolulu which led to Dr. Reynolds' arrest on July 1, 1958.

His group had decided unanimously to sail into the testing area. Near the Marshall Islands, 65 miles inside the zone mapped out by the A.E.C. for the U.S. testing of H-Bombs, the Phoenix was stopped by coast guardsmen and Dr. Reynolds placed under arrest. Reynolds was flown to Hawaii for trial, and the Phoenix — with all other members aboard — was towed by the Coast Guard to the atoll Kwajalein.

On September 26, Reynolds was sentenced to six months. As a matter of principle he decided to appeal. Hundreds in the United States sent contributions to the Phoenix Defense Fund for what they regarded an unusually important contest.

Dr. Reynolds proved to be no mean adversary; he knew both the real effects of H-bomb testing and his rights upon the seas. He was outspoken. He said he was won completely to the rightness of the Golden Rule's cause by attending the trial of the five-man crew. He added that he considered the interference with his sailing on high seas as an act of piracy, and the A.E.C. Administrative Decree under which all the arrests were made as illegal, highhanded and a violation of international law. That he was correct in these charges was later revealed when the higher court reversed the charges against him.

Aside from the legal questions, this nation's use of the illegally held area was a moral crime of the first magnitude against all the peoples living in a considerable area which surrounds the restricted zone. In addition, the United States was thus carrying out the worst possible policy in terms of our future relationships and interests with the peoples of Asia and all unprotected peoples who are likely to suffer from similar callousness and arbitrariness of any of the greater powers. The United

States would not have been in that area for any purpose whatsoever had the nation been acting democratically, or even honorably, in international affairs. No totalitarian power of right or left has committed an act more highhanded in world affairs, although some acts of aggression have been more destructive.

A broad and rapidly developing nonviolent movement of peoples against nuclear and biological-chemical warfare has been taking place especially in two countries, England and the United States. In England, most of this resistance has been under an organization now called the Committee of 100, of which Bertrand Russell has been a chief figure. In this country it is carried on under the national Committee for Nonviolent Action (CNVA); Omaha Action, against nuclear testing, and Polaris Action, against the atomic missile submarines, are two of the principal projects led by CNVA.

The use of vigils, or prayerful waiting at strategic places, has come into increasing use by the adherents of these groups. The outstanding one has been the long-time Vigil at Fort Detrick, the center of government research in germ warfare; after a year or so it was continued by Peace Action Center in Washington, D.C., on a periodic basis, along with various projects in Washington.

Another stirring and influential project was the San Francisco to Moscow March. Surprising to everyone was the favorable reception these unilateral disarmament advocates received from both official and nonofficial Russia. In this country, according to one report, the line of march was visited in advance and prepared for non-acceptance of the unilateral position on disarmament, but not so in Russia.

Some whose consciences have led them to protest against the state have done so by refusing to pay taxes. An ad hoc Tax Refusal Committee, with eighty to one hundred tax refusers against war, has existed for over fifteen years. It received national attention because of the tax refusal of the Reverend Maurice McCracken of Cincinnati. Many forums have been held on the conscience versus the state as a result of this strange case, which recalls the act of Thoreau in going to prison rather than consenting to pay taxes to a government which permitted domestic slavery.

There are several factors which made McCracken's case more than just one more person's protest. All Cincinnati knew that he was a loyal citizen; he was fully law-abiding; he was active in constructive civic contribution to the community. He was recognized as one of the most respected servants of the civic good. Further, he was a man greatly loved by both races because of the way he had lived and implemented year after year the full meaning of a human community, not merely in his own church and settlement house program but in the life of his city and the nation. The people of Cincinnati also knew that because of this, McCracken had been made a special mark by a form of smear propaganda which issued from the governor's mansion in Georgia.

His particular sin was mentioned by name as the establishing of a national "Friends of Koinonia." Sheets published by the specially formed "Georgia Commission on Education" were used to denigrate McCracken through the now well-known smear of an honorable and useful adult educational institution, the Highlander Folk School, where McCracken had helped in the summer school program. These sheets were distributed widely in Cincinnati by the Committee on Un-American Activities of the American Legion and by the Circuit Riders, a rough-riding, vigilante Methodist group. Pressure was brought by the same groups upon both the church and the government to act against McCracken because he refused to pay taxes for the support of war. For over ten years he had been refusing to pay such taxes, and the government had acted to collect from his bank account or out of his unpaid salary.

It is a matter of government policy in the cases of conscientious objectors to go after the money, not after the man. It is difficult to escape the conviction, held by most of McCracken's Cincinnati friends, that this case became an exception because of the unofficial forces which were the more responsible. It may be that the government became concerned that Maurice McCracken's lead for conscience should not be taken up by other pacifists. Since nothing has stirred pacifists the world over more than this courageous and steadfast stand of a single individual, it may prove to have been a tactical error on the part of the government.

Beginning on September 12, 1958, the Reverend Mr. McCracken began his refusal to respond to summons from the Internal Revenue Service to furnish the information he was withholding. The court took the case over and there followed a series of extraordinary episodes in which McCracken's consistent position was that he would not cooperate with a court in the effort to make him assist the Revenue Department in collection of taxes which would go for war purposes. He was charged with insanity, but three psychiatrists emphatically declared that he knew what he was doing and was of sound mind. Charged then with a continuing act of contempt because of his noncooperation, he was told that he could purge himself at will simply by voluntarily standing at the bar and pleading his case; the judge declared that he had the keys of the jail in his pocket. He remained in jail unmoved.

McCracken obviously, though unintentionally, had the court confused. The judge wanted the integrity of the court upheld by McCracken's one simple act of at least standing at the bar. The Revenue Department wanted the court to plead on McCracken's behalf and get on with the case. Finally, after some weeks, the judge gave in and the case went on without any cooperation on the part of the defendant. A jury found him guilty of the charge of "refusal to obey a summons." Thereafter, he was sentenced by Judge John H. Druffel to six months imprisonment and $250 fine. McCracken declared he would continue his noncooperation by not paying the fine and by not helping those who wished to appeal his case to the higher court. After his return from prison, he was suspended as a minister by the Cincinnati Presbytery.

What are the main points of the position of this man who thus stands singly against the state? Maurice McCracken insists that every man is bound by a higher law than a civil law supporting "a system which is evil and which threatens the existence of humanity." As one of his court-appointed lawyers said, "He is resolute. I believe he would stick by this if the penalty were death." His position as set forth in his own words is as clear and as simple as his single act of noncooperation:

> If I can say that Jesus would support conscription, that he would throw a hand grenade into a group of men, that he would drive men out of a cave with a

flame thrower, then I not only have a right to do these things but, as a Christian, I am obliged to do them. But if I believe that Jesus would do none of these things, then I have no choice, if I am a follower of his, but to refuse at whatever personal cost to support war. This means that I will not serve in the armed forces nor will I voluntarily give my money to help make war possible.

The only plea I wish to make is that our government stop its mad course toward destruction and that it respect the consciences of those who, in order to be true to themselves, cannot give tax money to war. This is the only plea I will make before the courts. What happens to our world is far more important than what may happen to me. In this spirit and for this plea I have again entered into a period of fasting and prayer.[9]

Maurice McCracken thus declared that he is obeying God rather than men. But he said also, in more modern terms, that his act represents the highest American citizenship of which he knows. In this way he follows the Gandhian conception of nonviolence as applied to the individual's responsibility to his country as a citizen: If he sincerely believes that his country is bent upon dashing itself over a precipice, from which there can be no possible recall, it is his duty to do all that he can to snatch it back.

No people have had a greater tradition of civil disobedience than the Americans — consider the War of Independence and the struggle of the North against slavery. The important and hopeful fact is that people are once more on the march with truth and justice, not only across our own nation but in India and elsewhere in the world. They are challenging unjust laws and arbitrary governments and courts. In the people's non-cooperation with any institution of or arrangement for their own debasement or oppression, jail sentences have become honorable as a choice of free men.

Civil disobedience is not nonviolence, although it may be imbued with nonviolence. Nonviolence has not been in the American tradition, but "Truth's yet mightier man-child leaps beneath the Future's heart." (James Russell Lowell). Those asserting their consciences against the state and the social order are taking the consequences with fortitude and equanimity, with love and sorrow for their fiercest opponents. This is democracy with its twin spirit, nonviolence. It points to the development of the forms of a new and nonviolent democratic society taking shape within the old.

> Truth rides the storms of all our
> senseless strivings,
> Twin horsemen of the Columbian
> apocalypse,
> Unfettered steeds of dawn,
> Bright spirits of all prophesying—
> Adventuring, experimenting Courage,
> Humble, forgiving Love,
> Asking not to be regular, approved,
> precise,
> Only to be true,
> Sane, human, just, compassionate;
> Embracing all mankind;
> Making free a world.[10]

THE EMERGENCE OF A NEW TRADITION OF CIVIL DISOBEDIENCE AND NONVIOLENCE

FOOTNOTES CHAPTER SIXTEEN

1. Mahader Desai, *A Righteous Struggle* (Ahmedabad: Navajivan Pub. House, 1951).

2. Rajendraprasad, *Satyagraha in Champaram* (Ahmedabad: Navajivan Pub. House, 1949).

3. *Harijan,* April 1, 1942, p. 116.

4. *Gandhi's Correspondence with the Government, 1942-44* (2nd ed. Ahmedabad, India: Navajivan Pub. House, 1945), p. 169.

5. *Harijan,* July 1, 1940, p. 214.

6. Noel Day, "No Hiding Place," 1964, in press.

7. Albert Biglow, *The Voyage of the Golden Rule, An Experiment with Truth* (Garden City, New York: Doubleday & Company, Inc., 1959).

8. Earl Reynolds, *The Forbidden Voyage* (New York: David McKay Company, Inc., 1961).

9. Maurice McCracken, Written statement, probably early November, 1958, sent by the Reverend McCracken from the Hamilton County jail, when under pressure to follow legal procedures, and before trial and sentencing, for distribution as his only plea, made to fellowmen, not to court. Used with his approval.

10. The author dedicates these lines to his friend, Maurice McCracken, and to the crews of the *Golden Rule* and the *Phoenix.*

CHAPTER 17

THE ROLE OF PACIFISM AND NONVIOLENCE IN NATIONAL DEFENSE

Pacifism, or the policy of adjusting differences among nations without recourse to war, is not synonymous with nonviolence. The pacifist opposes war; the pacifist who practices nonviolence is an advocate not only of peace but of man's responsibility to himself and to all his fellow men. The nonviolence which has become a movement in the United States is a struggle to end racism, not to end war, and is therefore not a pacifist movement. Even among pacifists themselves, there has as yet been no possibility revealed of an extensive movement of pacifism.

The West had a sizable minority of pacifists or war resisters in every country long before any of them became interested in taking the way of nonviolence. At present, a minority of pacifists have taken up nonviolence, but probably a substantial majority of those calling themselves pacifists do not yet approve of the nonviolent way or at any rate do not support the use of it. Still others violently repudiate it as not really pacifism, and some claim that pacifism is really nonresistance, because nonviolence is more violent than violence.[1]

Pacifism and nonviolence coincide in their advocacy of overt good will toward the opponent as a method of persuasion, but pacifism is concerned only with eliminating war between nations and with personal attitudes regarding war. Pacifism, nonviolence and democracy come together in the attempts of liberalized human beings to develop a rational and organized alternative to the political power struggle which now threatens the world with destruction.

Was Gandhi a pacifist? Was India under his leadership pacifist? Many pacifists now seem confused by the assumption of their opponents that because Indians (a few of them under Gandhi's leadership) once used nonviolence, by some magic of its influence India became pacifist. But the answer to both of these questions is No. There was nothing antiwar or even antigovernment about the Indian nonviolence; neither Gandhi nor his followers ever claimed to be pacifist.

The Nationalists used nonviolence to capture the government for India. Beyond that, the movement led to the adoption of a political form of democracy. The power had not been captured, as in Russia, by a faction; political opposition was therefore constitutionalized. But in this sense, the Indian revolution was no different in outcome from the Revolutionary War of the American Colonies. In only two respects did this new government of India go beyond the democratic governments of the West: (1) in granting the franchise to illiterates and (2) in legalizing civil resistance to unjust law or to arbitrary authority with nonviolent methods. These are important democratic landmarks, but they are not pacifism in any sense.

Is it just to claim that India and Nehru were ever in the pacifist camp, since independence? The answer again is No. There was never such a claim made. How, then, did this confusion arise? India became neutralist, that is, nonaligned and arguing for nonalignment as a better foreign policy. This meant, more vaguely perhaps, arguing positively for reliance upon world law and order and not upon nationalistic force as ways for achieving national interest, settlement of differences, or security and defense. This was obviously a more enlightened democratic world position than any of the Western democracies had taken. But it was not pacifism. It left India intact with all the paraphernalia of every modern, contesting, and ultimately warring nation. India was never, therefore, at any time a pacifist nation, any more than she was ever, as a nation, nonviolent.

The movement of war resistance has a long history going back not to India or nonviolence, but to the earliest wars in the United States, and much farther back among certain peace church groups in many countries. There have, however, been two developments since the outbreak of the Second World War which have tended to bring conscientious objection into the nonviolent camp.

One is the influence of the Gandhian movement, probably first brought into the American scene by the Kristagraha (Christian nonviolence) missionaries who were expelled from India during 1940.[2] Early in that year J. Holmes Smith, the first of these missionaries to be expelled, established the ad hoc Committee on Nonviolent Direct Action (CNVDA) which was active in New York City. By its teachings and activities, this committee directly influenced A. Philip Randolph and other leaders who later inspired, founded and led other movements, such as CORE and The Journey of Reconciliation. One peace group owing its origin and development directly to the Kristagraha influence is the Peacemakers.[3] It has been the history of Peacemakers that they have sparked other broader activities, such as the American Third Camp Movement with its significant publication, *Liberation,* and the Committee for Nonviolent Action (CNVA) which opposes nuclear armaments.

There have been two international pacifist bodies of rather long standing, with minorities in most of the countries. The Fellowship of Reconciliation (FOR) began in England during the First World War. This is a strongly religious movement, originally for peace through reconciliation, as the name suggests, today for very much more. The other, the War Resisters League (WRL) — called in England the Peace Pledge Union — with its War Resisters International, is secular and inclusive, as the name suggests, of any and every personal motive for repudiating war. As time has gone on the meaning of resisting war has deepened — at least in the determining thought of the organization — to include resistance to whatever produces war.

All peace movements were plagued by the popularizing that took place when, following the First World War, it was patriotic to be for peace. Then when the Second World War was foreseen, peace became a bad word. England was charged with becoming pacifist, and pacifism was charged with causing the unpreparedness that was disastrous in the early stages of the war.

Neither of those charges was true. When people argued that pacifism threatened the security of the West and weakened democracy against facism, they did not know the real meaning of pacifism. They implied that nations generally had become pacifist — a false use of that term. The United States was at that very time spending over a million dollars a day in preparing for the next war; England was similarly preparing. People in both countries were aiding Hitler to get his start against communism, for the next war was not expected to be against Germany. It is true that many people who had not previously taken that stand were for peace; many of them became members of the peace organizations and remained so until the outbreak of World War II. Nevertheless they did not strongly affect the actions of their countries or the course of events.

Today the outlook has changed. Militarism itself is forced to claim peace as its goal, for people will no longer support military preparedness unless they are led to believe that military superiority is the surest way to prevent wars. There is probably no American who does not, with the pacifists, desire peace. Peace is now the officially proclaimed foundation of all national policy.

Whatever other results this has had, it has purified pacifism and made it want to be something more than the vague and often deluded desire for peace. Pacifism is now something radically different from mere peace-seeking, and this is good — at least for pacifism.

The pacifist has been driven to rethink his faith and his role; he is emerging out of self-purification into a more dynamic and comprehensive war-resister, who seeks more and more to lay the axe to the roots of the violence in the structure of his society. He is, therefore, beginning to discover the deeper meanings of both violence and nonviolence. He is fond of expressing the change that has come into the philosophy of his pacifism by quoting the famous words of a French underground fighter who told of his postwar conversion to nonviolence: "There is no way to peace; peace is the way."

Nonviolence, which at first had been superficially and negatively borrowed by the pacifists from Gandhi and used in sporadic or personal ways, is becoming for the pacifist the basic philosophy of religion, of history and of economics. What the results of this change will be no one can foresee.

Gandhi's earliest world influence after his death was through a World Peace Conference which he had called just before his assassination. In 1949, ninety leaders from thirty-five nations spent half the month of December at the ashrams of Gandhi and the great poet, Tagore.

The Conference concluded in proposing the formation of "Satyagraha Units" of the nonviolent in each country. Members were to prepare themselves for the supreme sacrifice if that should prove necessary. Quoting Gandhi, the Conference stated: "The difference between war and Satyagraha amounts to this: While the former aims at coercion, the latter aims at conversion. In war one inflicts punishment upon the adversary: in Satyagraha one draws the maximum suffering without a trace of bitterness against the opponent as a human being."

The Satyagraha Units were to be "fully active during peace time" in a "constructive program" which would include social, economic, educational and administrative spheres, thus involving the actual building of the nonviolent structures of the present socioeconomic order. A preliminary International Liaison Committee was formed with volunteers representing eleven countries to get this "worldwide Satyagraha movement" started.

If Gandhi had been among them, he would have

insisted that a movement of nonviolence would have to be "homespun" — indigenous or grown from the grass roots — for each country. No such arbitrary formation of units was really needed; significant nonviolent revolutionary units already existed in several countries, notably India, South Africa and the United States. They owed their existence more or less directly to the influence of Gandhi — some to the sudden stimulus of his death. Important international liaison of these scattered movements has been going on ever since.

This international liaison among the scattered nonviolent groups led directly to the broader, more inclusive movement known as the Third Camp or the Third Way. (This is not the same as the Third Force, which was a proposal for the formation of a third bloc of powers.) The Third Camp people take the position of nonsupport of any militarized bloc of powers — communist, Western or any other. In Asia, in Africa, and to a lesser extent in Europe, people who are still far from ideological nonviolence but who are tired of war, distrustful of military defense and disillusioned with mere neutralism are joining forces with those committed to nonviolence.

All the world's people are casting about for some means by which the possibility of war can be eliminated. The masses already know "there is no hiding place." Within the consciousness of increasing millions, the presence of nuclear weapons has made ludicrous the notion of security through deterrence — the balancing of military strength. The futility and suicidal nature of increasing and extending military forces and nuclear weapons systems for defense, and the utter uselessness of any sort of civil defense against nuclear attack, have been starkly revealed.

The nuclear age is forcing man either to shape a kind of life in which resistance to anything will no longer be necessary, an obvious impossibility, or else to find a mode of resistance which is possible and effective. Gandhi's accomplishment in the first half of the twentieth century, an amazing performance of alternative revolution, is for democratic peoples the basic ingredient of the new world order of peace for which all sane men yearn. Nonviolence promises more hope for man than any other developing dimension in human relations.

Some governments have already been taken over by this popular revolution in thought; others will be in the years ahead. Nothing short of repudiating war as a solution to international problems can return to men a sense of security. This might well be called the nonviolent revolution in world defense.

It is only a matter of time until every diplomat and administrator will have to come to terms with this movement, designed to bring into existence more rational, humane world communities. Some administrations will awaken late, but with shame, to the realization that they have been advocating and defending an instrument of imminent self-annihilation. It will then be clear why certain nations, such as India, and men, such as Bertrand Russell, have refused to join "the right side" in this wasteful and futile dance of death. We will then wonder that we did not all join the United Nations long ago, instead of making that body a mockery in the eyes of all men by a mere pretense of membership.

In Finland a positive nonviolent (or an unarmed) defense department was developed and successfully experimented with over a considerable period. Under its aegis, a populace in one of the potentially most insecure positions in the West became among the most secure of peoples. Unfortunately, the Finns were induced to abandon this way and have suffered in consequence.

In England, too, nonviolence is being seriously investigated as a possible alternative to the policy of military deterrence. There, the term "unarmed defense" is used to suggest nonviolence as an alternative, not only as a way for the nation's successful defense, but as an international framework within which world peace can be considered a real possibility.

Commander Sir Stephen King-Hall, former naval staff officer who has led the movement for nonviolent defense in England, very frankly called for a Royal Commission study of nonviolence as a possibly more effective means of defense (1) for strategic reasons and (2) because the Government White Paper on defense declared that any further development of armed might for defense, especially along collective lines, could only lead to greater insecurity for England, if not to total destruction. The Government's own White Paper had clearly indicated an understanding of the implications of military deterrence as a safeguard against war. They would have to rethink everything. It was Commander King-Hall's use of the White Paper as his starting point which gave him such powerful influence among members of the Parliament.

This development fits well into the broader Third Camp movement among the peoples of Asia and Africa, whose position is that of escaping "a plague on both houses" and who have repudiated the very idea of armed blocs in the interest of a unilateral neutrality which is capable of favoring international solidarity.

Behind this philosophy is a demand for world order and peace under law. Its basis is a repudiation of the fundamental aggression upon which all overt aggression rests — the exploitation of the weak by the strong and the manifold arrogance by which imperialism supports itself.

People are turning away from war as a way of defense. They are turning more and more to nonviolent civil resistance as a way to end injustice and tyranny and move the world toward peace. On the positive side, they are working for renewed application of democratic and cooperative principles as a basis for developing a new and peaceful society.

I. F. Stone's Weekly of February 26, 1962, saluted about eight thousand youths who gathered in Washington, D.C., to protest the determination of the administration's leaders to continue and step up an insane and belligerent policy by retaliative testing of bigger and better bombs.

The attempt to secure and extend freedom with armies and military bases, strategic encirclement, containment or alliances for defense is to surrender the dynamic force of a popular will which is, at long last, attaining the realization that such stratagems simply won't work. In a struggle to preserve democratic values, the use of force as a countermeasure to any opposition is ultimately a source of weakness. Nonviolence is ultimately a source of enormous creative strength.

FOOTNOTES CHAPTER SEVENTEEN

1. The Niebuhrian break from pacifism, simply stated, followed this logic: Since resistance can be only by violence, and since some evils must be resisted by the lesser evil of violent resistance, pacifism is, therefore, impractical in this relative and violent world. Those who accept this logic assume the passive nature of pacifism as final. A second group stayed with pacifism and took the same position, but declared that the violent world must be faced with pacifism or nonresistance. They also argued that "nonviolence is more violent than violence."

Both these positions tacitly support all that the militarist himself holds: that the purpose of war is to put down evil, and the only method of resistance is violence (or that if you do resist, you are violent). These assumptions can be held only by those who do not understand the interrelationship of nationalistic aggressiveness and its war system, and the antidemocratic and anti-international aspects of this aggressiveness and system.

2. For the story of the Kristagrahis, of whom the author was one, see Appendix III.

3. An illustration of Peacemaker activities is given in Appendix IV.

CHAPTER 18

THE FULFILLMENT AND FUNCTION OF DEMOCRATIC CITIZENSHIP

The real issue facing the world is the struggle against organized violence by those working toward the enlightened, cooperative control of human destiny. Unknowingly man has enslaved himself and prepared the way to his own destruction. Human values are being ignored. Democracy is threatened with extinction. People throughout the world face a similar danger — the centralized control of their lives and destinies (whether by bureaucracies or by special privilege) — and are threatened by military destruction imposed upon them by the rivalry of world forces.

Armed might cannot defend the institutions of democracy without first nullifying them and then destroying them. Further, the strongest defense force in the world cannot make its nation secure in this nuclear age. All such solutions as the intensification of cold war, a showdown through an all-out shooting war, or even a victory in the sense that a particular "side" could dominate any other "side," are spurious and incredibly naive.

Power Bloc rivalry — rivalry among nations that cling to the war system and make war the final arbiter — is a way opposed in both method and objective to a democratic world community. This is true regardless of what either side in a cold war thinks it is struggling for;

indeed, even if one side in such a contest conceived of a democratic world community as its cause, its method would make the goal of democracy and world community impossible to achieve.

The essential method of democracy is peaceful change; without this method it cannot exist. Today world order under law has also become a necessity of democracy; force which supports democratic law, unlike sectional or unilateral might, is orderly and for the general welfare. Democracies require a force not of nations, but of people; a force employing not arms but nonviolence. Any evil which must be resisted must be resisted with the only finally effective method. Both violence and nonviolence as overt methods exist only because thought has found expression in action; the real nonviolence seeks to replace the thought which divides brother from brother with the thought that unites all men. Democracy is but part of this essential nonviolence which is the only possible answer to the violent structure of our present world. If this organized structure of violence in thought and life is not conquered, its violent deed, war, can never end.

It is clear that the people will not get peace and world order by waiting for their governments to act. Equally certain is the fact that since people are not able to depend on their governments, they must work in extra-governmental and international ways; they cannot use national means to establish international goals.

This does not mean giving up patriotism or one's government. It means harnessing them to the people's will in a way beneficial to the whole human family. Every nation's interests must become the world's and humanity's interests. We must live and endure, strive and achieve as the human race, or we shall not live or endure, strive or succeed at all.

The original character of our American citizenship carried all the implications of this universality; our citizenship cannot be fulfilled in its original character except through recognition of its world obligations. Democracy is government of, by and for the people, not government of nations — even of all the nations. Aggressive nationalism has detracted from and invalidated the first democratic principles; totalitarianism, under whatever name, is only its frankest and ugliest form.

What is required is not the aligning of people against their nations or governments, but a determination among all people to snatch their nations back from the precipice of annihilation engendered by the utilization of naked and lethal force, and a redirecting of these nations toward order and survival. There can be no higher democratic responsibility and obligation of citizenship in any nation than this. The call demands greater courage than has ever been known in war — the call to be honest and human at the same time, to accept any penalty of insecurity or suffering or death in freedom from either fear or rancor, to embrace all humanity as friends. There can be no higher democratic ideal, no finer expression of American loyalty and citizenship.

A people's revolutionary world movement means perhaps the deepest, most profound revolution in the history of modern democracy. The rising tide of popular sentiment against violent action must be organized within the present. To create peace and order, we must earnestly organize ourselves to carry democracy for the first time outside our national boundaries; we must establish it as our forefathers did before us within our nation, but we must use only nonviolence as our method of struggle; we must learn as soon as we can all that a nonviolent struggle involves, and familiarize ourselves with such nonviolent techniques as the educative, the democratic, the cooperative and community processes.

We cannot approach such a position without refusing, as the minimum essential of the democratic way, to support warmaking or aggressive behavior. We must not support nuclear suicide, nor alliances and pacts contrived to facilitate universal death or to spread the pall of disease, sterility and deformity through nuclear weapons testing.

More importantly, the positive side of this democratic revolution lies in the support of everything in the particular government's behavior which moves in the direction of world cooperation, world order and a shared world security under the beginning of world law and the enforcement of world law. Unilateral actions must thus be enacted in defense of the total interests of humanity everywhere — unilateral disarmament, unilateral strengthening of reliance upon world authority, and unilateral cooperation with the sane and moral forces in all regions and nations. People must make their nations "go it alone," if necessary, for world order and for world peace.

Whatever sets barriers against the world community must be boycotted nonviolently so that, lacking popular support, it will die. Whatever contributes to the minimum essentials of world community, without which mankind will not survive, must be made to live as the dynamism for a new democratic age. Resistance and cooperation are always the two essential sides in the use of nonviolence.

In his personal devotion to his country, the modern American — while continuing the same revolution in which his nation originated — has a distinct advantage over his forefathers who struggled against British tyranny. Gandhi's experiment in India revealed the availability of the method of peaceful persuasion not only to all people but in all areas of human need. He bequeathed to the world amazing new possibilities for popular struggle against injustice or against encroaching regimentation and tyrannical forms.

In a struggle that implements democracy's method of peaceful persuasion, method and goal converge. In each life, in each nation, in the international arena, no longer need the end justify the means; it is now possible to employ the right means to achieve humanity's goals. Such was the gift of Gandhi. His great achievement is not merely a milestone in democratic progress; it is perhaps a thousand-year marker.

In July 1940, the author, then resident in India, wrote to Gandhi to propose that Gandhi help develop a world nonviolent movement against the worldwide structure of organized violence which makes the sequence of wars following wars inevitable. The letter appealed to Gandhi to help develop nonviolent war to the finish against the whole structure of man's inhumanity to man; it suggested that nonviolent defense forces be developed for the precise purpose for which military force is being developed, and that such a development in India, where obvious preparation would make it possible, might lead to the organization of a vast Peace Army for the whole world.

Gandhi commented, "I gladly publish this letter. . . . I do not expect to lead any satyagraha army of the world. So far as I can see at present, every country will have to work out its own program. Simultaneous action is possible."[1]

In order to have world peace and world law, overt violence has to be ended. Overt violence will end only when the structure of world violence is no longer the dominant force both within and without the United Nations — when the strong themselves help to end the plunder of the weak. The United Nations must be changed to embrace such law and make it inclusive of all peoples, and support for its enforcement in all the world must be achieved. Otherwise another, more effective organization will arise in its place when the people are ready to demand peace and world order. There can be no people's world community or authority of any kind until the people themselves carry through their own world struggle with nonviolence. The democratic point of view requires democratically constituted law to give it reality; the cold war, whatever the pretexts employed, requires force as the basis of its reality. People will have to choose the way of nonviolent revolution if they and democracy are to survive.

Pressing one's nation into the democratic path, which is being so readily abandoned on every hand, will consist in a democratic revolutionary struggle of the first magnitude. Forces which are not those of the people or of their nations, but rather the forces of economic organizations and correlative superstates, will resist bitterly and brutally every attempt to halt their profiteering and aggrandizement. As in all ages, the old dying order will strike at the dynamic, advancing new order. Prisons may not, for a time, be large or numerous enough to hold the true patriots of the struggle for democracy.

The old order always dies hard, with a frantic struggle to survive. Ours cries with the passion of fanaticism for the old "patriotisms" which served it so well in the past. But today the new order of nonviolent world democracy is steadily being built. Nonviolence can be opposed with violence, but it can never be defeated with violence. The way is clear. The old order has left to it only the seeds of its death.

Violence is everywhere in evidence, it is true. But the age is reluctant to support violence. Autocracy is still prevalent, in chrome-fitted, streamlined forms. But the age is reluctant to support autocracy. Centralization characterizes every urban-political anachronism achieved by the Western order. But decentralization, born of the latest achievements of knowledge, brings release to the human spirit.

Among Americans today there are two movements working for world order and peaceful cooperation to be achieved through the necessary unilateral national surrender of specific measures of constituted authority. One of these is the world federalist movement; the other is the growing movement demanding unilateral disarmament. The latter, instead of implying no defense, argues rather for an adequate defense as the alternative to the present world threat of common suicide.

These are really but two sides of the one popular demand for world security, established through reason rather than through fear and passions, and resting upon popularly constituted democratic law. Both want a minimum democratic world framework within which co-existence and survival are possible for man. Unfortunately neither of the two has seen itself as related to the other. But if the unilateralists who resist national militarism do not see world order as the goal of their conscientious objection, they are quite unrealistic. And if the world federalists do not realize the necessity of the refusal to support national militarism as the primary condition for a world order that can "police" a world for coexistence, peace and justice, then they are not only unrealistic but also quite useless.

These two sides of one significant movement of nonviolence for world peace, though both are present and not insignificant in their isolated development, do not function with the great vitality which they could well possess, because they do not see themselves as parts of one whole and because they are not as yet seeking to combine the inevitable negative and positive aspects of every nonviolent reform movement.

The only miracle remaining to modern man is the one of people standing up in dignity, the dignity which makes active love available. A democratic revolution is a new way of new relationships among all peoples: a new way for solidarity, security and peace for all men. A world revolution of nonviolence can bring world order and, through such order, the coexistence and cooperation of the most disparate of social-economic orders or world views.

A nonviolent war against all aggression, the economic as well as the political, not only will prove more effective than all the world's armies, but can rapidly be made available, if the nonviolent of the world will put their minds and hearts to the matter. We can stake our future, our security and our lives on this war without violence, for without it there will remain no civilization: violence is no longer possible. Such is the challenge to the nonviolent in this violent world.

This democratic world revolution is now only in its earliest making, but it is as inevitable as any great reform impulse that ever began as a cloud smaller than a man's hand. Democracy will be implemented and extended by nonviolence. The goal toward which humanity's face is set is a world community; this is no longer "the city out of sight."

A world community under the control of the people means a world order for and by the people. It means a world of great diversity within unity. It means a world always in change, under the rule of searching, experimental man. It means a people ruled by no single idea or ideology, nor by any single group of men.

This great vision has never died; the courageous have kept it alive in their hearts. Today it shines again across our world. Minorities are again on the long upward march of humanity's maturation. All of the demoralizing, modernized, centralized forces of society, even with full assistance of all those "hounds of hell" which these forces have at last released upon mankind, cannot stop this twentieth-century march with truth.

"The one thing stronger than all the armies of the world . . . (is the) idea whose time has come."[2] Nonviolence is the idea that has come to men for such a time as this.

FOOTNOTES CHAPTER EIGHTEEN

1. The letter was published with Gandhi's comments in his magazine, *Harijan,* of July 28, 1940, VIII, No. 24.

2. Victor Hugo. See George Seld, *The Great Quotations* (New York: Lyle Stuart, 1960), p. 336, for a suggestion of the original of the quotation sometimes translated, "Nothing in the world is so powerful as an idea whose time has come."

APPENDIX I

THE SCHOOL OF LIVING

A brief account of the School of Living may serve to suggest how a school of living or its equivalent, serving the local adults as their own agency for study, planning and action on how to live richly and well, may furnish the foundation for grass-roots democratic planning.

Aside from its existence as a center of adult living and learning, the School of Living was a member homestead of the Bayard Lane Homestead Association. This community of sixteen families and the School was one of three "intentional" communities settled under the Independence Foundation by Ralph Borsodi, in what he regarded as a basic experiment in decentralist living.

Bayard Lane community is beautifully located on the sunny southern slope of the first range of the Ramapo Mountains near the town of Suffern, New York. Most of the male members of the community commute to their work in New York City. The School of Living was established in the community to point the way to them and to other "homesteaders" toward a partial independence for wage and salary earners through a measure of well-directed self-employment on the homestead through a step-by-step learning and development.

> . . . Borsodi . . . evolved a program of largely mechanized home production that is designed to bring consumer and producer together in one spot . . . Being a wage earner . . . . is entirely compatible with limited independence as a home owner and possessor of garden space. With a shrewd regard for conventional mores, Borsodi decided on a one-step-at-a-time program of conversion: he was looking first of all to make people home owners . . . . later to [get them to] keep chickens, goats and bees. . . .[1]

In 1941, Ralph Borsodi's resignation as Director of the projects which he had founded left the School without leadership. The Board of Trustees entrusted its administration to a group of which I was one. At the same time it accepted this group's

1. John Chamberlain, "Blueprints for a New Society: IV — Borsodi and the Chesterbelloc," *The New Republic*, January 1, 1940, p. 14.

"service fellowship" proposal — a sharing basis for the new staff organization which was in part a plan to meet serious financial needs. Thus mainly through the accident of circumstances there was launched a most interesting and thrilling experiment in homesteading practices and community cooperation.

As our hastily formed community family took over its responsibilities, we were faced against odds with re-establishing the Borsodi educational experiment.. In settling upon our policy in those first weeks, we decided to restore the School's early emphasis upon each of the two main foci of its original teaching: (1) It must be a homestead, that is, a home upon the land achieving a reasonably productive and satisfying family life; and (2) it must help to build into an integrated cooperative community the Bayard Lane settlement of which it was a part.

The first aim, homesteading, took us out into barn, field and garden, compost yard, orchard, and apiary; into the kitchen for every processing; and into all other places of homesteading practices, with increasing student participation as time went on. Everyone except the secretary worked four hours each day in some productive home activity. In this way, there was added to the increasing realization of our own subsistence, cash from home-processed foods through increasing assistance from students and guests. At the same time, this learning through experience was strengthening our appeal to the public and bringing new interest and support which we began to organize into a "National School of Living" as our membership association.

The second aim drove us out into our immediate neighborhood and beyond, first into memberships in the cooperative buying club, then into a place in its leadership; slowly but surely into a community place as neighbors among neighbors; and finally into becoming, for a growing constituency of neighbors, their recognized community center.

As we began our administration, the circumstances impelled us to lay hold of the resources we found available — both human and material. We brought the human and the material together, beginning within our own families; in doing so, we discovered a philosophy, age-old and profound. We found we were struggling against many of the mighty tendencies of the period (centralization — either bureaucratic or managerial —, segmental specialization, aggressive nationalism, regimentation, and others) through various countertendencies (civil liberties, intercultural integration, cooperation, the revival of the small community interest, formation of intentional communities, industrial democracy, and the like), toward a much needed reformulation of democracy appropriate for modern living. The story of how we first laid our hands to our humble tasks is the story, as well, of how we discovered this old philosophy which in our minds the new term "decentralization" came to represent.

All this while, the National School of Living was growing into a constituency at large of regular, though small, contributors, numbering about six hundred before we left the school at the end of our service in 1945. Our new organ, *The Decentralist,* was beginning to point a way appropriate for a mother-school of decentralist thought in a centralist crisis.

Our new thinking in larger and even world terms was not apart from the grass-roots realism of four former missionaries to India, driven out of that land as Kristagrahis when the Western imperialist order struck back at them and their brotherhood of equality and justice.[2] Now, with sleeves rolled up, those four with others planted gardens, harvested crops, made butter and cheese, received students from every part of the country, led folk dances, planned a cooperative development, and helped bring babies into the world. Our new thinking was inspired by all of this.

We noticed that more and more people coming to the School of Living were coming in groups — college groups, high school groups, summer camp groups, rural church groups both Protestant and Catholic, Quakers, pacifists and others. They asked us to set up seminars on decentralization and, often, on nonviolence. They were forcing us to interpret our way of life in national and world terms. We were increasingly doing this to the best of our ability in all these seminars and, through *The Decentralist* and *The National School of Living News Letter,* to our constituency at large. We were saying that

> Decentralization is a negative name for something very positive. Yet its negative form has special significance for this period. . . . What is transpiring in Europe and Asia today reveals the human race momentarily in conflict with an evil system more enslaving and degrading to human life than domestic slavery. . . . "Centralization" may be defined as that form of social organization in which control is ever more remote from man, render-

2. See Appendix III.

ing man servile and no longer sovereign, and reducing human personality to a status inferior to state or other organizations for social or economic control of human affairs. The builder does not grow. Totalitarianism is only an intensified, frank form of this evil. . . . This negative name cannot be escaped. But the decentralist needs to remember that his cause is the great affirmation of life.[3]

We were also helped in our interpretation by an awakening in rural and community living that we were discovering to be nationwide. There are three aspects of this awakening.

Interest in forming intentional communities is one of these aspects. The Borsodi venture in helping in the formation of such communities was inspired by the Single Tax Enclaves, which (though directly inspired by the great economist, Henry George) were inheritors of the early American utopian spirit. Government, under its various housing authorities, undertook the assisting of such planned communities and brought a number of them into existence. Many that have recently formed include almost every type that has ever existed. History has probably not recorded a period of greater experimentation along these lines — certainly not on the continent of Europe. Such communities, intentional and planned in nature, are to be found in almost every part of the West, and, to a lesser extent, wherever Western culture has penetrated, as in Japan and in Israel.

A second aspect of this community awakening is the renewed interest in existing, "casual" communities. Rural study groups are being renamed as community study groups to accord with the facts of change in many areas. Arthur Morgan's Community Service, Inc. at Yellow Springs, Ohio, has been organized to serve in this field. Arthur Morgan, the founder, had achieved national fame in two other fields — engineering and education — before he began this third and greatest career. Largely through his service organization and authorship of significant literature, to a considerable extent he pioneered this awakening of community interest.[4] Both Catholics and Protestants have

3. *The Decentralist,* I, No. 2 (October 1942), p. 1.
4. Arthur Morgan, *The Small Community* (New York: Harper & Bros., 1942). See also his *Industries for Small Communities* (Yellow Springs, O.: Community Service Inc.).

advanced into this field through their rural-life conferences, rural fellowships and town and country departments.

The third aspect of community awakening is seen in the population trend which indicates a movement of people toward nonfarming life upon the land. A trend called industrial decentralization is supplementing this population decentralization. Many of the later technological advances have helped to bear this fruit — decentralization as a Western trend — just as earlier technological advances bore the fruits of centralization when restricted by their own limitations and inspired by the desire for centralization.

Population specialists who have given attention to this trend, in contrast to census records which have scarcely registered it, say that the nonfarming rural living areas have registered this country's chief increases in population over a considerable period. Accurate studies showed that rural population was markedly increasing at the very time that farm population was markedly decreasing. It is therefore no longer correct to equate the terms "rural" and "agricultural."

While head of the Bureau of Economics of the Department of Agriculture in Washington, the late Dr. O. E. Baker made probably the most extensive studies of this population trend. He saw it as constituting the home for "a new civilization . . . whose form is embryonic," but at the same time as a challenge to the social scientist to do something concrete about its haphazard and neglected development. He saw the trend as an indication of failure, from the human and family points of view, of the Western "revolution in progress."[5] In some parts of the United States, as in much of New England, whole regions are taking the shape of this new civilization in embryo.

It will not be by trend or by chance that the revolution in progress (technology) will lead to the revolution of the human mastery of the material! But this conjunction of the best in rural and urban in a new pattern of living may prove the most significant development of even an atomic age. The need for human mastery may be met only by a philosophy and way of life, neither rural nor urban, relating people closely to the universal principles of soil, of life on the earth, of the human family on the earth and of intelligent control of human destiny.

5. "The Rural Family and Its Significance to Organized Religion," *The Christian Rural Fellowship Bulletin*, No. 43 (June 1939), p. 7.

For this, nothing less than a profound cultural upheaval will suffice.

It is no accident that the way of democracy is always the way of education in its profoundest sense. Our experiences in the School of Living revealed that the integrated community — inclusive of family interests and activities — is, as it always has been, the real educative force in stable societies. The sixteen Bayard Lane homesteading families gave evidence of the powerful influence of community. This evidence derives added significance from the facts that the community met with certain individual and group resistance throughout the period studied, and that the community spirit was never more than partially realized. A study made of the Bayard Lane Community showed that, after six years of existence, definite economic as well as cultural gains had been made and that a growing permanency had come about. Real roots were put down into both the physical and the cultural soil.[6]

6. Ralph T. Templin, "A School of Living." Unpublished report at Teachers College, Columbia University, 1946, pp. 125-130.

APPENDIX II

CODE OF DISCIPLINE AND STEPS IN SATYAGRAHA CAMPAIGN

CODE OF DISCIPLINE

The following points were laid down by Gandhi as a code for volunteers in the 1930 movement:

(1) Harbor no anger but suffer the anger of the opponent. Refuse to return the assaults of the opponent.

(2) Do not submit to any order given in anger, even though severe punishment is threatened for disobeying.

(3) Refrain from insults and swearing.

(4) Protect opponents from insult or attack, even at the risk of life.

(5) Do not resist arrest nor the attachment of property, unless holding property as a trustee.

(6) Refuse to surrender any property held in trust at the risk of life.

(7) If taken prisoner, behave in an exemplary manner.

(8) As a member of a satyagraha unit, obey the orders of satyagraha leaders, and resign from the unit in the event of serious disagreement.

(9) Do not expect guarantees for maintenance of dependents.

STEPS IN A SATYAGRAHA CAMPAIGN

The outline below is applicable to a movement growing out of grievances against an established political order. These steps could be adapted to other conflict situations.

(1) *Negotiation and arbitration.* Every effort to resolve the conflict or redress the grievance through established channels must be exhausted before the further steps are undertaken.

(2) *Preparation of the group for direct action.* Immediately upon recognizing the existence of a conflict situation which might lead to direct action, motives are to be carefully examined, exercises in self-discipline initiated, and the fullest discussion launched within the group regarding issues at stake, appropriate procedures to be undertaken, the circumstance of the opponents, the climate of public opinion, etc. This step often included, for Indian satyagrahis, purificatory fasting.

(3) *Agitation.* This step includes an active propaganda campaign together with such demonstrations as mass-meetings, parades, slogan-shouting.

(4) *Issuing of an ultimatum.* A final strong appeal to the opponent should be made explaining what further steps will be taken if no agreement can be reached. The wording and manner of presentation of the ultimatum should offer the widest scope for agreement, allowing for face-saving on the part of the opponent, and should present a constructive solution to the problem.

(5) *Economic boycott and forms of strike.* Picketing may be widely employed, together with continued demonstrations and education of the public. Sitting *dharna* (a form of sit-down strike) may be employed, as well as non-violent labor strike, and attempts to organize a general strike.

(6) *Non-cooperation.* Depending upon the nature of the issues at stake, such action as non-payment of taxes, boycott of schools and other public institutions, ostracism, or even voluntary exile may be initiated.

(7) *Civil disobedience.* Great care should be exercised in the selection of laws to be contravened. Such laws should be either central to the grievance, or symbolic.

(8) *Usurping of the functions of government.* Shridharani calls this "assertive satyagraha." Fullest preparations are necessary to make this step effective.

(9) *Parallel government.* The establishment of parallel functions should grow out of step (8), and these should be strengthened in such a way that the greatest possible cooperation from the public can be obtained.

The specific action which is to be undertaken in a given satyagraha movement will, of course, be determined by the nature of the circumstance itself. As in the extensive and intensive preparations for violent combat, much depends upon discipline, leadership, preparation, steadfast purpose, and the adaptation of basic principles and procedures to specific circumstances. An analysis of historic satyagraha campaigns in India indicates directions in which preparation for satyagraha might be developed to strengthen such movements and to avoid potential weaknesses. Gandhi and other Indian leaders accepted all who would join their campaigns. They developed tactics and rules as they moved to meet well-advanced situations of conflict. Had they been able to select their crusaders and to train them for their respective roles in the satyagraha operation, the movements might well have been even more dramatic. Even so, the degree of success with which they met is especially striking when one considers that they worked on an *ad hoc* basis, and that they dealt with a mass populace which had no prior understanding of the techniques involved and very few of whom had any consistent discipline in the application of these techniques.

APPENDIX III

THE KRISTAGRAHA MOVEMENT

Kristagraha, a Christian self-purification movement, was started in India by Christians who took active nonviolence as their way in wartime in 1939. London had declared India at war without broaching the subject to the Indians. This precipitated a dual crisis for India — the internal struggle which was to lead to the final victorious satyagraha campaign for independence, and a great international struggle, not of India's making or choosing, which violated the very genius of her movement.

Years of personal struggle in India had taught some of us that it was the white man who was most enslaved; the struggle for our own emancipation gave us this new insight into the greater enslavement and the sickness of the white race. It was our gradual achievement of this understanding about our own race — the "Europeans" as we were all known in India — which led my wife, myself and two other missionaries, Jay Holmes Smith and Paul K. Keene, to initiate a Christian self-purification movement.

This group asserted that it wanted to distinguish itself from the familiar compromised and pro-Western Christianity by following Jesus with utmost seriousness. It was devotion to this movement which led to the expulsion of every missionary involved in it — interestingly enough not by the government of India, but by our mission authorities. We had openly stood against racism, imperialism and aggressive nationalism as the forms of the initial, responsible aggression which produced our great wars, and which the white man had to end if there could ever be a world order able to establish permanent peace.

My perspective concerning this aggression had come from viewing the West, after years of absence, against my experiences in India. So for me, the story begins earlier — in 1933, while on a furlough between two terms of missionary service, with my first attempt to help develop the use of active love or nonviolence in the United States. The telling of this earlier story is important as an attempt to interpret the Western condition as viewed by oriental eyes, and to indicate the bearing of this condition on the earliest uses of nonviolence by Eastern or Western peoples.

After seven years in India, my wife and I were spending three months in travel and study of the Middle East and Europe on our way back to the States. It was our return to a West sick unto death: this was our impression. As missionaries in India, we had found that our greatest barrier to service was this "Christian civilization," as Indians called it — the dark backdrop against which all our offering was then viewed by them. We had observed, from a point of view different from that of most Americans, the steady deterioration of the white man's prestige throughout the East. We were not convinced that in the West, even Christendom had ever taken Jesus seriously. In Europe, America was editorially being called "Uncle Shylock" and blamed not only for the depression which had swept the Western World but for the spread of the conditions which had issued in the Great Depression.

The following year, travelling up and down this country, we viewed in a detached kind of way the strange sweep of the first New Deal election. There was something weird — as unnatural as the sepulchral aspect of all Europe — in this strange, seemingly unobstructed avalanche of mass humanity. The study of it as part of the mass movement phenomenon of a mentally sick West led me to recommend to western people the use of Gandhi's satyagraha or nonviolence.

In an article called "The All-Sided Sword," published in Boston's *Zion Herald* of December 14, 1933, I pointed out that thinking people desiring significant reforms had failed to speak the language of the people at any level of their growth. Even intellectuals were becoming less and less moved by reasoned appeals alone. Influence once wielded by advanced minorities had disappeared in a world keyed to mass production of opinion as of everything else. The election had revealed that aroused people will not turn in crisis to any of those limited groups whose specialty it is to face sincerely and to present rationally on behalf of people answers to the problems which confront them and thwart them at every turn. What hope was there then, the article asked, for the righteous minority to make a great human cause prevail?

No cause worth suffering and dying for is without hope! Suffering alone is a stirring which can go beneath the externals of our civilization, deep into life where all the finer qualities lie buried. My recommendation was to use Gandhi's "all-sided sword," of which Gandhi had said, "It can be used anyhow; it blesses him who uses it and him against whom it is used. Without drawing a drop of blood it produces far-reaching results. It never rusts and cannot be stolen." Given a just cause, this all-sided sword can cut deep and can prove irresistible.

It is the violence in our nature and in our ways which sets class against class or race against race, the article concluded. Thus the goal of every worthy achievement is pushed ever farther and farther from us. We must try the way of unconsciousness of class and race, as Jesus taught and practiced.

The following year, the method of the "all-sided sword" was seriously considered — perhaps for the first time in America — by a small group of people scattered over Southern Michigan. At the request of my Mission Board, I was spending a year speaking in the churches on India.

We were living in Ann Arbor. The University Director of the Wesley Foundation there was Gordon Halstead, working under the direction of his famous uncle, the Reverend Frederic B. Fisher, pastor of a large student church in Ann Arbor. Fisher, former Bishop of Calcutta, India, had resigned from the episcopacy in protest against the pro-Western complexion of the church. (He was the only Methodist bishop ever to resign. When told that a bishop could not resign, he said, "I'll show you.") Gordon Halstead had been expelled by the British Government from teaching in Lucknow Christian College, India, after he urged his students to support their nationalist nonviolent freedom struggle.

In Michigan, Halstead acted as Office Secretary for the small group we called New Abolition. Travelling over the state, I served as field worker. For the year that both of us remained in Michigan, we were able to gather in conferences a group of greatly concerned people.

The group reached certain agreement on the nature of the crisis: the West had already produced worldwide revolution. It was not possible intelligently to raise the question, "Whether or not revolution?" All that could be asked was, "What kind of revolution and with what methods?"

"We believed that active and positive nonviolence should be employed against this vast world system of Western exploitation, of which the depression was only a result; the opposite of this system, universal brotherhood, should be asserted. Both subtle and frank pretexts of superiority had led to arrogations of advantages of every kind. When hardened into societal structures, these had resulted in domination, exploitation, wars, unemployment, poverty, degradation and the like.

The New Abolition group felt that pacifism was weak in this country and throughout the West because it overlooked both the violence in the structure of Western society and its own essential resistance with nonviolence. In 1934, this small group committed itself to nonviolent revolution as the way for modern democratic man.

As my wife and I returned to India, the whole world seemed to be moving rapidly toward some dark and sinister travail. We served out another term, except for one year, but it could not be as before. We now identified ourselves closely with the Indian people; we committed ourselves wholly to nonviolence as our way.

In the end we were caught up in the Christian group in India which, as the New Abolition group had been, was stirred deeply by the old Western world of domination: of threats, counter-threats and invasions; of sword rattling in scabbard — that old world with its towering mountains of lovelessness which now seemed to be closing in all about people of both East and West. This group called its nonviolent movement Kristagraha.

If, as the late Krishnalal Shridarani says in *My India, My America*,[1] Kristagraha is the Western equivalent of satyagraha, and if its application is even more appropriate in a setting of democratic theory than it was in India, then its importance for the democratic West can be understood.

It was a memorable visit with Gandhi at which we discussed our purpose in founding this Christian movement for India's freedom through nonviolence. (Most Christians had remained aloof from the struggle or in many cases were pro-British.) We called the projected movement Kristagraha, or "Christ-force," but in the sense of engendering — hence "Christ dynamic in Christian living."

Gandhi said, "For me the Christ and Satya (Truth) are one and the same. You must hold them to this high moral principle." He said there were three things to observe: "Keep your movement pure (above-board and without guile); keep it moral (out of politics); keep it harmless (nonviolent in word and deed). Your success cannot be measured in numbers of adherents or grasp of power which worldly peoples and movements seek. Only one devoted person," he added, "if steadfastly loyal to nonviolence, can never be defeated nor his contribution prove vain."

The movement developed in and around Lucknow and was greatly influenced by E. Stanley Jones and his Ashram. When

1. (New York: Duell, Sloan & Pearce, 1941.) For a further account and interpretation of Kristagraha, see pages 303-309 and 342-345.

the war broke out in 1939, the name Kristagraha was first applied to distinguish these Christians from a Christianity which everywhere in India was embracing Western imperialism as its security and modus operandi. The responsible organizers were three Ashram leaders, Cyril Modak, Jay Holmes Smith and myself.[2] Modak was the originator of the name Kristagraha and the developer of the movement's ideas and purposes, as set forth in two handbooks, "The Kristagraha Movement" and "Modern India and Kristagraha."

After two conferences in Lucknow on "India in the Crisis," the group issued its statement on the war and peace called the "Kristagraha Manifesto: With Christ in the Crisis." The statement was translated into every vernacular by the nationalists and broadcast over India.

A storm of church disapproval broke over my head — I had signed as drafting chairman. There was no attack on John Wilson, an Indian, who signed as secretary. The missionary pledge, "to do nothing contrary to or in diminution of the lawfully constituted authority," was made the issue over which a nationwide controversy raged until the expulsion of the last missionary.

"Kristagraha Manifesto II: The Missionary's Stand with Christ" followed the first closely and was signed by four Methodist missionaries, Jay Holmes Smith, Paul K. Keene, my wife Lila, and myself. This statement repudiated not the pledge, but the official church interpretation and use of it, "to make us pro-government, even in relation to the noble nonviolent effort of the current nationalism to induce in that government a change of heart."

Though the government took no action against them, as revealed in later statements of both Bishops and government, the four signers of this second manifesto were expelled before the end of 1940 by the mission authorities. Jay Holmes Smith and Paul K. Keene accepted the Bishops' unanimous action and left at once. My wife and I resisted the expulsion and remained throughout the nine-month missionary pledge controversy. That

2. Cyril Modak, a Maratha poet, was a graduate of Drew University School of Theology and author of the book *India's Challenge to Christians* (Lucknow: Upper India Publishing House, 1940); he was Associate Acharia of the Lucknow Ashram. Jay Holmes Smith was the Acharia of the Lucknow Ashram. I had been a leader of discussion series for five summers in this Ashram's "Summer Ashram" in the mountain retreat, Sat Tal.

controversy was kept alive by the difference in policies of the Bishops in India and the Board of Missions in New York, which agreed with our position that the church should not itself interpret a missionary's act as against the state. As far as is known, the Bishops were supported by the whole of official Christendom in India in their claim that it was their responsibility to interpret a missionary's loyalty or disloyalty and to act accordingly.

In their first Manifesto, the Kristagrahis had defined Kristagraha as "that movement of the spirit of Christ in the hearts of men which leads them to offer resistance to whatever enslaves man or withholds from him his birthright of liberty, equality and justice. A Kristagrahi is one who commits himself to such resistance and, like his Master, relies only upon the force of God within him for safety and strength. . . . Kristagraha means the Christ way for the accomplishment of Christ's purpose, which is that the truth should make man free. True Kristagraha is a resolute campaign for right in every sphere of life and for all people."

Kristagraha spoke not just to India, but to the world. The challenge of the Kristagraha Manifesto is as apt today as at the moment of utterance.

> Nonviolence is more than mere method, just as violence is more than mere method. It inheres in the intention of equality just as violence inheres in the intention of inequality.
>
> We therefore repudiate the will to power over others as responsible for all the violence of whatever kind in the world. As Kristagrahis, we commit ourselves unflinchingly to the resistance of all such domination. . . . No world peace can ever be built upon the right of strong nations to continue the exploitation of the undeveloped portions of the world at will or force any kind of "protection," so-called, upon unwilling peoples. . . . Empire, therefore, must be repudiated. Its day is over! This is the crux of world peace!
>
> The very intention which divides one from his fellowman is violence. Therefore, we affirm that there is no inherently superior race or class or nation. All myths of special responsibility, "the white man's burden," Nordic destiny, and all other pretexts for exploitation, must be uprooted.
>
> We see two kinds of nationalism in the world, redemptive nationalism and aggressive nationalism. We take our stand with the former wherever it may appear

and against the latter as responsible for all our world turmoil. . . . We cannot help being intensely aware of the fact that this life and death struggle between aggressive and redemptive nationalisms is brought to a focus before our eyes in the present crisis.

Unlike aggressive nationalism, with its motive of exploitation, redemptive nationalism is a necessary stage toward a world organization for peace. Its passion is to liberate self, in order that all may be liberated. The oppressor is always as enslaved as the rest. He, too, has to be released. . . .

We see the nationalism of India as of the nature of this redemptive nationalism, and as inspiring the whole world to move toward the common goal of international justice. . . .

The hour has come when followers of Christ must stand with those who oppose aggressive nationalism in the interest of redemptive nationalism. . . .

It is because we see in the present crisis the ever-recurring judgment of God upon imperialist aggression that we are willing to offer our lives in this cause.

Before we left India in 1940, I wrote a letter to Gandhi which began,

. . . We are accepting this expulsion as God's closing of one door and the opening of another. We are content to trust His judgment as to the "effectiveness" of our work here or there. The present world is not in the mood to judge effectiveness. As the great Lowell expressed it,

We see dimly in the present
What is small and what is great;
Slow of faith how weak an arm
May turn the iron helm of fate.

I am hoping and praying daily that Congress may see that its supreme opportunity is not to win a doubtful political victory over a foe but, in an hour like this, to win the lasting friendship of all who love liberty, in England and all the world, by revealing the only adequate zeal for India's defense or defense of democracy in the world — *the nonviolent war to the finish against the whole structure of man's inhumanity to man.* Those who understand and love peace should build up a nonviolent defense force for the precise purpose for which military force is being established. . . . The great hope should be that such an army would lead directly and speedily to the organization of a vast Peace Army for the whole world.

In publishing this letter, Gandhi commented, in part, "Mr. Templin represents a growing number of Western Satyagrahis."[3]

On our memorable final visit with Gandhi, we knew we were taking farewell for the last time and that we were going into forced exile from India, the land of our adoption. Even so it was a happy occasion.

The visit took place in Gandhi's simple thatched hut at Sevagram. The conversation began in a jocular vein; Gandhi drew me out about futile attempts to learn to spin. He laughed heartily about "you Americans who want to get things done right now." He dilated in the same amused way about the delicate and elusive "art of spinning, which requires that one place in proper balanced proportion the desire to push ahead and the patience to hold back." One could sense that in twitting an American in this pleasant spirit, he was gently chiding the West.

When we arrived in New York City in December 1940, Jay Holmes Smith had already established the Committee on Nonviolent Direct Action of the New York Fellowship of Reconciliation. Later he settled in the Harlem Ashram; groups of nonviolent resisters began to open business firms on 125th Street to Negro employment, using the techniques that were extended in a nationwide movement by CORE two years afterward. At least one leader and founder of CORE has stated that it was in action with this early nonviolent action group that he was converted to nonviolence.

Paul Keene had become a professor of mathematics at nearby Brothers College, Drew University, but he gave up his teaching to be associated with us at the School of Living in Suffern, New York.[4]

The "American Kristagrahis" were formed early, but the organization did not take hold and was discontinued after a few meetings. Out of it, however, came the two anti-imperialist ad hoc organizations, the Free India Committee and the American Committee for Puerto Rican Independence.

3. *Harijan*, VIII, No. 24 (July 28, 1940).
4. See Appendix I.

APPENDIX IV

THE PEACEMAKERS' PROJECT IN PUERTO RICO

Nine Peacemakers, of whom I was one, represented their group in a Peace and Good Will Walk in Puerto Rico between Christmas and New Year's Day in 1959. The march was made in protest of the continuing "military occupation and Congressional Rule." Puerto Rico is governed under an Act of Congress, yet has no voting representation in either House. Washington takes no tax, for that would be taxation without representation; but Washington conscripts Puerto Ricans without representation!

The walk began at Guanica Bay where 60 years before American troops had landed and taken possession — as booty of the Spanish American War, in the name of a United States government which had not acted in the matter, and in violation of the independence charter under which Spain had shortly before granted the people full representation in the Spanish Diet. The Peacemaker group followed the army's route over mountains and across the island to San Juan. The walk culminated in a prayer vigil at the gate of the missile launching site which was then under construction at Roosevelt Road.

During the first two days of the walk, cars of the Security Police openly and continuously followed us. After that they were less in evidence — probably because of the extent of the publicity their actions had caused. The nine of us were well received by the people, to whom 20,000 of our protest pamphlets were distributed.

Our main emphasis was upon the traditional Peacemaker position of the use of nonviolence only. This was interpreted as the necessary resistance against any injustice or arbitrary arrangement, and, on the side of the exploitative or tyrannical group, as the grace of giving in and letting go. No political position was taken — merely the moral position that the Puerto Ricans must be given full scope in deciding their own destiny. This they have never had; the Act under which they wrote their present local autonomy Constitution offered them no alternative to their territorial status.

The questions most often asked us by the people pertained to U. S. military intervention. Some, like some of the people in this country, felt that defense was possible only by the establishment of strategically scattered bases from which ever more destructive missiles could be launched. To such persons there is little that one can say. We found that few Puerto Ricans believed that the presence of American military power, represented by the many bases, rendered them safe. On the contrary, most seem to agree with the group's statement of protest: that Puerto Rico is threatened with extinction by atomic bombardment because of the establishment of a key Intercontinental Ballistics Missile Base. This the simplest of them seemed readily to understand; this was the portion of the statement for which there was most interest and appreciation; it was the portion also singled out by several groups on the Island which published and circulated their own welcome to and appreciation of the March for Peace and Goodwill.

This was the second Puerto Rican Project.

INDEX